10,⁰⁰

The Sodomite in
Fiction and Satire
1660–1750

Between Men ~ Between Women
Lesbian and Gay Studies
Lillian Faderman and Larry Gross, Editors

The Sodomite in Fiction and Satire 1660–1750

Cameron McFarlane

Columbia University Press

NEW YORK

Columbia University Press
Publishers Since 1893
New York   Chichester, West Sussex

Copyright © 1997 Columbia University Press

Library of Congress Cataloging-in-Publication Data
McFarlane, Cameron.
The sodomite in fiction and satire, 1660–1750 / Cameron McFarlane.
        p.   cm.
Includes bibliographical references and index.
ISBN 0–231–10894–X (cloth). — ISBN 0–231–10895–8 (pbk.)
1. English fiction—Early modern, 1500–1700—History and criticism.   2. Gay men
in literature.   3. Homosexuality and literature—Great Britain—History—17th
century.   4. Homosexuality and literature—Great Britain—History—18th century.
5. English fiction—18th century—History and criticism.   6. Satire, English—
History and criticism.   7. Homosexuality, Male, in literature.   8. Sodomy in
literature.   9. Sex in literature.   I. Title.
              PR844.G34M38   1997
     823'.4093520664—dc21   97–35684
                                        CIP

Casebound editions of Columbia University Press books are printed on
permanent and durable acid-free paper.
Printed in the United States of America
          c 10 9 8 7 6 5 4 3 2 1
          p 10 9 8 7 6 5 4 3 2 1

Contents

Acknowledgments

I am grateful to the following friends and colleagues for their help, advice, and support: Henry Abelove, Alison Conway, Joel Faflak, Allan Gedalof, Dorothy Hadfield, Elizabeth Harvey, Wendy McIsaac, Jennifer Venn, and Lynn Wells. Special thanks go to Lisa M. Zeitz.

Research for this project was facilitated by a fellowship from the Social Sciences and Humanities Research Council of Canada.

A portion of chapter 2 appeared in *Masculinities* 3, no. 1 (Spring 1995).

The Sodomite in
Fiction and Satire
1660–1750

Introduction

ON JULY 1, 1663, Samuel Pepys recorded the following, somewhat notorious incident in his diary:

> . . . after dinner we fell in talking, Sir J. Mennes and Mr. Batten and I—Mr. Batten telling us of a late triall of Sir Charles Sydly the other day, before my Lord Chief Justice Foster and the whole Bench—for his debauchery a little while since at Oxford Kates; coming in open day into the Balcone and showed his nakedness—acting all the postures of lust and buggery that could be imagined, and abusing of scripture and, as it were, from thence preaching a Mountebanke sermon from that pulpitt, saying that there he hath to sell such a pouder as should make all the cunts in town run after him— a thousand people standing underneath to see and hear him.
>
> And that being done, he took a glass of wine and washed his prick in it and then drank it off; and then took another and drank the King's health. . . .
>
> Upon this discourse, Sir J. Mennes and Mr. Batten both say that buggery is now almost grown as common among our gallants as in Italy, and that the very pages of the town begin to complain of their masters for it.   (4: 209–10)

Having given this considerably detailed account of Sedley's debauchery and of the town's debauchery in general, Pepys then records his bewildered—and bewildering—response: "But blessed be God, I do not to this day know what is the meaning of this sin [buggery], nor which is the agent nor which the patient" (4:210). This passage from Pepys's diary raises a number of important questions for the project of gay studies of the Restoration and eighteenth century, questions ranging from the, perhaps, prurient (how many postures of lust and buggery *are* there?) to the more complex and far-reaching: how can Pepys have carried on this conversation with Mennes and Batten and then say he does not know what is meant by buggery? If he does not know what is meant by buggery, then how does he know that one of the participants may be described as active ("the agent") and the other as passive ("the patient")? *What did, or could, buggery mean during this period?* Certainly, the authorities seem to have had no clearer an idea than Pepys about exactly what it was that Sedley had done or was inciting: "It seems," writes Pepys, "my Lord and the rest of the Judges did all of them round give him [Sedley] a most high reproofe, my Lord Chief Justice saying that it was for him and such wicked wretches as he was that God's anger and judgments hung over us. . . . It's said they have bound him to his good behaviour (*there being no law against him for it*)" (4:209–10; my emphasis). If, on the one hand, the judges are inspired by Sedley's behavior to evoke the warning of Sodom and Gomorrah, they are on the other hand, as representatives of the law, unable to provide any specific reason for doing so. In matters of lust and buggery, the authorities share Pepys's strange combination of knowingness and uncertainty.

The following pages take as their object of study the representation of sodomy and of the sodomite during the Restoration and the first half of the eighteenth century.[1] To anyone unfamiliar with gay studies, it may seem odd to begin by suggesting that there is a certain vagueness about what the words *buggery*, *sodomy*, and *sodomite* refer to at this time. Anyone who is familiar with gay studies, however, will also be familiar (perhaps only too familiar) with Michel Foucault's often-quoted assertion in the first volume of *The History of Sexuality* (1976) that early modern sodomy is an "utterly confused category" (101). It is true that during the seventeenth century and into the eighteenth century the word *sodomy*, as Margaret Hunt points out, was used to "refer to such disparate activities as bestiality, heterosexual anal intercourse, *both* priestly celibacy and clerical concubine-keeping, an adult man's sexual abuse of a young girl, sexual intercourse between Christians and Jews, masturbation, coitus interruptus, birth control, pederasty, and luxurious consumption" (360). As a conceptual category, *sodomy* had a much broader sweep than we generally consider it having at present.[2] In the passage quoted above, for example, it is quite clear that Sedley's sexual debauchery is linked to—indeed, is inseparable from—his "Mountebanke sermon" and his slight against the King, at least in the minds of Pepys and the judges. Further, while Pepys, Mennes, and Batten obviously connect Sedley's behavior with buggery—and by buggery mean sex between males ("the very pages of the town begin to complain of their masters for it")—they express no surprise that Sedley should also be interested in having "all the cunts in town run after him." And finally, it is apparently to be taken as a matter of course that such behavior should flourish in countries other than England, especially in a (not incidentally) Catholic country like Italy. Hence Foucault's "utterly confused category": buggery and sodomy would seem to be part of, but might also simply denominate, a category of undifferentiated debauchery that included acts that we would call "homosexual" *and* "heterosexual" as well as behavior that could be deemed sacrilegious or a challenge to political authority and cultural purity.

But if Restoration and eighteenth-century sodomy was only "a category of forbidden acts" and their perpetrator "nothing more than the juridical subject of them," as Foucault suggests (*History* 43), in what way is either sodomy or the sodomite a subject for gay studies? As Carol S. Vance has asked of historically engaged gay research, "Is there an 'it' to study" (22)? The short answer is yes—and no. Yes, because while *buggery* and *sodomy*, especially in religious and legal texts, could and did denote a "confused category" of acts, in many other sources we find increasing evidence of a more narrow and specific usage, a usage in which these words refer first and foremost to sexual contact between two males; likewise, *sodomite* comes to refer specifically to a man who engages in a sexual act with another man. Indeed, as we shall see, the image of a male desiring another male gains a surprising cultural prominence during this period; like Sedley's debauchery, this image seems to come into "open day" to be witnessed by a "thousand people." And yet no, because we would be mistaken if we thought, therefore, that this move toward specificity had the result of making *sodomite* identical to *homosexual*, let alone *gay*.

To return one last time to Pepys's diary entry: even in this short passage about one incident we can discern a movement from the general to the particular in that, what starts out as a discussion of a general kind of debauchery ends up as a discussion of particular acts between masters and their pages. But what is the relationship between these two things? Are Pepys, Mennes, and Batten suggesting that masters buggering their pages is of a piece with Sedley's drunken behavior, or is it something different? And if different, is it different in *kind*, or only in *degree*? In other words, even as we note the growing number of specific references to sex between males at the end of the seventeenth and beginning of the eighteenth centuries, we should not lose sight of the "confused" background against which these references take place by too readily attributing a modern system of sexuality to the past. For it is this "background" that constitutes the system of signification within which representations of sodomy and of the sodomite were produced, circulated, and intelligible. Thus, unlike most of the gay historiography of the Restoration and eighteenth century (discussed below), this study does not begin with the assumption that the increased discursive presence of the sodomite during this period necessarily indicates the emergence of a proto-modern "homosexual identity," since such an assumption generally entails a movement toward decontextualization by which "sexuality" becomes separated from the political and cultural structures which inevitably produce and maintain it; instead, this study seeks to examine the diverse, though interconnected, ways that *sodomy* and *sodomite* were made to signify.

That is the short answer to Carol S. Vance's question; the remainder of this introduction will offer a more detailed consideration of whether there is an "it" to study, and of what "it" might be. I shall first consider a theoretical issue central to historical gay studies: the essentialism/constructionism debate. I shall then offer a brief survey of the most important gay historiography of the Restoration and eighteenth century. This work has focused almost exclusively either on recuperating a gay past hitherto "hidden from history," or on the emergence of a "homosexual subculture" and a "homosexual identity." Stimulating and archivally rich, this historical work has brought to light a number of documents that have established gay studies as a viable field of enquiry in the period. However, questions about the complexities of representation in these documents have yet to be more fully addressed. On the one hand, recuperative historiography, by positing a past that is not appreciably different from the present, assumes that *sodomy* and *sodomite* are always categories entirely obvious and known; one need not, therefore, examine these categories of representation themselves. On the other hand, the study of an emerging subculture, while often committed to demonstrating the alterity of the past, just as often naturalizes that alterity by constructing a teleological narrative of the gradual attainment of an integrated homosexual identity in which the Restoration figures as an originary moment of homosexuality "as we know it today," to borrow Eve Sedgwick's phrase (*Epistemology*, 44). Again, the range of meanings which *sodomy* and *sodomite* may set in motion is reduced to one. Finally, I shall suggest that the identity-inflected enquiry which presently characterizes gay studies of the Restoration and eighteenth century has precipitated a somewhat questionable means of reading historical documents that invites us to endorse homophobically charged depictions of male-male desire as a "gay heritage worth celebrating" (Norton 262), as the glass through which we might see ourselves, however darkly. On the basis of these criticisms, I shall outline the goals of this study and its means of proceeding, arguing for the necessity of moving away from the limiting discussion of selves and an abstracted sexuality to a more historically engaged discussion of representation and the social production and circulation of meaning.

Essentialism vs. Constructionism

It has been customary, though perhaps less so of late, to place discussions of the history of homosexuality within the theoretical frame

of the so-called "essentialist/social constructionist debate." As Jim
Ellis has observed, the ritual of invoking the essentialist/social constructionist debate "has mutated into a ritual of observing the ritual,
a weird sort of metaritual whose ultimate goal is to dismiss the necessity of going through the debate one more time" (175). My own discussion, I fear, falls into this second category, with the exception,
however, that it is undertaken with the knowledge that the debate is
likely to be with us always, even if only in some spectral form.
Variously characterized as "the hottest philosophical controversy to
hit psychology in years" (Weinrich 157), as "increasingly arid and
false" (Weeks 199), as "a controversy raging among those who study
the history of gay people" (Boswell, "Revolutions" 19), and as having
"outlived its usefulness" (Epstein 241), the essentialist/social constructionist debate would seem to engage precisely the question of
what "it" is we are studying. What is at stake is whether there is a
pure, natural, essential homosexuality that exists across history available for study, or whether the hetero/homo distinction is so modern
a regime of knowledge that it has no currency prior to the nineteenth-century sexological discourse which constructed it and
thereby constituted the very identities it purports to represent.[3] My
purpose in rehearsing the terms of the debate—or rather, impasse—
is not to adjudicate them and thus conclude the standoff, though it
will be plain where my sympathies rest. As Eve Sedgwick has per-
suasively, if dismally, argued, "such adjudication is impossible to the
degree that a conceptual deadlock between the two opposing views
has by now been built into the very structure of every theoretical tool
we have for undertaking it" (*Epistemology* 40). What I wish to stress,
however, is that coherent intervention (within the existing terms) is
also impossible to the degree that, in critical practice, the debate—
if we can even use that term—does *not* take such diametrically
opposed forms. Steven Epstein has argued that both essentialist and
constructionist views often exist oddly side by side in what he calls
the "folk understandings" of homosexuality:

> In a recent letter to Ann Landers, "Worried in Montana"
> expresses concern that her fourteen-year-old son may be

"seduced" into homosexuality (folk constructionism) by the boy's friend, who she has "no question" is gay, because of his "feminine mannerisms" (folk essentialism). Ann reassures the mother that the only way her son would turn out to be gay is if "the seeds of homosexuality were already present" (folk essentialism). At the same time, she questions the mother's certainty about the sexual orientation of the friend, claiming that it is "presumptuous" to label a fourteen-year-old as "gay" (folk constructionism). (242)

A similar, if more sophisticated, co-mingling of "essentialism" and "constructionism" exists in discussions of historical gay studies, especially those of the Restoration and eighteenth century. Indeed, the whole "debate" has become something of a Möbius loop in which one can sometimes hardly tell one side from the other, a fact which gives credence to Diana Fuss's claim that "essentialism underwrites theories of constructionism and that constructionism operates as a more sophisticated form of essentialism" (119).

The motive behind early attempts to write a "history of homosexuality"—a motive which clearly still exists—is encapsulated in the title of the collection of essays edited by Martin Duberman, Martha Vicinus, and George Chauncey, Jr.: *Hidden From History: Reclaiming the Gay and Lesbian Past* (1989). In their introduction, Duberman, Vicinus, and Chauncey sum up the goals of a humanistically oriented "homosexual history":

> Because the history of homosexuality has been denied or ignored, . . . gay people's hunger for knowledge of their past is strong. Having struggled to create a public presence for themselves in the world today, they seek to reclaim their historical presence. For many, gay history . . . helps women and men validate and understand who they are by showing them who they have been. (12)

Books like Noel I. Garde's *Jonathan to Gide* (1964), W. H. Kayy's *The Gay Geniuses* (1965), and A. L. Rowse's *Homosexuals in History*

(1977) first attempted to satisfy this "hunger for knowledge" by providing anecdotal narratives of a variety of historical personages ranging across two millennia. Neither very scholarly nor critical, these studies adopted an uncomplicated notion of what might count as "historical presence" and presupposed an unchanging, transhistorical homosexual type with whom readers might easily identify. "As an historian," Rowse writes, "it has always been my aim to get as close as possible to the lives of human beings, lay my finger on pulse and heart" (xii). As histories, these books have been justly dismissed as being *a*historical and anachronistic, even naïve.[4]

Subsequent attempts to write a history of this kind were more successful. John Boswell's remarkable *Christianity, Social Tolerance and Homosexuality* (1980), for example, raised the historical study of homosexuality to a stunning level of erudition and was instrumental in establishing the field as one of serious, scholarly enquiry. Nevertheless, Boswell's study remained vulnerable to the same objection as the earlier studies; subtitled *Gay People in Western Europe from the Beginning of the Christian Era to the Fourteenth Century*, Boswell's work argued that all Western societies have been made up of "gay people" and "non-gay people," and defined as gay any "who are conscious of erotic inclination toward their own gender as a distinguishing characteristic" (44)—though Boswell later decided that consciousness of this inclination as a distinguishing characteristic was not necessary ("Categories" 137 n.8). In a telling aside, Boswell notes that "the term 'sodomy' (*sodomia*) has been excluded from this study, since it is so vague and ambiguous as to be virtually useless (*Christianity* 93 n.2). Thus, despite its huge scholarly machinery, Boswell's study, like the earlier ones, still set out to write the history of something which was seen to be essentially outside of history, an unchanging, permanent "gay" essence.[5]

In 1968, Mary McIntosh had offered an alternate method of proceeding in her pioneering article "The Homosexual Role." Targeting medical conceptions of homosexuality, McIntosh argued that homosexuality in modern society is not an innate, or even acquired, *condition*, but a social *role*, a set of generally held expectations and assumptions. The crucial points McIntosh made were that, first, the "homosexual role" was a historically specific construction not evident before the end of the seventeenth century, and, second, that this role and the expectations which constitute it could exist and circulate regardless of whether any of these expectations were actually met. For example, McIntosh noted the disparity between the assumptions concerning the "homosexual role" (a fixed identity which marks people of exclusively homosexual desires) and Alfred Kinsey's findings concerning actual sexual behavior (188–92).[6] Perhaps, then, McIntosh suggested, the "homosexual role" which historians, sociologists and psychologists took as their starting point should itself be the object of study. How and why was it constructed? What purpose does it serve? Unfortunately, McIntosh's observations seemed to receive little attention until they were revived by historians influenced by the first volume of Michel Foucault's *History of Sexuality*. Arguing against the traditional notion that a "natural" sexual diversity is everywhere repressed by social restrictions, Foucault asserted that, since the eighteenth century, social practices and institutions have multiplied continually the forms of sexual expression, solidifying them "scientifically" into disparate categories:

> Through the various discourses, legal sanctions against minor perversions were multiplied; sexual irregularity was annexed to mental illness; from childhood to old age, a norm of sexual development was defined and all the possible deviations were carefully described. . . . The machinery of power that focused on this whole alien strain did not aim to suppress it, but rather to give it an analytical, visible, and permanent reality. (36, 44)

The point of Foucault's genealogical critique was to expose the power structures which were served by designating as "natural" (or "unnatural") those identity categories which were actually the *effects* of social institutions and discursive practices. Like McIntosh, Foucault advocated not the examination of the essential truths of sexual identity, but rather an examination of the structures that produced the category "sexual identity." Particularly galvanizing for gay studies was Foucault's assertion that the birth of homosexuality as an

identity could be dated as having occurred in 1870, a construction
of late nineteenth-century scientific and medical discourses:

> As defined by the ancient civil or canonical codes, sodomy
> was a category of forbidden acts; their perpetrator was noth-
> ing more than the juridical subject of them. The nineteenth-
> century homosexual became a personage, a past, a case his-
> tory, and a childhood, in addition to being a type of life, a life
> form, and a morphology, with an indiscreet anatomy and pos-
> sibly a mysterious physiology. Nothing that went into his total
> composition was unaffected by his sexuality. It was every-
> where present in him. . . . The sodomite had been a tempo-
> rary aberration; the homosexual was now a species.   (43)

It would be difficult to overestimate the influence of Foucault on
gay studies. But within the terms of the essentialist/social constructionist debate and its focus on selfhood, that influence has often taken
a limiting and insular form, and the radical thrust of Foucault's—and
McIntosh's—arguments has been ignored. Instead, since Foucault
made the above statement, a great deal of gay historiography has been
attempting to offer a more precise dating of what Sedgwick calls "The
Great Paradigm Shift" (*Epistemology* 44), a more exacting narrative of
the development and establishment of a "homosexual identity." In
order to do this, historians have generally assumed a correlation
between an identified group and personal identity and have thus
sought evidence of "homosexual subcultures." Using this method,
Alan Bray, Randolph Trumbach, Leo J. Boon, Theo van der Meer,
and Michel Rey, among others, have moved the conceptual shift
which Foucault places in the nineteenth century back to the end of
the seventeenth century, where Mary McIntosh had originally placed
it. James Saslow and Guido Ruggiero, however, have moved it even
farther back and have argued for the existence of subcultures and of
an identity in the Renaissance: "Renaissance terms for homosexuality," Saslow writes, "imply a nexus of ideas amounting to a rudimen-
tary psychological theory" ("Homosexuality" 97). And, examining a
poem by Richard of Devizes, Warren Johansson has argued for the

existence of a homosexual subculture in medieval London. "[T]he 'gay subculture' of the large cities of the twentieth century," writes Johansson, "is not a new creation, but grows out of many centuries of subterranean history. That the London of 1192 was not very different from the London of 1982 should give students of social history a fresh incentive for uncovering traces of the continuity of the sexual underground in Western Europe" (162).

We would seem, then, bizarrely, to have come back, even via constructionism, to John Boswell's medieval "gay people." This is the circular trap of the essentialist/constructionist debate and of the identity-inflected research it encourages. If the debate has been found wanting, if it has unproductively circled back upon itself, it is because essentialism v. constructionism has too frequently structured enquiry as though the only question to be asked is when did a recognizable homosexual identity "emerge." As such, all enquiry within the terms of this debate operates on a system of presence or absence; its touchstone, its referent, is inevitably, on *both* sides, an essentialized homosexual identity which is said either to exist, to be "emerging," or not yet to exist. Thus while histories which document the "emergence" of *the homosexual* would seem to de-essentialize that sign by marking it as historically specific, the word *emergence* marks it as having always been there awaiting complete expression. For example, Alan Bray, at the beginning of his enormously—and justly—influential *Homosexuality in Renaissance England* (1982) states that to "talk of an individual in this period as being or not being 'a homosexual' is an anachronism and ruinously misleading" (16). Yet the argument with which Bray later supports this statement is that there was a "cleavage . . . between an individual's behavior and his awareness of its significance," and he goes on to warn historians to "be watchful for signs, however difficult to detect, that for someone involved in a homosexual relationship the nature of that relationship might not have been as obvious to him as it is to them" (68). The we-all-know-what-that-means tone of this passage effectively reinstalls the essentialized homosexual identity that Bray is supposedly trying to dismantle. The problem with the essentialist/constructionist debate and its unwillingness, or inability, to relinquish the minoritizing (to use Sedgwick's term) focus on a normative identity category—which is "there," or not yet "there"—is that it can prevent us from asking questions about the "larger" social processes that invest terms like *homosexual, sodomite, lesbian,* and *gay* not only with personal meaning but also with social and historical meaning, questions about how these terms operate, and how they intersect with other social structures that produce meaning. In other words, the search for identity's emergence can prevent us from asking questions about representation and the way that representational practices order the world. The tendency to appeal to an abstracted, self-defining homosexuality is nowhere more present, more persistent, than in gay studies of the Restoration and the eighteenth century, and it is to this work that I now turn.

GAY STUDIES AND THE EIGHTEENTH CENTURY

Margaret Hunt offers the following description of the metanarrative which often structures historical gay studies:

> the standard narrative of the history of homosexuality in the West (perhaps most visible in "history of homosexuality" or "introduction to lesbian/gay studies" courses) still sees the Greeks as confusing teases, treats everything up through the early modern period as foreplay, finally gets down to it with Whitman and Havelock Ellis, and climaxes with the Mattachine Society and the Stonewall riots. (361)

Hunt's sexual metaphor is not merely witty; it accurately captures the emphasis on teleology that directs, explicitly or implicitly, the research which focuses on homosexual subcultures and identity. In exemplary Darwinian fashion, Homosexual Identity emerges from a primordial confusion, struggles for definition, and finally and inevitably attains its integrated and idealized modern form: sodomite becomes molly becomes invert becomes homosexual becomes gay. Within this narrative, the Restoration and eighteenth century have assumed pivotal and foundational status as that point at which homosexuality shuffled off its cloak of confusion to don the garment of recognizable modernity. "[A] profound shift occurred in the conceptualization and practice of male homosexual behaviour" (Trumbach "Sodomitical Subcultures" 118); "the early eighteenth century marked a basic watershed in the conceptualization of homosexuality" (Dynes xvi); compared to only fifty years before, this period "is brilliantly different" (Bray 80). The premise that a radical change occurred in the organization of same-sex sexuality at the start of the eighteenth century has given rise to a great deal of historical research—statistical studies of judicial restraints,[7] the examination of particular individuals (Lord Hervey, for example) or groups (court circles, university clubs),[8] and, most prominently, the documenting of the emergence of a visible homosexual subculture (discussed below).

There is no doubt that this research has been profitable. Not only has it established gay studies as an important field of enquiry in eighteenth-century studies, but the excellent archival research of scholars like G. S. Rousseau, Michael S. Kimmel, and Randolph Trumbach has proven enabling to everyone working in the field. Nevertheless, the combination of an emphasis on a radical conceptual shift and the pressures of an aggressively teleological framework has led to a number of interrelated problems which may be said to characterize gay research of the period. Paradoxical though it may seem, it is exactly in documenting what is supposedly so specific to the Restoration and eighteenth century that historians have reified an abstracted and essentialized homosexuality. The intense preoccupation with the dramatic emergence of a specific, visible subculture and a proto-modern identity has carried with it the assumption that the preceding diffuse, more "confused" structures of sexuality were eclipsed and rendered obsolete. But it is precisely this conception of eclipse and supersession that enables the normative, teleological narrative described above to chart the inevitability of homosexuality "as we know it today." The extent to which historians have appealed to a pure, original, genuine homosexuality which lies outside of its cultural articulation, even while attempting to document a "profound shift" in that cultural articulation, will be clear if we consider some specific examples.

Before turning to these examples, let me stress that the questions I shall raise here are not meant as a repudiation of the work of these historians. My own work is, clearly, dependent upon and enable by theirs; that is, their work provides the conditions of possibility for me to pose the questions I wish to explore.

The bursting into visibility of a distinct "homosexual subculture" has been most extensively written about by Randolph Trumbach and Alan Bray and, in a popular rather than scholarly mode, by Rictor Norton. Although each of these writers brings his own distinctive approach, they are, ultimately, engaged in a similar project and, therefore, they all present us with a similar problem. Because each of these historians is, in his own way, attempting to document the cultural *visibility* of homosexuality in this period, they each necessarily operate with a fixed and abstract notion of what "homosexuality" is: that is, they know what they are *looking* for. Further, being able to *see* "homosexuality" depends upon the idea that textual representation is nothing but the transmission, reflection, reproduction of the "real" world. As Joan Scott has cogently argued, when "evidence" is

> conceived through a metaphor of visibility or in any other way that takes meaning as transparent, [it] reproduces rather than contests given ideological systems. . . . [T]he project of making experience visible precludes critical examination of the workings of the ideological system itself, its categories of representation, . . . its premises about what these categories mean and how they operate.   (400)

The metaphor of visibility can preclude the examination of representational practices and of the politics of representation.

Randolph Trumbach has argued, over a number of articles, for the emergence of a sophisticated sodomitical subculture in early eighteenth-century London, a subculture complete with identified walkways and parks, gestures by which men might signal their interests to each other, and meeting places—called "molly houses"—where "mollies" could gather in relative safety. Trumbach cites contemporary accounts which indicate that the patrons of molly houses often used a specialized argot and engaged in deviant, effeminate behavior: the use of feminine names, mock-marriages, mock-births, and transvestism. In order to analyze this effeminate subculture, Trumbach has developed what he calls an anthropological approach, drawing on studies of same-sex relations in several non-European societies. This approach seems initially to be promising, offering, one would think, the kind of concrete cultural context for analysis that would resist assimilation into a normalizing narrative. Indeed, Trumbach himself writes that "we ought to study the historical forms of sexual behaviour . . . because sexual behaviour (perhaps more than religion) is the most highly symbolic activity of any society. To penetrate to the symbolic system implicit in any society's sexual behavior is therefore to come closest to the heart of its uniqueness" ("London's Sodomites" 24).

Trumbach argues that the ethnocentric and moralistic bias of many anthropologists has prevented them from noticing that Western European society has been unique in objecting to all forms of homosexual behavior ("London's Sodomites" 1–9). Outside of Western Europe, sexual relations between men were allowed for in one of two ways:

> Other world cultures allowed adult men to take the "dominant" role in homosexual acts without stigmatizing them in any way or denying them access to women. But males who took the passive role were allowed to do so only if in either the temporary status of boy or adolescent or the permanent adult status of transvestite. ("Sodomitical Subcultures" 115)

However, Trumbach understands Western Europe to be unique only in its objections to forms of homosexual behavior, not in the forms themselves. Although enacted within an illicit subculture, "Western homosexual behavior," he states, "has *always operated within the terms of the two worldwide patterns*" ("Gender" 151; my emphasis). Trumbach ascribes to same-sex relations a universal structure which asserts itself whether it is allowed a licit place in culture or not. In the 1660s, '70s, and '80s, he argues, sodomy was the province of the libertine rake who enjoyed sexual relations with both women and adolescent males. Sodomitical rakes were not at all effeminate in their behavior or dress and, far from being held in contempt, "they were secretly held in awe for the extremity of their masculine self-assertion" ("Birth" 131). By the end of the century, however, sodomy was associated not with the assertive, masculine libertine but with the effeminate molly who was presumed to have a total lack of interest in women, and who was consistently connected with transvestism. In the emergence of the molly-house subculture, then, Trumbach sees a shift from the adult/adolescent model of homosexual relations to the transvestite model, albeit a transvestite model which did not allow for an unstigmatized active partner.

To understand this shift from one worldwide pattern to the other, Trumbach asserts that the emergence of the effeminate molly must be considered within the broader context of gender roles in general. In other cultures with an adult male transvestite role, he tells us, that figure serves as a bridge between male and female roles where those roles are not greatly differentiated. The emergence of the English molly "would therefore indicate that male and female roles had begun to grow more nearly equal. This is confirmed by the development at that time of the companionate marriage and the domesticated family" ("Birth" 140). Yet, what Trumbach presents here as cultural analysis seems to be rather a necessity which he himself infers from the presumed universal structure of same-sex sexuality. For even setting aside the assumption that the "companionate marriage" and "domesticated family" might mark a flowering of gender equality, Trumbach's own argument would rather seem to suggest a climate in which gender roles became more rigidly separated, in which it became culturally impossible to imagine a masculine male desiring another male. However, what Trumbach does draw our attention to, importantly, is that the representations of sodomy and of the sodomite in the late seventeenth and early eighteenth centuries are fissured, disjunctive, are not easily reducible to the status of documentation of a stable social reality. For example, what difference does it make if we note that sodomitical rakes appear only in poetry which, at least initially, circulated within a small coterie while "descriptions" of the mollies circulated widely within the popular press? Why is it that masculine, sodomitical rakes are almost invariably represented as aristocratic and the effeminate mollies are almost invariably represented as middle or lower-middle class? What questions about the production and reception of texts and about the ways in which class and sexuality intersect do we need to ask?

Alan Bray's *Homosexuality in Renaissance England* has proven to be a productive foundation for some of the most interesting gay and lesbian work now being done in Renaissance studies.[9] It has not yet, however, proven to be as enabling for Restoration and eighteenth-century studies. Like Randolph Trumbach, Bray also documents a radical change in the social forms and institutions of homosexuality at the end of the seventeenth century. And, like Trumbach, Bray describes the emergence of a sodomitical subculture. Unlike Trumbach, however, Bray, obviously influenced by Foucault, concentrates for the most part on an analysis of the terms and categories of signification through which the sodomite was represented. This would seem to be precisely the sort of study that I am advocating (and, indeed, it is), but it is also precisely the kind of study that Bray seems to abandon when he arrives at the end of the seventeenth century.

Covering a much larger historical period than Trumbach, Bray argues that in Elizabethan and early Stuart England, references to sodomy usually appear in conjunction with references to other forms of "sexual excess"—incest, adultery, rape. The reason for this grouping, Bray argues, is that sodomy formed only one part of a general notion of debauchery and sin—a temptation to which everyone was potentially subject because of his or her fallen nature. Most interestingly, Bray notes that references to sodomy often appear in distinctly other-worldly contexts; sodomites were frequently linked together with werewolves, sorcerers, and basilisks (19–25). The sodomite was part of "the symbolic universe of Elizabethan and Stuart England" (21). Within this symbolic universe, Bray argues, sodomy "was not a part of the chain of being, or the harmony of the created world, or its universal dance. . . . It was none of these things because it was not conceived of as part of the created order at all; it was part of its dissolution" (25). The sodomite thus represented a principle of demonic disorder. So extreme was the apocalyptic characterization of the sodomite that Bray suggests that it was unlikely that people who actually engaged in or observed "homosexual" behavior ever made any cognitive connection between their behavior or perceptions and the demonic figure of the sodomite which appeared in sermons, tracts, and pamphlets (67–70).

I have already noted how Bray actually deploys a normative idea of homosexual identity even while denying it existed. As Elizabeth Pittenger notes, the mental closet which Bray presupposes for his Renaissance subjects is a curious one since at some level he has had to put them there first (167). What this closet does enable, though, is the spectacular "outing" of homosexuality which Bray performs when his study reaches the Restoration and eighteenth century. Now we discover that, with the emergence of the molly-house subculture, "the picture is radically different" (80); the homosexual "could not avoid knowing . . . what he was" (93): "while the archetypal figure in which the Elizabethans and Jacobeans embodied their ideas of homosexuality had little direct relation to the *facts* of social life, this was by no means true of the molly: that figure was part of everyday experience" (109; my emphasis). In the passage just quoted, we see that Bray posits a disjunction between the "facts" of social life and the form in which they are given representation—for the Renaissance. Restoration and eighteenth-century accounts of male-male desire, in contrast, appear as accurate, empirical accounts. It is true that the discourse of sex at the end of the seventeenth century, like a great many other discourses, became more secular. But why should a secular discourse suddenly indicate a direct and transparent correspondence between word and object? Why should a secular discourse have no "symbolic" force? Bray does say that the last chapter of his book, the one which deals with the Restoration and eighteenth century, "is not put forward as a complete description" (10), and it is Bray's own persuasive critical acuteness, demonstrated elsewhere in his book, that stimulates the examination of the ways in which the secularized sodomite remained part of a "symbolic universe."

The last work I turn to, Rictor Norton's *Mother Clap's Molly House: The Gay Subculture in England, 1700–1830*, is the least scholarly, most popular of the works here examined. It demonstrates neither Trumbach's breadth of research nor Bray's analytical adeptness. I choose to include it, however, because it throws into such sharp relief the problems involved in ignoring the complexities of representation. Norton's study clearly situates itself within a metaphor of visibility, its aim being to "look back through the veil of repression, and discover a gay heritage worth celebrating" (262). As the word "gay" indicates, Norton is concerned with finding in the eighteenth century a homosexual subculture which closely approximates (his) ideas of a gay community which might exist today—and he finds "evidence" of it everywhere: "As early as 1703 the mollies seem to have overrun the city" (117). But it is precisely Norton's relation to the "evidence," and his discussion of it, which reveals the legerdemain involved in the project of documenting the *visibility* of "homosexuality" in the past and positing the emergence of an "identity." The problems become clear in the book's brief introductory section: "I am more interested in how the mollies lived than what people thought about them. . . . Almost all our evidence about homosexuals during this period was written by people who hated homosexuality" (12–13).

If these texts were not written by the mollies themselves (not that that would necessarily make them more "accurate"), by what means does Norton separate "how the mollies lived" from "what people thought about them"? How does he distinguish between what is "description" and what is "bias"? Comparing descriptions of molly houses, Norton asserts that Ned Ward's entry "Of the Mollies Club" in *The Secret History of Clubs* offers us "more trustworthy evidence" than can be found in other accounts (97). But how has he made this distinction? *Is* it "more trustworthy"? One might think the fact that *The Secret History of Clubs* also includes an account of "The Farting Club" should give us pause.

Norton does point out one useful detail: the evidence of same-sex desire is never far removed from the evidence of homophobia. This alone might make us stop and think before we naturalize historically distant representations of such desire as transparent and inevitable. For when we do so, what other structures are we allowing to stand uncontested?

Sodomitical Practices

If the foregoing makes anything evident, it is, I hope, that the following study will not approach the sodomite as an uncomplicated forerunner of the homosexual. Nor will this study make any programmatic statements about what sodomy and the sodomite *were*, no statements like "the sodomite equals 'x.' " Thus what is to be examined is not *sodomy* and *sodomite* in and of themselves (whatever they were), but what I shall call, borrowing a phrase from Ned Ward's "Of the Mollies Club," *sodomitical practices*.

Unlike Ward, the sodomitical practices I shall be examining are representational practices—the nexus of ideas, relations, behaviors, discursive practices, and meanings that could be set in motion under these signs. It will not be my goal to assess the "truth" of these representations (an impossible task in any case); rather, I am interested in examining the cultural work which these representations performed. A more adequate examination of the diverse meanings which *sodomy* and *sodomite* could be made to bear would render the idea of the radical rupture less plausible by showing how a continuing "confusion" inheres in apparent "specificity;" it would also return these terms to the specific cultural and political worlds in which they were made to signify in order to show how meaning is controlled. In this respect, the study of sodomitical practices is enabled by Foucault's *History of Sexuality*; for it was Foucault who first indicated the "confusion" of the term *sodomy*, that it was not a self-evident category, but that it was discursively constituted and reconstituted and that these discursive formations enabled specific, often violent, political structures. My use of Foucault, however, is not dogmatic. For example, unlike Foucault, I will argue that one could "be" a sodomite, that the term did indicate an identity, at least inasmuch as people were *identified* as such. That is to say that sodomite indicated a social, though not necessarily a personal, identity: like "fop" or "witwoud," sodomite indicated a social type. But this is not to reinstate the proto-homosexual. For if one "was" a sodomite, that is not all one "was." The sexual aspect of the term fails to be exhaustive because the term itself encompasses so much more. Thus the point is not simply that one could "be" (called) a sodomite, but that one could "be" (called) a sodomite *and* an anarchist *and* a papist *and* a threat to trade. To study sodomitical practices is to study how these various concepts intersect, displace, and define each other, to realize, as Jonathan Goldberg has pointed out, "sexuality is only phantasmatically cordoned off to some private sphere; in truth, sexuality structures and destructures the social" (*Queering* 6). To study sodomitical practices is also to realize that the structuring and destructuring of the social is a struggle that takes place in and for representation, and to insist on the productive nature of discourse. The study of sodomitical practices is also enabled by the work of scholars from areas other than Restoration and eighteenth-century studies. Renaissance studies has been particularly rich in this respect. Despite my earlier criticisms, Alan Bray's *Homosexuality and Renaissance England* remains an essential starting point, and Bray's arguments have been expanded and refined in such fine studies as Jonathan Goldberg's *Sodometries: Renaissance Texts, Modern Sexualities* and Gregory W. Bredbeck's *Sodomy and Interpretation: Marlowe to Milton*. These works have begun to detail the ways in which *sodomy* is implicated in the various "spheres of cultural production" in the Renaissance, as Goldberg puts it (23), and vice versa; that is, they have begun to elucidate the complex ways in which the discourse of sodomy is inextricably bound up in the discourse of cultural order and intelligibility. As Bredbeck points out, the discursive " 'space' of sodomy is, in actuality, coterminous with a vast range of other terms of 'difference' within culture" (89). My study is also indebted to Jonathan Dollimore's *Sexual Dissidence* and to his astute explication in that book of how the concept of perversion is integral to the concept of order itself.

Treating the "emergence" of a secularized sodomite and of the molly at the end of the seventeenth and beginning of the eighteenth centuries as a discursive event is not, as some may protest or fear, to argue for a kind of linguistic determinism. Nor is it to evacuate from the field of study that which may be said to constitute it by asserting that male-male desire is simply a phantasm of language. As Joan Scott points out, subject positions, "social types," are discursively produced "and experience is a linguistic event (it doesn't happen outside established meanings), but neither is it confined to a fixed order of meaning" (409). Discursive systems are never self-identical: there are contradictions *between* them and contradictions *within* them which render them "vulnerable to appropriation, transformation, and reincorporation in new configurations" (Dollimore 87). The discursive system which repudiates sodomy as foreign and simultaneously laments its supposed proliferation, for example, ultimately produces what, in its own terms, should not exist: the domestic sodomite. It thus "affords the opportunity for transgression *in and of its own terms*; transgression is in part enabled by the very logic which would prevent it" (Dollimore 88; original emphasis). This is to say that sodomitical practices constitute the discursive field within sodomitical desire can be, not simply excoriated, but also articulated.

This will sound like Foucault's conception of "reverse discourse." Foucault argues that we should not "imagine a world of discourse divided between accepted discourse and excluded discourse" (*History* 100). However, he continues, "discourse can be both an instrument and an effect of power, but also a hindrance, a stumbling-block, a point of resistance and a starting point for an opposing strategy":

> There is no question that the appearance in nineteenth-century psychiatry, jurisprudence, and literature of a whole series of discourses on the species and subspecies of homosexuality . . . made possible a strong advance of social controls into this area of "perversity"; but it also made possible the formation of a "reverse" discourse: homosexuality began to speak in it own behalf, to demand that its legitimacy or "naturality" be acknowledged, often in the same vocabulary, using the same categories by which it was medically disqualified. There is not, on the one side, a discourse of power, and opposite it, another discourse that runs counter to it.   (101)

I am not suggesting, however, that such a fully developed reverse discourse existed in the eighteenth century. We do not find the sodomite and the molly speaking on their own behalf, demanding they be accepted. What we do find, instead, are occasions when the demarcation, the distinction, between the representer and the represented, between the observer and the observed, between subject and object begins to blur, to collapse. This is less a reverse discourse than what Jonathan Dollimore would term a "transgressive reinscription," a repetition of conventional categories of representation which simultaneously displaces conventional understandings of them and allows for new meanings (33, 285–306). Transgressive reinscription is, in Dollimore's words, a kind of "return of the repressed and/or suppressed and/or displaced" which moves male-male desire "from the margins to the centre, from construction to presence but a presence still in terms of, or working in terms of, the initial construction" (33, 227).

This movement "from construction to presence but a presence still in terms of . . . the initial construction" is, in miniature, the trajectory pursued in the following pages through an examination of the representation of the sodomite. Chapter 1 will trace the discursive emergence of the sodomite as a secularized social type in the late seventeenth and early eighteenth centuries, drawing on a variety of texts in order to chart a rhetoric of sodomitical practices. The chapter proceeds through a series of binary oppositions that are typically invoked in the ordering of the social world. Chapter 2 examines the way that these sodomitical practices are deployed—often incoherently—at times of social upheaval. Focusing on works by Rochester, Thomas Gordon, the *Poems on Affairs of State*, and some anonymous works, this chapter argues that the development of a secularized vision of the sodomite provided a compelling figure onto which a variety of social anxieties could be displaced. Thus, the sodomite is often made to bear a meaning that is only partly sexual and appears, instead, as a refigured and condensed representation of a variety of class, economic, and political transgressions. This is only possible, I will suggest, because the very conception of the sodomite is always already implicated in these other types of transgression. Focusing on works by Smollett, Chapter 3 looks at the instabilities within the discursive field of sodomitical practices that make transgressive reinscription possible. Repeatedly shunned and repudiated in Smollett's work, the sodomite nevertheless repeatedly returns as the object of a fascinated representation across Smollett's *oeuvre*. I argue here that the depiction of the sodomite can become the focus of the very desire it means to police and negate. My final chapter offers a startling example of transgressive reinscription in an extended reading of John Cleland's *Memoirs of a Woman of Pleasure*. Reading this "classic" of hetero-eroticism back through its sodomitical scene, I show how the novel offers its reader a position from which to engage in homoerotic fantasy by eliciting from the reader what we might call the sodomitical "gaze."

The following pages represent a number of attempts; or, more precisely, in the following pages I attempt to do a number of things. First, this study is an attempt to expand the discussion of sodomy in the Restoration and early eighteenth century beyond the context of the "molly house subculture"; it is an attempt to open up discussion and, more simply, to open discussion. Second, I have attempted to strike a balance between amassing textual examples of sodomitical practices and avoiding tedious repetition. What this probably means is that some readers will wish there was a greater iteration of detail and others will wish that there was less than there is; however, I have tried, particularly in chapter 1, to provide a relatively broad base of textual evidence. Finally, I began this introduction with Pepys's uncertainty about what buggery could possibly mean; the following pages will attempt to offer some answers.

Chapter One
Sodomitical Practices

This Sin [is] *being now Translated from the* Sadomitical [*sic*] *Original, or from the* Turkish *and* Italian *Copies into* English.

—The Tryal and Condemnation of Mervin,
Lord Audley, Earl of Castle-Haven, 1699

The
PLAY
of
SODOM,
A
TRAGEDY.
As it was lately Acted on the Stage of *France*, and now occasionally Translated into *English*

—Title-page of *The Play of Sodom*, 1707

Gabriel Lawrence was indicted for committing, with *Thomas Newton*, aged thirty Years, the heinous and detestable Sin of Sodomy, not to be named among Christians.

—Select Trials at the Sessions-House in the Old-Bailey, 1742

HISTORICALLY, THE representation of sodomy has been marked by nothing so much as sodomy's troubled relationship to representation itself. Represented as unrepresentable, named as that which cannot be named, sodomy is *peccatum illud horribile, inter christianos non nominandum*—the horrible crime not to be named among Christians, even when, as we see above, it is named.[1] "It is the Action of a *Man* to *beget* a *Child*, but it is the Act of a *Beast*, nay worse, to _____ I scorn to stain my Paper with the Mention," writes one eighteenth-century pamphleteer (*Plain Reasons* 23), employing a construction that John Stirling in his *System of Rhetoric* (1733) designates as "aposiopesis" and describes as follows: "*Aposiopesis* leaves imperfect Sense;/ Yet such a silent Pause speaks Eloquence" (7).[2]

Denied in its assertion, asserted in its denial, sodomy would seem to confound the "orderly" workings of representation, particularly in light of the late seventeenth-century project of stabilizing and clarifying verbal representation so that there might be a direct transference of "the Trayne of our Thoughts, into a Trayne of Words," as Hobbes put it (101)—a project summed up by Thomas Sprat in *The History of the Royal Society* (1667) as the delivering of "so many *things*, almost in an equal number of *words*" (in Vickers 172). Into this harmonious system where thoughts, things, and words all correspond, sodomy is an interloper, a *translation*, the origin of which seems at first to be, predictably, France, Italy, or Turkey. But even in those places sodomy is only an *act*, a *copy*: the "Sadomitical Original" is without location, is in fact unlocatable precisely because sodomy was thought to be outside the order signified by the general correspondence of thoughts, things, words, and locations. *Sodomy* signifies confusion by confusing signification.

As the enactor of disorder, the sodomite was a conduit for the chaos beyond representation, "the point of entry into civilization," as Dollimore puts it, "for the unnatural, the aberrant, the wilderness of disorder which beleaguered all civilization; a disorder in part, but rarely only ever, sexual" (239). It is not surprising, then, that Alan Bray should find the sodomite—a site at which disorder (unrepresentable) is given shape (representation)—linked with such figures as werewolves, basilisks, and witches in the Renaissance. As a "crime," sodomy was a crime against neither persons nor property; it was instead, like bigamy or treason, a crime against order and, in the Renaissance, order was conceived—at least theoretically—to proceed from and to be ratified by the divine. Order and the authority which maintained it came down from above via the familiar hierarchy that had God at the top, then the monarch, the Church, the nobility, and so on down through the various ranks. If Bray finds references to the sodomite in what he calls an other-worldly "mythology" (21), it is because the order to which the sodomite represented a threat was itself "other-worldly" in nature and not, therefore, vulnerable to any merely mundane challenge. What lay outside divine order was demonic chaos, and sodomites, werewolves, basilisks, and witches formed a consortium of cosmic evil poised against creation. As such, sodomy, as an act, was initially and logically policed by the ecclesiastical, rather than the temporal, courts.

The appearance at the end of the seventeenth century of a secularized sodomite, rather than signaling a radical break with the past, inflects and redefines an already existing cultural discourse of sexual behavior and order. What changes by the end of the seventeenth century, I suggest, is less the conception of sodomy itself than the conception of that order against which sodomy was thought to be a threat. Although almost from the beginning of the Reformation in England parliament had begun to pass legislation against behavior that had previously been punished only by the ecclesiastical courts—effectively making these acts crimes against the order of the state rather than the order of God[3]—this process of secularization was intensified by the tumultuous events of the seventeenth century until, finally, order and the authority that established it were understood, not only practically but theoretically, to originate in the social body and the needs of people rather than to descend hierarchically from above. Indeed, at the end of a fifty-year period that had seen the execution of Charles I, the restoration of Charles II, and the Glorious Revolution, it could hardly be otherwise. As George deF. Lord comments:

> When Englishmen found that they could pull down kings and set them up again, the myth of Divine Right became a polite fiction. Opposition writers of the Restoration were not slow to discover flaws in the "ancient rights." . . and they went back to Henry VIII to suggest that these had their real origin in purely human urgencies. As one satirist wrote of Charles II,

> The virtues in thee, Charles, inherent
> (Although thy count'nance be an odd piece)
> Prove thee as true a God's viceregent
> As e'er was Harry with the codpiece. (xxix)

Of course, Divine Right remained something more than a mere "polite fiction," but, as J. R. Western has detailed, the basis of monarchy was the subject of considerable debate in the closing decades of the century, and both the Tories and the Whigs believed that the rights of the king and the rights of the people were complementary, not opposed (5–45).

In her study, *Players' Scepters*, Susan Staves shows that the idea that kingship was being secularized into a kind of executive position, the authority of which was conferred only by the people, and that actual sovereignty was being transferred from the monarch to the people, is evident "even in that most conservative of institutions, the law" (94). For example, after the Glorious Revolution, treason laws were modified to acknowledge the right to resist a tyrannical sovereign and acts that would have been prosecuted previously as high treason became, by the 1690s, lesser crimes like sedition, riot, or libel. "Since anyone could be the object of libel but only the sovereign the object of treason," Staves writes, "this redefinition treated the king less as a quasi-divine figure and more as an ordinary person" (96).

Eager to ensure both the rights of "subjects" from infringement and the maintenance of social stability, satirists from the Restoration on were quick to expose the only too *human* failings of monarchs. Once stripped of his traditional divinity, the king in fact could be conceived of as a threat to, instead of a symbol of, order, as was so clearly the case with James II. Despite the Whig bias of his study, G. M. Trevelyan accurately captures the change in perspective when he describes the expulsion of James as an effort "not to overthrow the law but to confirm it against a lawbreaking King" (5). Whether a love of law is what truly motivated the rebels is of less significance than the fact that this rhetoric could appear credible. That this rhetoric could appear credible was due to the growing idea that "the public good was that of the individual citizens added together, so that the people's grievances were a reliable guide to what was wrong in the state" (Western 27). In contradistinction to the deposing of James's father, in 1688 the country was not plunged into civil war.

In a similar fashion, this same period saw the enfeebling of the ecclesiastical courts. It was not simply the case that parliament con-

tinued to pass legislation on matters that had previously been exclusively the province of the spiritual courts, but in 1641 parliament
stripped the ecclesiastical courts of their powers generally and the
Court of High Commission was abolished. In 1642, bishops and arch-
bishops were denied a vote in the House of Lords and, later, were
deprived of their titles and lands. As Staves notes, despite the fact that
the Restoration brought with it the demise of most of the interreg-
num legislation, "the ideas that animated the legislation were not
necessarily repudiated when it was repealed" (15). Charles II, J. R.
Western comments, was to some extent "the heir of Cromwell as well
as of his father" (5). The bishops, for example, were restored with
Charles, but, significantly, the Cavalier Parliament endorsed the
weakening of the ecclesiastical courts and, in 1663, ratified the aboli-
tion of the Court of High Commission, though it was briefly revived
by James. The temporal courts thus became the guardians of public
morality and, as we saw in the case of Sedley, took it upon themselves
to police and punish behavior that was not yet even subject to legal
prohibition. "The order of society was to be defined and defended by
the state, not by the church" (Staves xiv).

Relatedly, it is worth noting Mark Kishlansky's argument that there
developed over the course of the seventeenth century a politicization
of culture, a growing tendency to view the world in political terms
rather than, say, in terms of common human generalities. "This is not
to suggest that before then English people lived in an apolitical or pre-
political world," Kishlansky writes,

> that they did not understand power relations, or the nature
> and forms of government. But it is to suggest that they did
> not view their world through a political prism at the begin-
> ning of this period and that they did so by the end. Not sur-
> prisingly, it was the events of the middle of the seventeenth
> century which, if they did not initiate the process, certainly
> accelerated it. (339)

Further, Kishlansky suggests that even the supposed return to ortho-
doxy after the Restoration served only to emphasize a political per-

spective of the world since the conscious attempt to undo the previous twenty years resulted in an almost constant attention to political forms in broadsides, tracts, and sermons (355–56). Kishlansky is not arguing, I think, that this "political prism" entirely displaces more traditional understandings of the world and its operation. For example, as J. Paul Hunter has shown in *Before Novels*, providence books, which interpret the world in terms of divine organization, were extremely popular at the end of the century. However, as Hunter also notes, the interpretations that providence books gave to certain events were often divided along party lines (221). The politicization of culture, then, did not displace older discursive structures as much as it subsumed them and recast them through a new emphasis on specific social forms.

The changes that I am outlining here are essential to an understanding of the discourse of sodomy at the end of the seventeenth and beginning of the eighteenth centuries, particularly to an understanding of the extent to which this discourse represents a continuity with, and not simply a departure from, what went before. The appearance of a secular sodomite at the end of the seventeenth century has been seen to signal the emergence of something radically new. But while the secular sodomite and his counterpart, the molly, may represent something new, they are only new within a changed context of how these figures might signify. The images we find during this period do not spring out of nowhere; they redefine the long history of sodomitical images discussed by Bray and others. In fact, it is probably more accurate to say that these images constitute less a vision of a secular sodomite than a secular vision of the sodomite.

For sodomy, as we shall see, was still conceived of as a threat to order, the sodomite still the "point of entry" for a chaotic disorder. But as order itself was now understood to originate within the social body, so too were the threats to order given a social embodiment and identified as social types: the plotter or secret conspirator, the insurrectionary, the foreigner, the papist or Jesuit, the corrupt government minister, the crafty stock-jobber, the enervated and supercivilized indulger in luxury, the freethinking libertine—all were, at one time or another, connected with sodomy and the sodomite. Although these figures may be identified as distinct types in Restoration and eighteenth-century writings, they exist in a rather fluid system of interchangeable signification. Conspirators were likely to be papists and sodomites with foreign connections. Papists were likely to be sodomites in league with foreign governments plotting the overthrow of Protestant rule. Corrupt government ministers would indulge all of their luxurious habits like sodomy, habits no doubt acquired on trips abroad, and thus render the state vulnerable to foreign spies. This fluid system of signification is concisely illustrated in John Oldham's third "Satyr Upon the Jesuits" (1679). In this poem, Loyola tells his followers to give unwavering obedience to the Pope,

> Tho' he be Atheist, Heathen, *Turk*, or *Jew*,
> Blaspheamer, Sacriligious, Perjured too:
> Tho' Pander, Bawd, Pimp, Pathick,[4] Buggerer,
> What e're Old *Sodoms* Nest of Lechers were:
> Tho' Tyrant, Traitor, Pois'ner, Parracide,
> Magician, Monster, all that's bad beside.   (ll. 91–96)

These figures all cluster together in such a way that one of them always seems to imply the others, and the grouping of papists, plotters, libertines, and sodomites constitutes no less a "mythology" than did the grouping of witches, werewolves, and sodomites. However, what is at stake is no longer creation but, rather, the nation.

In a satire attributed to Henry Carey, *Faustina: or the Roman Songstress, A Satyr on the Luxury and Effeminacy of the Age* (1726), for example, foreign travel is blamed for having corrupted the once "Noble Race of *British* Youth" (4). Now only enervated voluptuaries, the British have cast aside all "Manly Arts" to embrace foreign fashions and Italian opera: "Curse on this damn'd, *Italian*, Pathic Mode," exclaims the satirist, "To *Sodom* and to Hell the ready Road" (5). In *Faustina*, foreign luxury from papist Italy ("Who may, for ought I know, be singing Mass") is linked with sodomy because it will weaken the people and, ultimately, undermine England by luring citizens away from the practices of nation building:

They talk not of Army, or our Fleet,
But of the Warble of CUZZONI sweet,
. . . .
Nay, there are those as warmly will debate
For the Academy, as for the State;
They care not, whether Credit rise, or fall,
The Opera with them is all in all.   (6)

Army, navy, and trade abandoned, England will be undone by a foreign invasion which comes via the "Pathic Mode" of Italian opera. Well, why prolong the inevitable, the satirist wonders:

Let us to them our Wealth, our Dwellings yield,
And graze with savage Brutes in open Field:
Let's to our pristine State return once more,
And leave these foreign Minstrels all our Store;
And when we've learn'd to speak *Italian*, then,
If they so please, we may come home again.   (11)

Faustina offers us a good example of the way in which, even as seemingly concrete cultural associations appear to accrue to it, sodomy continues to function primarily as a symbolic concept. On the one hand, the road to Sodom is marked by specific social manifestations: an "effeminate" interest in dress, the supposed spreading of the Continental custom of men kissing each other in greeting, the oddities of Italian opera itself, which showcased the castrato—a figure that was, to borrow a phrase from G. S. Rousseau, "a type of sodomite *manqué*" ("Pursuit" 141). On the other hand, the satirist is clearly more interested in the body politic than in any particular body. As Judith Butler has pointed out, the construction of stable bodily contours—physical and social—"relies upon fixed sites of corporeal permeability and impermeability" which establish cultural coherence (*Gender* 132). The fear expressed in *Faustina* is that England is becoming passive (pathic), subject to a dangerous and contaminating permeability: Italian opera is coded as sodomitical because it is a conspicuous site at which foreign culture is seen to penetrate the social body of England. And although Faustina was an actual prima donna of the time, one cannot help but note the felicity of her name for the satirist, recalling, as it does, Faustus and suggesting a discursive continuity between an older theological perspective and an apparently different secular perspective—destructive commerce with demonic powers now refigured as vitiating contact with foreign culture.

The purpose of this chapter is to give an account of the various ways in which sodomy and the sodomite were given a cultural, as opposed to cosmic, legibility. To do this, I bring together a number of documents in order to chart a set of terms and associations—the "sodomitical practices"—upon which the rest of the chapters in this study will repeatedly draw. The divisions I make here between modes of representing the sodomite are, of course, critical rather than actual; that is, while I separate terms for ease of discussion, they should be understood to form a complex signifying system in which the various associations with sodomy inflect, reinforce, recall or, sometimes, contradict each other. This chapter, then, constitutes a kind of composite portrait of the sodomite at the end of the seventeenth and beginning of the eighteenth centuries. What emerges from this is, on the one hand, a figure (as in personage) of some cultural coherence, a social type; more frequently, however, the sodomite is deployed as a figure (as in trope) of cultural *in*coherence. With that in mind, the chapter concludes with a consideration of the idea of a subculture by looking at the most frequently cited "account"—Ned Ward's "Of the Mollies Club."

Order/Confusion

Monster of men, who altered Nature's course,
The stream ran backwards, and found out the Source.

— Nathaniel Lee, *The Tragedy of Nero* (1675)

I begin with the fear that order might fall into confusion, that the world could be turned upside down, and that "Nature's course" might somehow be reversed. Inversion—and the chaos that will inevitably result from upsetting the order of things—is the structuring principle of almost all representations of the sodomite, the one element that holds together what can otherwise be quite disparate depictions. This composite portrait of the sodomite, therefore, moves through a number of binaries: order/confusion, natural/unnatural, civilized/uncivilized, manliness/effeminacy, domestic/foreign. While contemporary theoretical impulse often encourages us to jump immediately beyond binaries via a deconstruction that would collapse the two terms of a binary structure into each other by showing that they are interdependent, and to dismiss inversion as a trope which merely maintains the binary it appears to threaten, I choose to uphold these binary structures—to start with, at least—for two reasons.

First, I wish to reemphasize the power that binaries have in the organization and understanding of the social world; second, given the social power of binaries, I wish to insist that inversion has a kind of threatening power which a purely deconstructionist argument might disallow. The binary oppositions through which the social is interpreted are invariably value-laden. One term in the binary is dominant, prized, encouraged; the other is subordinated, repudiated, feared. The possibility of inversion, therefore, can never be looked upon as simply the neutral maintaining of binary logic, at least not by any who feel they have a stake in the dominant term. In addition, as Jonathan Dollimore has remarked, because "in any historical instance [a] binary holds in place more than it actually designates, its inversion typically has effects beyond itself" (66). The lines quoted above from Lee's tragedy, for example, are spoken by Agrippina to her son, Nero, at the start of the play, just after he has ordered her execution. What kind of man would order the death of his own mother, his own "Source"? A sodomite, of course; as soon as Agrippina has been taken out to her death, Nero forgets all about her and exults in his love for "Sporus, now Lady, once Lord of [his] heart" (32). The "backwards" tendency of Nero's affections inverts marriage bonds, familial bonds, and introduces a disorder into the state that sets the tragedy in motion and precipitates the downfall of Rome.

The act of sodomy itself is most frequently designated as a disordered, inverted, or "preposterous" act. Sodomy is "transposing nature" (*Poems on Affairs of State* 2:194);[5] "a back stroke trecherous and base" ("Jenny Cromwell's Complaint" 381); "this backward Way," "contrary" (Ward 299, 300); "a Paradox" (Dunton 95); "prepost'rous Venery" (*Almonds* 4); "preposterous," "preposterous addresses," "the *contrary Road*," an "*Extreme* of a contrary Nature" (*Plain Reasons* 10, 12, 14, 21); "backward" (*A Treatise, wherin are Strict Observations* 31); "absurd," and a "project of preposterous pleasure" (Cleland 156–57). The idea of sodomy as backward, inverted, and preposterous carries with it the sense of things being not simply out of place or out of order, but out of control. The *OED* definitions of "preposterous" reflect this sense in their rapid movement from inversion to chaos and evil: "1. Having or placing last that which should be first; inverted in position or order. 2. Contrary to the order of nature, or to reason or common sense; monstrous; irrational; perverse." In *The Sodomites Shame and Doom* (1702), a "Minister of the Church of England" urges potential sinners not to give way to "Bestial . . . *Disorders*," since to do so would be to instigate disorder's spread. The author of *A Treatise, wherin are Strict Observations upon That detestable and most shocking Sin of Sodomy* (1728) agrees:

> If all were to go on at this rate, God must begin a new Creation, and the King wou'd not have Subjects to defend his Throne. Women wou'd not stay with you, but violently destroy themselves, and your vile corrupt Seed would raise such a Sett of Devils in their room, if it should take Root, as wou'd torment you worse than the Damn'd. (32)

In this passage we see again that, despite the move toward secularization, sodomitical discourse never actually loses its religious dimension; the confusion of sodomy affects the divine, and the political, and the social realms. Indeed, the very mention or thought of sodomy is sufficient to give rise to a vision of civilization in miserable disarray:

> it could not fill us with greater Disdain, to see a Man eating *Humane Excrements* with *Dogs*, or the most *stinking Carrion*

with *Swine*, than to consider your most abhorred *Sin* and *Shame*.

And this is the reason why your hateful Sin is seldom reproved in *Sermons* or *Books*, namely, because the *Jakes* is so foul that it cannot be toucht without offending the Company by the intolerable Stench of it.

(Sodomites Shame and Doom 2)

The mere mention of sodomy might unleash an infectious, uncontrollable confusion that has the power to collapse the distinction between humans and animals and to transform churches into foul jakes. In fact, Lee Edelman has argued that sodomy came to be construed as "a behaviour marked by a transgressive force reproduced, not merely designated, by naming or discussing it. For it constituted, more than an assault upon the flesh, an assault upon the logic of social discourse" (174); simply to speak of it is to "reenact a 'sodomitical' disturbance" (183). Hence, of course, the long list of what Sedgwick calls "substantive uses of space-clearing negatives" (*Epistemology* 202)—"the sin not to be named," "things fearful to name"—and of the kind of typographical concealment called "gutting": "S—d—y," "S——y," "B——y," and even "He-L—ry." These are precisely the type of representational inversions with which I started: codes which indicate what they do not name, and name what they insist they do not.

As the vehicle for this potential confusion, the sodomite would seem to carry disorder about with him, lacking, according to the "Minister of the Church of England," a "steddy Resolution" (2). "I am excessively disordered!" cries Captain Whiffle in Smollett's *Adventures of Roderick Random* (1748) as he flings himself into the arms of Simper, and one knows that his ship will soon be disordered too (196). Generally, the sodomite is presented as a conduit for, rather than simply the source of, confusion, at once the effect of and effecting a disorder beyond himself. The author of *Plain Reasons for the Growth of Sodomy* contrasts sodomites with mythologized British forefathers "train'd up to Arts and Arms" and "subject to Order and

Correction" (3, 4). With the advent of modern indolence and imported luxury, however, it is not to be wondered at that there are men with "so crazy a Constitution" (9). And Ned Ward imagines that the sodomite can only be the result of some kind of confused, mistaken copulation:

> Sure the curs'd Father of this Race,
> That does both Sexes thus disgrace,
> Must be a Monster, Mad, or Drunk,
> Who, bedding some perposterous [*sic*] Punk,
> Mistook the downy Seat of Love,
> And got them in the Sink above;
> So that, at first, a T–d and They
> Were born the very self same Way.   (299)

Produced by disorder and confusion, the sodomite then goes on to produce it himself: "From whence they draw this cursed Itch,/" Ward's lines continue, "Not to the Belly, but the Breech" (299). *Plain Reasons* similarly imagines sodomites to be continually attempting to lead others to "Ruin" (15).

Sodomy and the sodomite thus function as figures of an insidious kind of confusion. The result of something imagined to be outside of, and encroaching upon the social order—say, foreign culture as in *Faustina*—they then begin to undermine the social fabric from within as internal means through which a threatening otherness can operate. Sodomy and the sodomite also function as rather flexible figures for confusion. For just as sodomy is conceived of as creating a wide variety of social disorders, so can a wide variety of social disorders be conceived of as being sodomitical. The sodomite can, therefore, stand as a refiguration of almost any kind of perceived threat. This is a point taken up in chapter 2.

NATURAL/UNNATURAL; CIVILIZED/UNCIVILIZED

Significantly, being "outside" the hegemonic order does not signify being "in" a state of filthy and untidy nature. Paradoxically, homosexuality is

almost always conceived within the homophobic signifying economy as
both *uncivilized and unnatural.*

—Judith Butler, *Gender Trouble*

The natural/unnatural and civilized/uncivilized binaries are two of
the most frequently invoked structures with reference to sodomy's
and the sodomite's potential to enact a frightening inversion. As
Judith Butler points out, male-male sex always ends up on the
devalued end of these binaries. Sodomy is the crime *contra natu-
ram* just as it is also a "beastly" act. However, the natural/unnatural
and civilized/uncivilized binaries are also two of the most complex
and slippery structures.

As Raymond Williams has remarked in *Keywords*, "Nature is perhaps the most complex word in the language" (219), and Arthur O.
Lovejoy calls "nature" a "verbal jack-of-all-trades" (69). In *The
Sodomites Shame and Doom*, sodomitical acts are said to be "contrary
to the *Light of Nature*" (3), "nature" here meaning the system or order
of the world, or, perhaps more specifically, the system which directs
and orders the world. In this same pamphlet, sodomitical acts are also
said to be "of a *debasing, defiling*, and *damning* Nature" (2). In this
case, "nature" refers to the essential quality or character of something.
This second use of "nature," apparently, need not be consonant
with—indeed, the point here is that it is not consonant with—the
first. The sodomite both defiles nature and *is of* a defiling nature. Or,
to put it another way, *The Sodomites Shame and Doom* suggests that
there is a nature which is natural and a nature which is unnatural.

The civilized/uncivilized binary can be similarly mobilized in
opposite directions. In *Faustina* we saw that the satirist was concerned that civilization was being undermined, not because men
were turning to activities that were nasty and brutish but, on the
contrary, because they were becoming so very civilized, excessively
interested in art and "high" culture. Strangely, he imagines that this
will lead to a regression into the "pristine State" of nature in which
men are undifferentiated from "savage Brutes." Just as nature can be
unnatural in *The Sodomites Shame and Doom*, in *Faustina* civilization can have an uncivilizing effect.

The matter is further complicated by the fact that, while the natural/unnatural and civilized/uncivilized binaries are often presented as operating independently, together they form the poles of yet another powerful binary: nature/culture or nature/art. Within the logic of this larger structure, then, to become "civilized" should mean to become "unnatural"; to become "uncivilized" implies a lapsing into the state of "nature." Yet nature and culture do not exist in anything like a stable relationship to each other, and one's understanding and deployment of the nature/culture binary will differ wildly depending, for example, on whether one imagines nature to be a state of Hobbesian disarray which culture holds at bay, or a state of Newtonian perfection which culture emulates. Different still, nature might designate a state of innocence and purity, and culture, a state of distorting, decadent corruption. Thus culture can either be the opposite of nature (in a number of different ways) or it can be rooted in nature, nature providing the model for culture. Representations of the sodomite draw upon all of these models of the nature/culture binary, often simultaneously.

On the one hand, the sodomite is frequently represented as having sunk into a filthy and bestial nature associated with dirt, mire, offal, and animality. Sodomy is a "Brutal Fact," "a Brutal way" (*Women-Hater's*), and a "Beastly way" (*A Full and True Account*). Sodomites have "Brutal Lusts" (*Women-Hater's*), "filthy Lusts," "Bestial *Inclinations*," are like "Unclean Beasts" (*Sodomites Shame and Doom* 1), and commit "odious Beastialities, that ought for ever to be without a Name" (Ward 284). Arthur N. Gilbert has suggested that the sodomite was linked with a filthy and bestial nature because of his association with anality and thus with the animality/mortality of the body: "[t]he sodomite was wedded to the bowels and thus to the bowels of the earth where men rotted and decayed" ("Sexual Deviance" 98; see also "Buggery" and "Conceptions"). This would seem to be borne out by the fact that a number of satires and pamphlets, like *The Sodomites Shame and Doom*, John Oldham's "Upon the Author of the Play call'd Sodom," and *A Treatise wherin are Strict Observations*, do link sodomy and the sodomite with the jakes and excrement. Yet as often as the sodomite is associated with a brutish

and beastly nature, actual brutes and beasts are just as often held up
as examples to show that sodomy is unnatural, as in these lines from
Dunton's "The He-Strumpets":

> . . . To act a Vice so full of Shame,
> That Brutes wou'd fly, and blush to name:
> For even Goats are grown so poor,
> That *He* with *He* does never Whore.
> There's Mr. *Puss* does caterwaul
> With none but Sow-Cats on the Wall,
> For Boar-Cats—he does hate 'em all.
> The *Town-Bull* he does never prove
> His Mettle in the *He-Alcove*,
> The modest *Cow* has all his Love.
> The very *Horse* so much does smother
> His wanton Tail from *Rampant Brother*,
> That one Horse never rides another.
> And *Sparrow*, tho' a Whoring Tit,
> Did ne'er *He-L——ry* commit.   (95)

This passage is not without its ambiguities, clearly: if the goats "are
grown so poor,/ That *He* with *He* does never Whore," one imagines
that previously—perhaps when times were better—he with he did.
And if the horse has to "smother/ His wanton Tail," would it not seem
to be the case that that "*Rampant Brother*" has his eye on it? Dunton,
of course, like other satirists, overrides these ambiguities by dint of
repetition, and the point is made over and over again that "The
brawny Boar will love his Sow;/ The Horse his Mare; the Bull his
Cow" (Ward 300). The sodomite, then, is indicative of both a dirty,
uncultivated nature and, conversely, of something not to be found in
nature at all, nature providing, in this case, a model for culture.

The third model of nature/culture through which the sodomite
is represented is that in which nature designates a state of innocence
and purity, of what is right and inevitable, and culture, a state of
decadence and corruption. It is important to note that nature in this
model has less to do with trees and animals than with tradition, con-

vention, and nostalgia for a "simpler," more "wholesome" time. This model makes explicit, then, what is implicit in the others: whether conceived of as adverse to culture or as culture's source, the idea of nature is deployed in order to endorse specific cultural practices. That this model of nature/culture is really culture/culture is nicely expressed in Pope's lines, "Learn hence for Ancient *Rules* a just Esteem;/ To copy *Nature* is to copy *Them*" ("Essay on Criticism" ll. 139–40). In its simplest form, this construction involves merely designating any cultural innovation as a distortion of nature. In *Mundus Foppensis: or, The Fop Display'd* (1691), a foppish interest in dress and modern fashion is presented in terms of art against nature and, of course, is linked with sodomy:

> Bless us! what's there? 'tis something walks,
> A piece of Painting, and yet speaks:
> Hard Case to blame the Ladies Washes,
> When Men are come to mend their Faces.
> . . . .
>
> And then they study wanton use
> Of Spanish Red, and white Ceruse;
> The only Painters to the Life,
> That seem with Natures self at strife;
> As if she only the dead Colours laid,
> But they the Picture perfect made,
> . . . .
>
> And only what renews the shame
> Of J. the first, and *Buckingham*.   (10–13)

The reference to James I's sodomitical relationship with the Duke of Buckingham is invoked in order to indicate that "unnatural" lust must be at the root of an "unnatural" interest in dress.

 Almonds for Parrots (1708) rehearses the same idea of art against nature, and asserts that art, not nature, produces "a true Hermaphrodite" and sodomitical lusts (5): "For *Nature* ne'er made Men so soft and fair,/ And yet adorn'd their Heads and Beards with Hair./ But *Art* surpasses *Nature*; and we find/ Men may be transform'd into Women-kind" (5). Extravagant dress is a perversion of nature by art equivalent to, and therefore indicative of, "base prepost'rous Venery" (*Almonds* 4). Obviously, however, neither of these satirists is advocating a return to nakedness; rather, they advocate a return to social customs said to be more natural. The more extreme version of this nature/culture model works in the opposite direction. Instead of viewing one particular "decadent" custom as a perversion of nature indicating sodomy, sodomy is seen as indicating the decadence and degeneracy of the entire culture which must either return to nature — i.e., idealized tradition — or face inevitable destruction. This is the warning of the destruction of Sodom and of the fall of Rome. The lament for a wholesome, authentic past legitimated by nature, but now corrupted by the sickening artificialities of culture, makes up the substance of the Preface to *The Tryal and Condemnation of Mervin, Lord Audley, Earl of Castle-Haven*; *The Play of Sodom*; *Faustina*; and *Plain Reasons for the Growth of Sodomy*.

The manifest inconsistencies of the natural/unnatural, civilized/ uncivilized, and nature/culture binaries attest to — and account for — the power and resilience of these structures. Because both nature and culture mobilize a number of meanings, they can be called upon as vehicles of approbation and condemnation in a variety of contexts with equal conviction. These inconsistencies combine with sodomy's long history as *the* crime against nature, as well as its long association with a gross and bestial nature, to mark the reconstitution of the sodomite as a social figure at the end of the seventeenth century. Sodomy can be invoked, then, to damn by association almost any cultural practice as "unnatural" and "uncivilized."

MANLINESS/EFFEMINACY

Randolph Trumbach has offered, over a series of articles, what is probably the most thorough examination of the relationship of manliness and effeminacy to the sodomite (see especially "Birth of the Queen"). To briefly recount his findings: Trumbach argues that in the 1660s and 70s, the sodomite was most likely to be associated with the masculine, aristocratic rake or libertine who had sex with both women and adolescent males, usually his page. Within this milieu, sodomy was not at all conceived of as feminizing but, rather, represented the summit of masculine self-assertion. By 1700 and into the eighteenth century, however, according to Trumbach, sodomy came to be seen as a specifically *de*masculinizing act, and the sodomite himself as an effeminate, hermaphroditic outcast—a "he-strumpet," as Dunton calls him—totally uninterested in women and frequently connected with transvestism. The reason that Trumbach gives for the emergence of the effeminate "molly" is that "male and female roles had begun to grow more nearly equal. . . . The molly was therefore a wall of separation between the genders" ("Birth" 140). I do not wish to dispute Trumbach's well-researched assertion that, before 1700, one does not tend to encounter the cross-dressing molly and that, after 1700, the masculine, sodomitical rake more or less disappears. However, we need, I think, a more nuanced account of this shift than Trumbach is able to provide, an account which asks, for example, *who* made these different associations with sodomy and how might we account for exceptions? In Smollett's *Adventures of Roderick Random,* to take one instance, Capt. Whiffle is presented as being extremely effeminate, but the other sodomite in this same novel, Earl Strutwell, is not particularly effeminate at all. Why should this be? We might begin by looking at Trumbach's argument that the link between sodomy and effeminacy indicated that male and female gender roles were growing more equal.

In an interesting article on effeminacy and English satire, Susan C. Shapiro makes the following observation:

Although *known* homosexuality always implied "effeminacy," . . . the reverse is simply not the case. "Effeminacy" traditionally was associated with weakness, softness, delicacy, enervation, cowardice, delight in luxurious food and clothing—all those qualities that oppose the essential attributes of the warrior, the most "manly" of men. But just as frequently, "effeminacy" was used to connote some deviant form of *hetero*sexuality: subservience to a wife or mistress, lecherousness, or the compulsive pursuit of sexual experience to the neglect of more "manly" activities, . . . or conversely, such personal vanity and

self-absorption as to preclude any but the feeblest interest in
sexuality at all.   (400–1; original emphasis)

Shapiro points out here that the manliness/effeminacy distinction
translates into power/weakness, activeness/passivity. Effeminacy, in
other words, has less to do with what a man might adopt—frilly
clothes, rarefied notions—than with what he abandons—power,
mastery, control. This is why the plainly dressed man subservient to
his wife and even the lecherous, compulsive "sex maniac" can be
described as effeminate: they have both relinquished that mastery
over the self and others that characterizes manliness. The ideologi-
cal underpinning here, obviously, is the conventional masculinist
gender hierarchy that constructs men as active, powerful, and dominant, and women as passive, weak, and subordinate in all things
including, and I stress this, sexual intercourse.

This brings me to a second point about Shapiro's comments, and
to Trumbach's assertion about gender roles vis-à-vis the sodomite.
Shapiro—and others, for she is not alone in doing this—is misleading, I think, in the distinction that she makes between the application of "effeminacy" to "homosexuality" and to "some deviant
form[s] of heterosexuality." She is misleading because *sodomy is
always represented as a deviant or confused form of "heterosexuality."*
Within the conventional, masculinist signifying economy, an act of
penetrative sexual intercourse is always already gendered. Sex,
despite appearances, always takes place between a masculine, penetrative "male" and a feminine, penetrated "female," and these gendered positions remain absolutely, irrevocably separated. "Men"
penetrate; "women" are penetrated. For a man "[t]o be penetrated
is to abdicate power" (Bersani 252), is to become effeminate, is to
become a woman. Hence John Dunton, even though he does not
attribute any typically effeminate characteristics to the sodomite,
designates him as a "He-Strumpet," a "He-Whore," and a "He-
Concubine"—the hermaphroditic terms supplementing/trans-
forming the apparently masculine, male body of the sodomite,
which simply fails to signify satisfactorily the "truth" of the gender
conferred upon it by the sexual act.

The obsessive emphasis on transvestism in other depictions functions as a more emphatic version of Dunton's terminology. Sex between two males simply cannot be sex between two males. By interposing a rhetorical hermaphrodism in the scene of male-male sex, writers can maintain the preeminence (i.e., impenetrability) of the male body proper which sodomy threatens to erase and, therefore, can maintain the gender hierarchy. Because Trumbach conceives of manliness/effeminacy only in terms of the absence or presence of overt, external signifiers (masculinity, of course, being unmarked), rather than as a system of power, he accords the gender hierarchy more malleability than is warranted. As a consequence he fails to note not only the stability of the gender hierarchy, but also how, as a power structure, it can be mapped onto other axes of power like class. Trumbach also fails to note that the privilege of claiming for oneself a powerful masculinity seems always to rest, significantly, with whoever is holding the pen.

So who associated sodomy with powerful, libertine rakes? The answer is powerful, libertine rakes. When Trumbach argues for a connection between sodomy and masculine self-assertion, he does so by citing lines like these from Rochester's misogynistic "Love a woman? You're an ass!"(c. 1672):

> Then give me health, wealth, mirth, and wine,
> And, if busy love entrenches,
> There's a sweet, soft page of mine
> Does the trick worth forty wenches.   (ll. 13–16)

The libertine speaker of this poem presents himself as triumphantly powerful enough to do without women and still satisfy his sexual desires. One must immediately pause, however, and say that it is doubtful that Rochester's poetic vision represents as widely held a view as Trumbach's argument seems at first to imply. The poem from which I have just quoted, for example, though written about 1672, was not actually published until 1680, after Rochester's death and his death-bed repentance. Indeed, even Trumbach ultimately attributes this type of libertine self-fashioning to only a "relatively small circle" ("Birth" 130). He might have added that when libertine poems were read outside of the small circle of their authors they tended to shock their audiences as, of course, they were meant to do. In any case, whether we see it as a wide or as a narrow view, to argue that libertine poems associate sodomy with masculinity is only to tell half of the story, to identify unreflectingly with the "I" of the poem, and to forget all about the "page." What is interesting about the libertine poems and the later accounts of the mollies is not so much how they differ, but rather how they participate in precisely the same gender dynamics.

Although Rochester's libertine verse often appears to construct an entirely male sexual economy, his poems, as Harold Weber has recently shown, never move outside of what George Chauncey has called the "heterosexual paradigm," continually reproducing the active/passive, masculine/feminine structure of the sex-gender hierarchy (see Weber, "Drudging"; Chauncey, "From Sexual Inversion"). In these poems, sweet, soft pages and "well-looked linkboy[s]" ("Disabled Debauchee" l. 38) are interchangeable with women, their "worth" measured in terms of the "tricks" of "wenches." That the sexual act confers gender, that "men" penetrate and "women" are penetrated is made clear in the following lines on the penis from "The Imperfect Enjoyment" (c. 1672–73):

> Stiffly resolved, 'twould carelessly invade
> Woman or man, nor ought its fury stayed:
> Where'er it pierced, a cunt it found or made–   (ll. 41–43)

"Men make women," Harold Weber comments; "the penis [is] representative of a phallic power that alone establishes gender" ("Drudging" 104). It does not matter what the penis penetrates: what it penetrates is always a "cunt." Libertine poets like Rochester maintain the masculine preeminence of the aristocratic male body by maintaining a rhetorical and structural, if not actual, "heterosexual" economy of desire in their poems. Further, these poems also demonstrate how the misogyny of the gender hierarchy is mapped onto the hierarchy of class:

> In Rochester's poetry the economic underclass [pages and linkboys] functions as an image of the sexual underclass, both defined by their inferiority to the aristocratic male narrator. . . . In terms of sexual power, women are always the ones who are fucked, . . . defined by the passivity that renders them subordinate to men. . . . [L]ower class substitutes, firmly fixed in an economic system . . . , can stand in for women precisely because they do not question the distinction between active and passive, superiority and subordination.
>
> (Weber, "Drudging" 114)

While he neglects to mention the sexist and classist means by which it is achieved, Trumbach is partly correct when he says that libertine depictions of sodomy are about masculine self-assertion. But that masculine self-assertion is dependent upon a gender and class hierarchy that remains immutable. One can only argue that libertine sodomy is not at all feminizing by participating in that hierarchy to the extent that the pages and linkboys become unworthy of notice. For all their apparent sexual freedom, libertine poetics articulate a set of highly conservative assumptions about gender and class.

Depictions of the "he-strumpet" and of the effeminate molly certainly appear to position sodomy within an entirely different frame of reference. Expressions of rakish triumph are replaced by an examination of "*Delicata Insania*" or "Effeminate Madness" (*Castle-Haven*, Preface). The physical body, so present in libertine poems, now gives way to laundry lists of its outrageous coverings: "Gowns, Petticoats, Head cloths, fine lac'd Shoes, Furbelow Scarves, Masks, and compleat Dresses for Women" (Wild 32). And, perhaps most important, the first-person narrator of rakish sexual experience is replaced with a "detached," distanced observer.

I stress the importance of the position of the writer in these texts for, just as discussions of the libertine sodomite have tended to efface the position of the page, so too have discussions of the effeminate sodomite tended to efface the position of the satirist or pamphleteer. When we bring the writer back into the picture, what we discover is that, for all their manifest differences, these texts articu-

late exactly the same gender dynamics as did the libertine poems.
These texts, too, are about masculine self-assertion. That is, these
satirists and pamphleteers do not dismantle the position of the masculine writer vis-à-vis a feminized other that we see in Rochester's
verse as much as they appropriate it, and sometimes in a clearly
sexualized manner.

In John Oldham's "Upon the Author of the Play call'd Sodom," for
example, the speaker of the poem feminizes the playwright of *Sodom*
by characterizing him as a "Green-sick Girl" (l. 30) and as a type of
he-whore or he-strumpet: "Sure Nature made, or meant at least
t'have don 't,/ Thy Tongue a Clitoris, thy Mouth a Cunt" (ll. 31–32).
However, the poem then continues "How Well a Dildoe would that
place become,/ To gag it up, and make 't forever dumb!" (ll. 33–34).
The satirist here assumes exactly the position of Rochester's libertine
speakers: one man wielding phallic, penetrative power over a feminized, penetrated other. In *Plain Reasons for the Growth of Sodomy*,
the author constructs himself in a similar manner, albeit more
obliquely. After railing against the custom of men kissing in greeting,
the author informs us that he has made "a solemn Vow, never to give,
or take from any Man a *Kiss*" (15). His reason is that men kissing each
other is "the first *Inlet* to the detestable Sin of *Sodomy*" (12). Clearly,
the "*Inlet*" of kissing prefigures the eventual penetration/feminiza-
tion of the male body by sodomy. Through his vow, then, the writer
presents himself as impenetrable, as masculinely whole, in opposition to the only too penetrable bodies of the men he discusses. Just as
the libertine's assertions of his own masculinity depend upon his first
feminizing his page, later assertions of sodomitical effeminacy
depend upon the writer first establishing his own sexual power over
the object of his satire.

As well, *Plain Reasons* reminds us of the intimate connection
between gender and class structures:

> I am confident no Age can produce any thing so preposterous
> as the present Dress of those Gentlemen who call themselves
> pretty Fellows. . . . 'Tis a Difficulty to know a Gentleman from
> a Footman by their present Habits: The low-heel'd Pump is an

Emblem of their low Spirits; . . . the Silk Wastcoat all belac'd,
with a scurvy blue Coat like a Livery Frock. . . . I blush to see
'em Aping the Running Footmen, and poising a great Oaken
Plant fitter for a Bailiff's Follower than a Gentleman.   (10–11)

To slide down the scale of gender and become a "pretty Fellow"
is to slide down the scale of class and become a servant rather than
a master. The fixity with which active/passive, masculine/feminine
maps onto a hierarchy of class accounts even for what seem to be
exceptions in the representation of the sodomite after 1700, those
where sodomitical interests do not entail an accompanying effeminacy. The swooning *Captain* Whiffle may be effeminate, but the
predatory *Earl* Strutwell is not. And in *Love Letters Between a certain
late Nobleman and the famous Mr. Wilson* (1723), it is the impoverished Mr. Wilson, and not the powerful nobleman, who gets connected with transvestism. Unlike the mollies who are almost always
depicted as being middle class, sodomitical figures who have a powerful class position tend not to be represented as effeminate.

Again, my point here is not to suggest that there is no difference
between a Rochester poem and Ned Ward's account of cross-dressing mollies; clearly there is. This may have less to do with a change
in the conception of sodomy *per se*, however, than with the fact that
the position of the rake became less tenable as one moves into the
eighteenth century (see Weber, *Restoration Rake-Hero* 179–221).
What I want to emphasize here, however, is that we cannot simply
apply the terms "manliness" to one and "effeminacy" to the other as
though these terms were purely abstract and descriptive, unconnected to the structures of power that organize almost all social relationships. All representations of sodomy and of the sodomite, before
and after 1700, involve a misogynistic assertion of masculine power
and preeminence over a repudiated, feminine weakness.

Tyranny/Slavery

As we have just seen, the representation of sodomy and of the
sodomite was inextricably bound up in the power structures which
organize society; it is not surprising, therefore, that sodomy could

come to stand as a figure for power relations themselves. And, given the order/confusion and natural/unnatural binaries through which sodomy was represented, it is not surprising that sodomy should stand as a figure for confused, unnatural power relations. If "heterosexual" relations, as naturalized through the gender hierarchy, provided a model for a "proper," "natural" balance of power, sodomy, as a deviant form of "heterosexuality," provided a model for power relations which were dangerously out of balance. In political terms, the active/passive distinction of the sexual partners translates into tyranny/slavery.

In Nathaniel Lee's *The Tragedy of Nero*, from which I quoted earlier, Nero's unnatural thirst for power is linked explicitly with his unnatural love for Sporus (this is Nero speaking):

> Virtue's a name, Religion is a thing
> Fitter to scare poor Priests, than daunt a KING.
> Swift, as quick thought, through every art I range:
> Who but a GOD, like me, could Sexes change?
> Sporus be witness of my Mighty art;
> Sporus, now Lady, once Lord of my heart.   (32)

Ranging swiftly through every art, Nero is clearly marked by an instability unwanted in a ruler and, as the capitalization makes clear, he moves quickly from considering himself a "KING" to considering himself a "GOD." He scorns the restraints of virtue and religion, and his unbounded aspirations are reflected in his desires which similarly refuse to acknowledge the bounds of "nature." *Sodom; or, the Quintessence of Debauchery* (c. 1672–73), attributed to Rochester, takes the analogy between sodomy and tyranny one step farther: Bolloxinion, the King of Sodom, not only indulges in sodomy himself, but he decrees that sodomy must be the rule of the realm. Ironically, he makes his decree in the language of liberty, and describes it as a throwing off of unnecessary restraints and bars to pleasure:

> Let other Monarchs, who their scepters bear
> To keep their subjects less in awe than fear,

Be slaves to crowns, my Nation shall be free—
My Pintle only shall my scepter be;
My Laws shall act more pleasure than command
And with my Prick, I'll govern all the land. (57)

This passage makes explicit the connection between the sexual order and the political order as Bolloxinion's pintle and scepter are one and the same. While Bolloxinion insists that his prick enacts "more pleasure than command," the subsequent action of the play is designed to convince us of the opposite, that the decree is actually an assertion of phallic power by which he gains a tyrannical control over his courtiers. Indeed, each of his courtiers is now forced to take his turn rendering up his "arse" for the "Royal Tarse": "In and untruss," Bolloxinion orders them at the end of Act 1, "I'll bugger you by turns" (64). Throughout the play, Bolloxinion insists that he has given his subjects unparalleled liberty, but he is repeatedly characterized by the other characters as a "Tyrant." (I discuss this play at length in chapter 2 with reference to debates about the king's prerogative.)

Of course, to submit to tyranny, as do Bolloxinion's courtiers, is to become slavish, and slavish, in this case, means pathic. " 'Tis all I wish," Pockenello, one of the courtiers, says obsequiously, "that Pockenello's Arse/ May still find favour from your Royal Tarse" (61). We already saw in relation to *Faustina* how, as Mary Douglas puts it, the body can stand as a model "for any bounded system. Its boundaries can represent any boundaries which are [perceived to be] threatened or precarious" (in Butler, *Gender* 132). The body politic, like the (male) body, establishes its integrity by maintaining its impenetrability. In *Faustina*, Italian opera was represented as an assault on the English nation, a kind of cultural tyranny which rendered all unresisting opera-lovers "Pathic." The consequence, according to the satirist, would be the enslavement of the English people, reducing them to a bestial existence or, at best, a form of cultural colonization by which the English would become foreigners in their own country. *Plain Reasons for the Growth of Sodomy* conceives of the usurpation of the English stage by opera from Italy—"the *Mother* and *Nurse* of *Sodomy*" (12)—in the same way. Whereas men used to go from a "good *Tragedy*, fir'd with a Spirit of Glory" and ready to stand up for their native rights, they now sit "indolently and supine at an OPERA" (18). The writer goes on to compare the state of England to the state of the Roman Empire in its declining years when, rather than fight their country's enemies, men would relinquish "their Liberty to preserve their *Effeminacy*" (19).

Sodomy, then, can represent a perversion of the "natural" balance of power—either the exertion of a power that ought not to exist (tyranny), or a repulsive submission to that which ought to be resisted (slavery). Because sodomy is conceived of as a deviant or confused form of the "natural" power hierarchy of "heterosexual" relationships, it can be a particularly useful figure, enabling the critique of a specific manifestation of power while leaving the power hierarchy itself intact.

Procreation/Sterility

. . . the Sodomites, that endeavour to destroy the World backward, whom [sic] God has so beautifully created, by stopping Procreation. . . . Were all of us to have gone backward the unnatural Way, the World would have been depopulated long ago.

—A Treatise, wherin are Strict Observations

When Foucault calls sodomy an "utterly confused category," he does so because the word has been used to designate a wide variety of acts. These acts do, however, have something in common: they are non-procreative. Injunctions against sodomy have always emphasized that sodomy "frustrates" reproduction, the only "true" aim of sex. As Jonathan Dollimore reminds us, the word "buggery" itself "derives from the religious as well as sexual non-conformity of an eleventh-century Bulgarian sect which practised the Manichaean heresy and refused to propagate the species" (237). Sodomy was a casting of one's seed among the rocks, a refusal of the divine injunction to go forth and multiply. According to John Dunton, sodomy entails the loss of "Nature's End":

Then *Sodomy* is the Abuse
Of either Sex, against the Use
Of Nature, —that shou'd Babe produce.
When Men with Men–act what's unchast,
The Children (Nature's End) are lost,
And the main End of Woman's crost.
When Tails the Whore, and are uncivil,
They get no Children! —but the *Devil*.   (94)

Here we see once again the neat slide of "nature" into "culture," nature legitimizing the cultural constitution of the female body as primarily and compulsorily a reproductive body, the production of children its "main End." In frustrating nature, then, sodomy also frustrates those social structures said to derive from nature. As a "sterile" practice, sodomy can therefore figure any social practice also condemned as sterile, and as far back as 1598, Francis Meres associated usury with sodomy, saying that both were against nature and that both were "sterill and barren" practices (see Bredbeck 5).

In the expanding mercantilist economy of the end of the seventeenth and beginning of the eighteenth centuries, however, the link between the "proper" circulation of reproductive desire and the "proper" circulation of money and productive labour was something more than figurative. As Louis A. Landa has demonstrated, the most cherished maxim of mercantilist economic writers was that people are the riches of the nation:

"Fewness of people is real poverty; and a Nation wherein are Eight Millions of People, are more than twice as rich as the same scope of Land wherein are but Four. . . . "

People . . . are "in truth the chiefest, most fundamental, and precious commodity . . . *capital material* . . . *raw* and indigested. . . . "

"Nothing makes Kingdoms and Commonwealths, Mighty, Opulent and Rich, but multitudes of People; 'tis Crowds bring in Industry."

"... all that is valuable in a nation ... depends upon the
number of its people...."   (see Landa 102–5)[6]

As a sexual act that does not lead to the production of the "precious commodity," the "capital material," of people, sodomy stands
as a threat to the economic growth of the entire nation. The correspondence between the sexual economy and the economy of
expanding mercantilism finds expression in descriptions of non-
procreative sexual acts, like sodomy or masturbation, which use a
vocabulary of wasting or squandering of productive vitality, indolence, and loss of issue, reproducing marketplace anxieties about saving, spending, production, and consumption. It is precisely this correspondence that John Cleland draws rather wittily upon when he
has Mrs. Cole, for whom sex *is* business, say that she objects to
sodomy since it tends to take out of the mouths of womankind
"something more precious than bread" (159). In *Plain Reasons for
the Growth of Sodomy*, sodomy is seen more seriously as the ultimate
and inevitable consequence of a decline in mercantilist values. In
the glorious past, we are told, a man was fit for "serving his King, his
Country, and his Family;" his "Application to Business keeps him
from Debauch, and his success so Spurrs him on, that he soon sees
a fine Provision made for himself and his Family; and his (perhaps
small) Patrimony amply augmented" (5). Modern indolence, however, has negated this situation of increase and, instead of applying
himself to business in order to augment his fortunes, the "Man of
Clouts dwindles into nothing, and leaves a Race as effeminate as
himself; who, unable to please the Women, chuse rather to run into
unnatural Vices one with another" (9–10; cf. Edelman 121–28).
Sodomy, then, as a "sterill and barren" practice, at once endangers a
productive economy and replicates bodily an exhausted, unproductive economy and its dwindling into nothing.

The association between sodomy and sterile, exhausted social
practice recalls the link between sodomy and a destructive decadence which precipitates the ruin of the state:

From at least the biblical story of Sodom and Gomorrah, scenarios of same-sex desire would seem to have had a privileged,

though by no means an exclusive, relation in Western culture
to scenarios of both genocide and omnicide.... [T]here is a
peculiarly close, though never precisely defined, affinity
between same-sex desire and some historical condition of
moribundity, called "decadence," to which not individuals or
minorities but whole civilizations are subject.   (Sedgwick,
Epistemology 127–128)

Paradoxically, then, sodomy *can* be conceptualized as a productive
sexual act. But, as a confused or inverted form of "heterosexuality,"
sodomy occasions the birth not of life but of death, a death capable
of engulfing an entire society. Sodomy is thus, in Lee Edelman's
phrase, "the definitional act of de-generation" (99).[7] Representations
of sodomy and of the sodomite rehearse again and again their apocalyptic potential to "turn a Fruitful and Pleasant Country, into utter
Barrenness and Desolation" (*Castle-Haven* Preface). From the story
of Sodom—what we might call the foundational text of "sodomitical
practices"—the sodomite has stood as a figure antithetical to the concerns of founding, developing, and maintaining the nation.

DOMESTIC/FOREIGN

How famous, or rather how infamous Italy *has been in all Ages, and continues in the Odious Practice of* Sodomy, *needs no Explanation.*

—*Plain Reasons for the Growth of Sodomy*

Nor, of course, does it ever get one. Nevertheless, sodomy is repeatedly represented as coming from elsewhere, a kind of foreign infec-
tion erupting within the social body, but the source of which is definitely outside of that body.[8] Just as the representation of sodomy
and the sodomite is refracted through the social structures of the
gender and class hierarchies, it also intersects with a discourse of
xenophobia, a xenophobia directed particularly toward the Catholic countries of France and Italy. Anti-foreigner satires from the end
of the seventeenth and beginning of the eighteenth centuries
repeatedly depict England as the beleaguered abode of Protestant
purity continually assaulted by corrupt foreigners, a sentiment
which has its most hysterical manifestation in the fears of the Popish

Plot (1678–1681). Almost from the start of the Restoration, Charles's court was perceived as being overly "Frenchified," the result of his years spent in exile. In addition, from 1670 until Charles's death, the "exalted role of the King's chief mistress" (Falkus 144) was occupied by the French Catholic Louise de Kéroualle, Duchess of Portsmouth, who, it was thought, exercised a powerful influence over the king. That de Kéroualle should have dominated Charles made their relationship, like sodomy, a confused form of "heterosexuality," and was therefore connected with a perversion of power relations. One satire against de Kéroualle dreams of the "day that sets our monarch free/ From butter'd buns[9] and slavery./ This hour from French intrigues, 'tis said,/ He'll clear his Council and his bed" (*POAS* 2:168). Another has Charles, "Silly and sauntering," going from "French whore to Italian":

> A pretty set he has at hand
> Of slimy Portsmouth's creatures. . . .
> Who would reform this brutal nation,
> And bring French slavery in fashion.   (*POAS* 2:167–68)

The death of Charles in 1685 did nothing to alleviate the fears of French influence in the Court since it brought Charles's Catholic brother, James, to the throne. As well, 1685 also saw the revocation of the Edict of Nantes by Louis XIV, an act which had two major consequences. First, the revocation was seen as a blow to European Protestantism causing England to see itself even more as the last bastion of hope and liberty; second, the revocation resulted in a large influx of Huguenots which ultimately intensified anti-French feelings (see *Baboon* below). Even when anti-French sentiments died down, there were other ready targets to hand. The Glorious Revolution, of course, was undertaken to secure Protestantism, but it did so by installing a Court that was perceived to be full of foreign favorites (see Rubini). And later, as we have already seen, the ascendancy of Italian opera was understood to strike right at the heart of English values. Representations of the sodomite implicate him in all of these perceived foreign threats, or, more precisely, the sodomite comes to stand as the domestic embodiment of foreign corruption. The extent to which this is the case will be clear if we look briefly at a typical antiforeigner satire.

The Baboon A-la-Mode. A Satyr Against the French, written by "a Gentleman," appeared in 1704 and subjects the French, "the common Scourge of Human Kind," to "just Poetick Fury" (2). Unlike the staid, reasonable English, the French embody an "empty, fluttering" disorder:

> So roving and inconstant is his Thought,
> That when into the Shape of Words 'tis brought,
> So quick they tumble from his opening Mouth
> They one another bruise in coming forth. . . .
> Their Tongues not only wag, but Hands and Feet;
> Each Part about them seems to move and walk,
> Their Eyes, their Noses, nay, their Fingers talk.   (3)

Like the sodomites, the French enact through their bodies a strange, disturbing confusion, and, also like the sodomites, the French participate in a distortion of nature, signified by an effeminate interest in dress: "Their Modes so strangely alter Humane Shape,/ What Nature made a Man, they make an Ape" (4). The effeminacy of the French, however, is most clearly revealed in their passive, grotesque submission to the "Arbitrary Power" of their "Haughty TYRANT":

> They tamely-passive quietly submit,
> And part with what by Nature is their Right.
> They'd rather live in Want and Slavery,
> Than make one brave Attempt for Liberty.   (6–7)

Too kindly taking pity on the tyrannized French, the English welcomed fleeing Huguenots with open arms, but "they Returns of Gratitude have made,/ By Undermining of the Nation's Trade" (8). The discourse of xenophobia that one finds in The Baboon A-la-Mode corresponds almost exactly to the discourse of sodomy as we have looked at it thus far, working through the same structures of order/confusion, natural/unnatural, manliness/effeminacy, tyranny/slavery, and even procreation/sterility if one takes into account the undermining of trade. Jonathan Dollimore has suggested that one consequence of a culture's extreme xenophobia is the "paranoid search for the internal counterpart of external threats" (155). Indeed, *The Baboon A-la-Mode* makes this quite clear:

> Yet stay a while, my over-hasty Muse,
> Whilst French you blame, the English you accuse;
> And whilst you would expose th'Original,
> You too severely on the Copy fall:
> 'Tis so—but *so like Enemies they seem,*
> No Wonder if the Satyr aim'd at them.   (5; my emphasis)

Its source always projected onto the "elsewhere," the act of sodomy introduces the alien into the social order and the sodomite thus becomes a substitute alien—so like the enemy—reproducing internally foreign corruption and danger as domestic perversion and deviance.

The domestic/foreign binary returns us, too, to those representational structures that formed the epigraphs to this chapter in which sodomy was seen to enact its corrupting disturbance precisely at the level of discourse and representation, reminding us of Lee Edelman's assertion that, more than an assault upon the body, sodomy was "an assault upon the logic of social discourse" (174): "*This Sin* [is] *being now Translated from the* Sadomitical *Original, or from the* Turkish *and* Italian *Copies into* English." At its simplest level, the discursive "assault" of sodomy involves the displacement of good, plain, English "sense" by alien words and notions:

> Cloaths is a paltry Word *Ma foy*;
> But Grandeur in the French *Arroy.*
> *Trimming*'s damn'd English, but *le Grass*
> Is that which must for Modish pass.

To call a Shoe a Shoe is base,
Let the genteel *Picards* take Place,
. . . .
So strangely does *Parisian* Air
Change English Youth, that half a year
Makes 'em forget all Native Custome,
To bring French Modes, and *Gallic* Lust home.

(*Mundus Foppensis* 14–15)

More seriously, sodomy disrupts the linearity of the chain of discourse that provides the foundation for reason and order: "they have little else in their Heads or Mouths, than *Casto* and *Culo* which they intermix with almost every Sentence, (a beastly and withal most stupid Interjection!) for, let them be talking on never so serious a Subject, these two Syllables must come in, though never so foreign to the Purpose" (*Plain Reasons* 17–18). The sodomite, then, through the continual introduction of what is "foreign," frustrates the very discursive structures through which one imposes order and sense on the world, disrupting the "Trayne of Words" and inverting, as we have seen, representational practices to the degree that sodomy can be named precisely by not naming it. Sodomy and the sodomite are alien to the workings of "logic" and order and their manifestation in language. Always "foreign to the Purpose," always "so like Enemies," sodomy and the sodomite lurk outside the "normal" (i.e. normative) English social world.

The sodomite, then, produces a threatening confusion in an otherwise stable social order, or may be produced by the confusion of an already destabilized order. Having sunk into a bestial and filthy nature—marked by his supercivilized, luxurious tastes—the sodomite is immediately identifiable by his outrageously effeminate mannerisms, except, of course, when he does not have any. Given to passive, slavish submission, when he is not tyrannically powerful, the sodomite is representative of an obviously foreign corruption, despite his appearance at the centre of the domestic scene. Clearly, the sodomite is a highly flexible figure of signification, allowing for the mobilization of a variety of ideas in opposite directions. Surveying sodomitical practices, we see that they are, to borrow a turn of phrase from Gregory Bredbeck, "not so much a system of words designed to articulate a specification of sodomy" as they are "a specification of sodomy designed to articulate a system of words and ideas" (13).

Sodomitical practices conflate three of culture's most intensively policed structures—gender, class, ethnicity—enabling the condensation of a number of transgressions into one sign. The sodomite is thus, perhaps, *the* demonized other, capable of standing in for almost any manifestation of evil or disruption and made, through the adaptable signification of sodomitical practices, to bear the blame for it all. In the Renaissance, according to Alan Bray, sodomy "was not conceived of as part of the created order at all; it was part of its dissolution. . . . What sodomy and buggery represented" was a "disorder in sexual relations that, in principle at least, could break out anywhere" (25). At the end of the seventeenth century, sodomy, as we have seen, still represents this principle of disorder; however, it is a principle of disorder that has become relocated—alarmingly—in the social scene itself. To further explore the effects of this relocation, I turn now to the idea of a sodomitical subculture.

Sodomitical Subculture

One thing would seem to be clear: as the crime that was not supposed to be spoken of, sodomy, at the end of the seventeenth and beginning of the eighteenth centuries, was spoken (or rather written) of quite a bit. What are we to make of the increased discursive presence of the sodomite? What were the effects of this presence? It will likely seem that my discussion thus far, emphasizing as it has the sodomite as a discursive figure or trope, has tended to eclipse any discussion of the sodomite as an "actual" social figure. As I indicated in the Introduction, the excavation and reconstruction of the "real," "actual" subculture is not the goal of this study. Further, it should be clear by now, I hope, *why* it is not my goal. Whatever the sodomites "were" or "did" is available to us only through the textual representations that we have of them. The project of historical reconstruction is dependent upon reading the texts that we have looked at as traces of the subculture they purport to depict rather than as traces of the culture which produced the texts. In other words, that project is dependent upon a fairly easy equation between discursive presence and cultural reality.

But, as the survey of sodomitical practices indicates, *sodomy* and *sodomite* are sufficiently overdetermined as to be irreducible to any one particular cultural reality. This is not to say that the designation "sodomite" had no worldly effects: looking at the sodomy trials in *Select Trials* one encounters again and again the sentence "The Jury found the Prisoner guilty. *Death.*" Indeed, to the contrary, I have been suggesting that sodomitical practices *did* have worldly effects, effects felt most brutally by those who were labeled sodomites, but which extended beyond—though definitely included—the workings of a minority oppression. In fact, to read vitriolic satire as mere description is to miss this point, to ignore the investment that satire as a genre has in social surveillance and regulation.

Let me give an example from closer to our own time to clarify what I mean by the distinction between discursive presence and cultural reality. In the 1950s in America, "communist" attained a remarkable discursive centrality and functioned in a way not dissimilar to "sodomite" in the Restoration and eighteenth century. Not immediately recognizable when seen on the street and given to meeting in secret, the communist embodied the complete antithesis of every value that made the nation strong, representing internally a perceived external (in this case Russian) threat. No doubt there were communists in America in the 1950s; they may even have met in secret, and it is likely that they were opposed to the national policies of the United States. But would anyone really suggest that the spate of innumerable Hollywood B-movies with titles like "My Mother Was a Communist" provides us with documentary evidence of the workings, the ideas, the identity of an "actual" communist underground? What these filmic representations give us is not insight into the communist movement itself in the 1950s, but rather insight into the place that the figure "communist" occupied in the cultural imagination. As well, the function of these film texts was obviously not transparent description; rather they exerted a social power and control through an incitement to vigilance, vigilance over not only "known" communists, but over everybody—even one's mother. And while we may easily recognize that the widespread discursive presence of the communist did not necessarily reflect a cultural reality, no one could argue that it did not have worldly effects.

Similarly, one might consider the idea of the "Elizabethan Underworld." As depicted in a vast number of pamphlets, plays, and satires, the "Elizabethan Underworld" was made up of a colorful array of thieves, vagabonds, rogues, and con-artists who formed a highly organized anti-society, much more organized than the forces of law and order, poised to overthrow the established society. This underworld was thought to have a complex system of rules and regulations, recognized leaders, and even its own specialized language, the "thieves' cant" or "rogues' lexicon." While the detailed "descriptions" of the underworld have impressed even some twentieth-century historians into believing in its existence, as A. L. Beier has recently shown, the "literature of roguery" bore little resemblance to any actual underworld of vagrant crime (see Beier 123–45). However, as Beier also shows, despite the fact that the underworld was nowhere near as large nor as organized as it was depicted as being, the dissemination of the idea that it was large and organized enabled the government to react vigorously, responding "in ways that significantly extended state authority" (147), and this extension of state control worked to curb the movement of everyone, not just those who "were" vagrants.

It is useful, I think, to keep these examples in mind when approaching the idea of a sodomitical subculture in Restoration and eighteenth-century England, to remember that discursive presence does not necessarily indicate an undistorted cultural reality. So, do I think that there *were* sodomites at the end of the seventeenth and beginning of the eighteenth centuries? Quite definitely. Do I think that there may have been a relatively organized sodomitical subculture? Quite possibly. And do the representations we have provide us with access to the workings of that subculture and to a new "proto-homosexual" identity, or subject position, behind it? Quite unlikely. Like the films about degenerate communists, these texts tell us more about the place of the sodomite in the cultural imagination than about actual social practice—much less what sodomites may have thought or felt themselves. When we read the documents from this period as indicating the emergence of a "homosexual" identity what we are often doing is collapsing what is actually an external element (satirical attack) into the internal element that we are hoping to find (the sodomite's "identity"). That is, we read accounts of the sodomites as though they were *self*-representations, records of subjectivity. Indeed, many works of historical reconstruction often subtly reveal this sliding from the external to the internal in their titles—"Attitudes Toward Deviant Sex," "Attitudes Toward Homosexuality," "The Pursuit of Sodomy"—*toward* and *pursuit* indicating that what is sought does not actually lie in the texts at hand but is elsewhere, out of reach. Rather than attempting to reconstruct the "actual" subculture from these texts, it is perhaps more useful to view these texts as themselves constituting the "social role" of the sodomite—in Mary McIntosh's sense of that term—and to ask what was the function and effect of these representations and their assertion that there was an *organized* group of sodomites.[10]

The most frequently cited "description" of the sodomitical subculture is Ned Ward's "Of the Mollies Club" which forms chapter 25 of *The Secret History of Clubs* (1709). It is therefore worth looking at in detail here. Though consistently mined anthropologically for details about the subculture, the ascription of a descriptive function to Ward's text simply cannot account for the sheer excessiveness, the overdetermined nature, of the depiction he provides:

There are a particular Gang of *Sodomitical* Wretches, in this Town, who call themselves the *Mollies*, and are so far degenerated from all masculine Deportment, or manly Exercises, that they rather fancy themselves Women, imitating all the little Vanities that Custom has reconcil'd to the Female Sex, affecting to Speak, Walk, Tattle, Curtsy, Cry, Scold, and to mimick all Manner of Effeminacy, that ever has fallen within their several Observations; not omitting the Indecencies of lewd Women, that they may tempt one another by such immodest

Freedoms to commit those odious Beastialities, that ought for
ever to be with out a Name.   (284)

Ward begins, then, by asserting the existence of a Molly Club in
town. He does not tell us how he has discovered it, nor where it is,
since he is bizarrely "unwilling to fix an Odium upon the House"
(285). Nor does Ward tell us where *he* is that he is able to take down
this "description." Is he hiding in the back? Whatever the case,
Ward presents himself as familiar with the "usual Practice" of the
mollies (285). The sodomite here, obviously, is distinguished by his
effeminacy, having "degenerated from all masculine Deportment,"
degenerated marking the inflection of this account through the gender hierarchy. As David F. Greenberg has noted, it is remarkable—
or at least odd—that accounts like Ward's describe *all* the patrons
of a molly house as effeminate cross-dressers (*Construction* 333).
However, as we have already seen, the depiction of male same-sex
desire seems always to involve the imposition of an at least rhetorical hermaphrodism. Men *as men* cannot desire other men *as men*.
Ward's depiction, of course, simply raises the problem it attempts to
solve in a different guise: if the mollies all "fancy themselves
Women," how is it that they tempt one another by acting like "lewd
Women"?[11] Ward, probably, is more intent on presenting the mollies as distorted travesties of gender, as having degenerated from the
proper order of things, than on accounting for desire. Indeed,
except for brief allusions in the opening and closing, Ward's
account is remarkably desexualized. Interestingly, however, in presenting the mollies as travesties of gender, Ward suggests, perhaps
inadvertently, that behavior is not so much a product of nature, but
that it is "reconcil'd" to a particular "Sex" merely by "Custom."

Having informed us that the mollies meet every night so as to have
every opportunity to lead the unwary astray, Ward then continues:

it is their usual Practice to mimick a Female Gossiping, and fall
into all the impertinent Tittle Tattle, that a merry Society of
good Wives can be subject to, when they have laid aside their
Modesty for the Delights of the Bottle. Not long since, upon

one of their Festival Nights, they had cusheon'd up the Belly of
one of their *Sodomitical* Brethren, or rather Sisters, as they
commonly call'd themselves, disguising him in a Woman's
Night-Gown, Sarsnet-Hood, and Nightrale, who, when the
Company were met, was to mimick the wry Faces of a groan-
ing Woman, to be deliver'd of a joynted Babie they had provided for that Purpose, and to undergo all the Formalities of a
Lying in. (285)

What are we to make of this bizarre event? Nothing like this
appears in the trial accounts. Indeed, compared to Ned Ward, the
trial accounts are rather bland, though some do mention the mim-
icking of female voices (see *Select Trials* 1:105–7, 158–60, 280–82,
329–30; 2:362–72; 3:36–40). Rictor Norton sees this as "spectacular
evidence" of the mollies' "female identification" and asserts that
this ritual "almost certainly originated as an act of imitative magic
designed to cast off sickness or evil spirits" (97–98). It is unclear to
me, I confess, how these two assertions fit together. I would suggest, instead, that what we are meant to see here is the mollies'
gleeful mocking of the very practice they are in the process of frustrating. As the reintroduction of the word "*Sodomitical*" serves to
remind us, producing children is precisely what the mollies will
not be doing. "Thou unnatural Monster," exclaims the author of
*A Treatise wherin are Strict Observations upon That detestable and
most shocking Sin of Sodomy*, "Is this the Return of Gratitude to
the Fair-Sex for giving thee Birth? . . . Cou'd they have suppos'd
the Favour wou'd be return'd Backward. . . ." (31–32). Given, as we
have seen above, that the sodomite was consistently depicted as
thwarting reproduction and, hence, society itself, the mock-birth
scene here gains its force as a sort of "adding insult to injury." Not
content to merely frustrate the foundation of society, the mollies
reenact it as sport. Ward, in fact, goes on to emphasize the dese-
cration of social and religious practice that is taking place:

The Wooden Off-spring to be afterwards Christen'd, and the
holy Sacrament of Baptism to be impudently Prophan'd, for

the Diversion of the Profligates, who, when their infamous
Society were assembl'd in a Body, put their wicked contrivance
accordingly into practice.   (285)

This passage recalls the earlier construction of the sodomites as dev-
ilish creatures, suggesting that they are almost like a coven, performing perverted versions of sacred ritual. But it also characterizes
the sodomites as secret plotters, planning "wicked contrivance[s]" to
put into practice.

"Of the Mollies Club" then describes at length how, "for the further promotion of their unbecoming Mirth" the mollies all took
turns talking about "their Husbands and Children" (286). It is, undoubtedly, the description of the mock-birth, and the long recounting of "tea-table" chat about "Husbands and Children" that have
led modern readers to think that Ward is here positing effeminacy,
or "female identification," as Norton puts it, as the hallmark of a
new sodomitical "identity" that marked the subculture. What this
ignores, however, is that Ward, at the end of his account, actually
reverses the assertions that he makes at the beginning:

> Thus, every one, in his turn, would make a Scoff and a
> Banter of the little Effeminate Weaknesses which Women
> are subject to when Gossiping, o'er their Cups, *on purpose to*
> *extinguish that Natural Affection which is due to the Fair Sex*
> [my emphasis], and to turn their Juvenile Desires towards
> preternatural Pollutions.   (288)

Whereas female impersonation seemed at first to be a distinguishing characteristic of the sodomite, an expression of identity, it is
revealed ultimately to be a ruse, a means of stamping out "that
Natural Affection" they would otherwise have. Whereas the mollies
seemed at first to abandon their manliness and "degenerate" into
effeminacy, they now reassert their manliness through a misogyny
that forms the foundation, apparently, of their "preternatural Pollu-
tions." Ward thus manages to depict the mollies misogynistically as
grotesquely effeminate, as having "degenerated" from true manli-

ness, and then, in a neat turn, to displace that misogyny onto the mollies themselves. It is the mollies, not Ward, who "Scoff" at the "Effeminate Weaknesses" of women. This ending seems to imply that the mollies, oddly, or perhaps just more wickedly, have to labor at their sodomitical passions; that is, they work to thwart the "proper" direction of desire, just as they intentionally profane a variety of social practices "for the further promotion of their unbecoming Mirth."

The fascinated attention that historians have paid to the mock-birth and gossiping has also led them to ignore the last few lines of "Of the Mollies Club," lines which are almost never cited, but which are, perhaps, the most significant. Despite Ward's opening assertion—"There are a particular Gang of *Sodomitical* Wretches, in this Town"—this account concludes by designating the molly subculture a thing of the past:

> Thus, without detection, they continu'd their odious Society for some Years, till their Sodomitical Practices were happily discover'd by the cunning Management of some of the Under Agents to the *Reforming-Society*; so that several were brought to open shame and punishment; others flying from Justice to escape the Ignominy, that by this means the Diabolical Society were forc'd to put a period to their filthy scandalous Revels. (288)

"Of the Mollies Club" functions ultimately, then, less as an empirical "description"—as its manifest inconsistencies make quite clear—than as an endorsement for the "Reforming Society," an example of a threatening deviance eradicated by effective and powerful forces of order.[12] The idea of a subculture, operating dangerously "without detection" and luring "unwary Youth to the like Corruption" (285), argues for the existence of a locus of conspiratorial disruption. "Of the Mollies Club" is thus an argument for the need for the continued policing and surveillance of the social scene, for its "cunning Management." The relocation of sodomitical disorder to the social world paradoxically enables the heightened regulation of a variety of social practices. As Sedgwick points out, the secularization of the sodomite not only set "the terms of a newly effective minority oppression" but also made available a new and potent tool "for the manipulation of every form of power that was refracted through the gender system—that is, in European society, of virtually every form of power" (*Between* 87). For just as sodomy comes to be marked by a number of social behaviors, so a number of social behaviors could be stigmatized as being sodomitical and subjected, therefore, to regulation, censorship, and punishment. The relocation of sodomitical disorder to the social scene does not just enable increased regulation of social practice, it demands it.

As we shall see in the next chapter, the increased discursive presence of the sodomite as a "social type" enables the continual reassertion and relegitimation of authority, a relegitimation which occurs primarily through a process of displacement. We have just seen an example of this displacement in Ned Ward: in "Of the Mollies Club" the misogyny of the gender hierarchy—a violence which is integral to "order" itself—is displaced onto the mollies who "extinguish that Natural Affection which is due to the Fair Sex." Misogyny thus becomes not at all central to the social order; it is, rather, said to be the province of a marginal group who are disrupting and perverting that order. The forces of order, here embodied in the Reforming Society, can not only disavow misogyny, then, but can actually present themselves as working to eradicate it. This process of disavowal and displacement is central to the representation of the sodomite and is the subject of chapter 2. Looking at two texts which characterize social crisis as sodomitical—*Sodom; or, the Quintessence of Debauchery* and *Love Letters Between a certain late Nobleman and the famous Mr. Wilson*—chapter 2 will offer a more particular account of the operation of sodomitical practices, suggesting that the figure of the sodomite as a social type does not simply facilitate the displacement of disruption from its source, but is, in fact, constituted through that act of displacement. The chapter begins, though, with a reading of the destruction of Sodom in Genesis 19 as the text which underwrites sodomitical practices.

Chapter Two
The Sodomical State

AND THERE came two angels to Sodom at even; and Lot sat in the gate of Sodom; and Lot seeing *them* rose up to meet them; and he bowed himself with his face toward the ground; 2 And he said, Behold now, my lords, turn, in, I pray you, into your servant's house, and tarry all night, and wash your feet, and ye shall rise up early, and go on your ways. And they said, Nay; but we will abide in the street all night. 3 And he pressed upon them greatly; and they turned in unto him, and entered into his house; and he made them a feast, and did bake unleavened bread, and they did eat. 4 But before they lay down, the men of the city, *even* the men of Sodom, compassed the house round, both old and young, all the people from every quarter: 5 And they called unto Lot, and said unto him, Where *are* the men which came in to thee this night? bring them out unto us, that we may know them. 6 And Lot went out at the door unto them, and shut the door after him, 7 And said, I pray you, brethren, do not so wickedly. 8 Behold now, I have two daughters which have not known man; let me, I pray you, bring them out unto you, and do ye to them as *is* good in your eyes: only unto these men do nothing; for therefore came they under the shadow of my roof. 9 And they said, Stand back. And they said *again*, This one *fellow* came in to sojourn, and he will needs be a judge: now will we deal worse with thee, than with them. And they pressed sore upon the man, *even* Lot, and came near to break the door. 10 But the men put forth their hand, and pulled Lot into the house to them, and shut to the door. 11 And they smote the men that *were* at the door of the house with blindness, both small and great: so that they wearied themselves to find the door. 12 And the men said unto Lot, Hast thou here any besides? son in law, and thy sons, and thy daughters, and whatsoever thou hast in the city, bring *them* out of this place: 13 For we will destroy this place, because the cry of them is waxen great before the face of the LORD; and the LORD hath sent us to destroy it. 14 And Lot went out, and spake unto his sons in law, which married his daughters, and said, Up, get you out of the place; for the LORD will destroy this city. But he seemed as one that mocked unto his sons in law. 15 And when the morning arose, then the angels hastened Lot, saying, Arise, take thy wife, and thy two daughters, which are here; lest thou be consumed in the iniquity of the city. 16 And while he lingered, the men laid hold upon his hand, and upon the hand of his wife, and upon the hand of his two daughters; the LORD being merciful unto him: and they brought him forth, and set him without the city. 17 And it came to pass, when they had brought them forth abroad, that he said, Escape for thy life; look not behind thee, neither stay thou in all the plain; escape to the mountain, lest thou be consumed. 18 And Lot said unto them, Oh, not so, my lord: 19 Behold now, thy servant hath found grace in thy sight, and thou hast magnified thy mercy, which thou has shewed unto me in saving my life; and I cannot escape to the mountain, lest some evil take me, and I die: 20 Behold now, this city *is* near to flee unto, and it *is* a little one: Oh, let me escape thither, (*is* it not a little one?) and my soul shall live. 21 And he said unto him, See, I have accepted thee concerning this thing also, that I will not overthrow this city, for the which thou has spoken. 22 Haste thee, escape thither; for I cannot do any thing till thou be come thither. Therefore the name of the city was called Zoar. 23 The sun was risen upon the earth when Lot entered into Zoar. 24 Then the LORD rained upon Sodom and upon Gomorrah brimstone and fire from the LORD out of heaven; 25 And he overthrew those cities, and all the plain, and all the inhabitants of the cities, and that which grew upon the ground. 26 But his wife looked back from behind him, and she became a pillar of salt. 27 And Abraham gat up early in the morning to the place where he stood before the LORD: 28 And he looked toward Sodom and Gomorrah, and toward all the land of the plain, and beheld, and, lo, the smoke of the country went up as the smoke of a furnace. 29 And it came to pass, when God destroyed the cities of the plain, that God remembered Abraham, and sent Lot out of the midst of the overthrow, when he overthrew the cities in the which Lot dwelt. 30 And Lot went up out of Zoar, and dwelt in the mountain, and his two daughters with him; for he feared to dwell in Zoar: and he dwelt in a cave, he and his two daughters. 31 And the firstborn said unto the younger, Our father *is* old, and *there is* not a man in the earth to come in unto us after the manner of all the earth: 32 Come, let us make our father drink wine, and we will lie with him, that we may preserve seed of our father. 33 And they made their father drink wine that night: and the firstborn went in, and lay with her father; and he perceived not when she lay down, nor when she arose. 34 And it came to pass on the morrow, that the firstborn said unto the younger, Behold, I lay yesternight with my father: let us make him drink wine this night also; and go thou in, *and* lie with him, that we may preserve seed of our father. 35 And they made their father drink wine that night also: and the younger arose, and lay with him; and he perceived not when she lay down, nor when she arose. 36 Thus were both the daughters of Lot with child by their father. 37 And the firstborn bare a son, and called his name Moab: the same *is* the father of the Moabites unto this day. 38 And the younger, she also bare a son, and called his name Benammi: the same *is* the father of the children of Ammon unto this day.

—Genesis 19

This narrative of sodomy, attempted sodomitical rape, pandering, death, destruction, drunkenness, and incest—listed in the apparatus at the back of my King James's as a "Favourite Bible Story"—is, as Robert Alter has recently reminded us, set within a larger narrative concerned with the founding of a nation (see "Sodom as Nexus"). The destruction of the Cities of the Plain occurs between God's covenantal promise of seed to the founding father, Abraham, in Genesis 17 and the fulfillment of that promise with the birth of Isaac in Genesis 21. Sodomy thus figures largely right at the very beginning of the Patriarchal History and functions as a social as well as a sexual designation: Genesis 19 is the story of a community judged and destroyed. J. P. Fokkelman has argued that the entire book of Genesis is concerned with survival, progeny, fertility, and continuation, a concern reflected in God's repeated commandment to "[b]e fruitful and multiply" (1:28, 8:17, 9:1), and in the generational chapters (5, 10, 11, 25, 36, 46) in which lists of names suggest the successful execution of this commandment (see Fokkelman 40–44). Particularly important in this respect is what Fokkelman calls "God's twofold blessing or promise to the patriarchs":

> God promises the patriarchs numerous offspring and the land of Canaan as a permanent home. Clearly, offspring are not safe without a fixed habitat, and promises of land are useless if there is no procreation. The two parts of the promise/blessing therefore presuppose each other and are intertwined.   (42)

In other words, Genesis, as the protohistory of the nation of Israel, links inextricably the idea of nation with procreation, each "naturalizing" the other. Significantly, however, Genesis also warns that neither the existence of the nation nor procreation can be taken as a matter of course. Sarah, for example, like the other matriarchs, Rebekah and Rachel, is barren until God intercedes. The foundation and continuity of the nation, then, is enabled only by God and is dependent upon his continued blessing. Positioned between the promise of progeny to Abraham and Sarah—the father and mother of nations and kings (17:6, 16)—and the fulfillment of this promise, the destruction of Sodom functions as a warning and counterexample. While the birth of Isaac involves the miraculous transformation of barrenness into fertility under God's smiling eye, the narrative of Sodom vividly displays the opposite: the equally awesome transformation of fertility into barrenness occasioned by God's displeasure. It is fitting, then, at least thematically, that the sin which has aroused God's displeasure should be an "unnatural" (i.e., unnational or nonprocreative) form of sex.

It was common in the late seventeenth and early eighteenth centuries—particularly after the fire and the plague of 1666—for satirists to refer to London as another Sodom, as a place where sin was so rampant that judgment could not but fall upon the city and, likely, the entire nation. The analogy between Sodom and England does, of course, predate the late seventeenth century. Michael Warner, for example, has shown the early seventeenth-century Puritans "referred to Sodom as an example of judgment and a warning for England; they referred to themselves as a possible 'saving remnant' of the kind Abraham bargained for with God; and they referred to the American migration as the journey of Lot into Zoar" (19). Warner also remarks, however, that "sexual proscription was not the overt content of [this] language about Sodom" (19). In the Restoration, the "language about Sodom" is overtly sexualized. "Let Sodom speak, and let Gommorah tell,/ If their curs'd walls deserv'd their flames so well," writes Charles Sackville, Earl of Dorset, in "A Faithful Catalogue of Our Most Eminent Ninnies" (1688), comparing the present state of London to that of the biblical cities (*POAS* 4:191). Dorset's comparison arises from a sense of general debauchery among the "Most Eminent," general in the sense that, as Norton points out, the brothels of Salisbury Court were referred to as "Sodom" and "little Sodom" (32).

However, the comparison between London and the Cities of the Plain most frequently involved an assertion of the growth of sodomy between men. "Nostradamus' Prophecy" (1672), for example, predicts that disaster will come "When sodomy is the Prime Minister's [i.e. Buckingham's] sport/ And whoring shall be the least crime at court" (*POAS* 1:187); and "The Women's Complaint to Venus" (1698) fears that London has been "overrun/ By Sparks of the Bum/ And peers of the Land of Gommorah" (167). These two satires suggest a movement toward a hierarchy of debauchery: there may still be whoring, but it is the "least crime at court," and the complaining women we are asked to sympathize with are in fact "Poor Whores" who now may as well be "Nuns" (167). *The Play of Sodom* (1707), a brief dramatic version of Genesis 19, makes explicit that what is at stake is the "Nation's Fate":[1]

Nay, if our Sins are grown so high of late,
That Heaven scarce can long adjourn our Fate;

By Raining scalding Showers of Brimstone down,
To Burn us, as of old, the lustful Town:
. . . .

But where Lust reigns, it shews a Nation's Fate
Is given up, and past for reprobate.   (3)

The narrative of Genesis 19 is foundational for the "sodomitical
practices" we are looking at in this study.

It has, of course, been argued that the sin of Sodom was not
male-male sex at all but, rather, that it was a serious breach of hospitality.[2] This argument has been most fully expounded by Derrick
Sherwin Bailey in his book *Homosexuality and the Western Christian Tradition* (1955). Bailey argues that when the men of Sodom
surround Lot's house and demand that his visitors be brought out
that they might "know" them (v. 5), they do not mean "engage
in sex with," but merely "get acquainted with" (2–4). What the
Sodomites are guilty of is inhospitality to strangers. More recently,
Bailey's arguments have been supported by John Boswell. Boswell
suggests that on the basis of the text there are four possible reasons
for the destruction of Sodom: "(1) the Sodomites were destroyed
for the general wickedness which had prompted the Lord to send
angels to the city to investigate in the first place; (2) the city was
destroyed because the people of Sodom had tried to rape the
angels; (3) the city was destroyed because the men of Sodom had
tried to engage in homosexual intercourse with the angels . . . ; (4)
the city was destroyed for inhospitable treatment of visitors sent
from the Lord" (*Christianity* 93). Although Boswell says that the
second possibility is the "most obvious," he actually argues for
acceptance of the inhospitality interpretation and suggests that a
sexual dimension to the story is minimal, if present at all (93–97);
the narrative ought to be understood within the context of numerous Old Testament and folk stories that insist upon hospitality to
strangers as a sacred duty.

Both Boswell and Bailey remind us, importantly, that Genesis 19
is a story about the disruption of social order and duty. However,
one cannot divorce the social order entirely from a sexual economy

here. For if there is some uncertainty about the exact manner in which the Sodomites wish to "know" the heavenly messengers in v. 5, it seems to become less uncertain in v. 8 when Lot offers his daughters to the crowd as substitutes for the visitors and emphasizes the fact that they are virgins. While the source of social disorder may not be explicitly stated here, Lot's solution to the problem is: he attempts to restore social order by offering to restore a more acceptable circulation of women's bodies among men, to restore, that is, an order which is disrupted by the similar circulation of men's bodies.

We do well to recall the complicated history of Genesis 19 that John Boswell details. However, eighteenth-century commentators express few doubts about the nature of the sin of Sodom and Gomorrah. Matthew Henry, in his mammoth *Exposition of the Old and New Testament* (1706), is quite sure what caused the destruction of the city:

> It was the most unnatural and abominable wickedness that they were now set upon, a sin that still bears their name, and is called *Sodomy*. They were carried headlong by those vile affections (Rom. i. 26, 27), which are worse than brutish, and the eternal reproach of the human nature, and which cannot be thought of without horror by those that have the least spark of virtue and any remains of natural light and conscience. (122)

Unnatural, abominable, vile affections, brutish, against the light of nature: here is the language of sodomitical practices that we have already encountered. Having set up the scene in this way, Henry then offers the following "Practical Observation" on this episode: "Note, Those that allow themselves in unnatural uncleanness are marked for the vengeance of eternal fire" (122). To Henry, the destruction of Sodom is clearly an example of God's judgment against sexual sin, against "[b]urning lusts against nature" (125). Henry also sees a clear link between the sexual and the social: commenting on v. 4, he connects sodomy with the collapse of not only the natural order, but also the civil order:

Here were old and young, and all from every quarter, engaged
in this riot; the old were not past it, and the young had soon
come up to it. Either they had no magistrates to keep the peace,
and protect the peaceable, or their magistrates were themselves
aiding and abetting. Note, When the disease of sin has become
epidemical, it is fatal to any place, Isa. i. 5–7.   (122)

Like a horrible contagion, unnatural lust spreads, corrupting all
members of the social body and eradicating the distinction between
the peaceable and the unpeaceable, the magistrates and the crimi-
nals. Genesis 19 shows what might destroy a community, and the
monitory function of the story is highlighted, as I have already indicated, by its position within the narrative of the founding of a nation.

However, Genesis 19 is only *in part* about the destruction of a
people. Lot, as the one righteous man in Sodom, is delivered from
the conflagration along with his family—though the unbelieving
sons-in-law, one assumes, are consumed in the fire and brimstone
(v. 14), and Lot's wife is, of course, turned to a pillar of salt (v. 26).
Lot and his two daughters flee first to Zoar and then, overcome with
fear, to a cave in the mountains. Here in the mountains, Lot's
daughters fear that the entire world has been destroyed (v. 31); they
therefore put into action a plan to preserve the seed of their father.
On two consecutive nights, they give their father wine to drink and
they each lie with him: "Thus were both the daughters of Lot with
child by their father" (v. 36). From the unions of Lot and his daughters spring two peoples, the Moabites and the Ammonites.

This chapter, then, which begins with the destruction of a people, ends, revealingly, with the founding of a people, revealingly
because these two oppositional events—the destruction of a people
and the founding of a people—are both occasioned by "unnatural"
sex, or "abominations" as these acts are characterized in Leviticus
(18:7, 22, 26, 27). Indeed, Matthew Henry, in his commentary,
describes the actions of Lot's daughters in almost exactly the same
language he used to describe the actions of the Sodomites: "their
project was very wicked and vile, and an impudent affront to the very
light and law of nature" (127). Henry further links Lot's daughters

with the Sodomites by suggesting that they were motivated by the "fire of lust," though there is no indication in the text that lust was their motive (127). Scandalously, Genesis 19 reveals that the practice of founding a nation can involve acts similarly as interdicted as those which are said to destroy a nation—but with one significant difference: while nation-destroying "abominations" are rendered spectacular (the destruction of Sodom is framed by Abraham's "before" and "after" gaze [18:16, 19:28]), the "abominations" which build a nation are marked by a disavowal. In contrast to the Sodomites' rowdy demand to "know," we are told twice that Lot "perceived not when [his daughter] lay down, nor when she arose" (vv. 33, 35). Whatever Lot may or may not have perceived, however, he "knows" his daughters well enough. If Genesis 19 shows Sodom as an "anti-nation" because of its corruption, it also shows that a nation—perhaps *the* nation—may be rooted in a like corruption.

It will of course be objected that the Moabites and the Ammonites *are* marked out for a kind of destruction because of the "abomination" of their origin. Certainly they do figure later in the Patriarchal History as the enemies of Israel and, in Deuteronomy, the Moabites and Ammonites are denied entry into "the congregation of the Lord" because they did not help the Israelites in their exodus from Egypt (23:3–4). Thus Robert Alter writes:

> the two peoples . . . will carry the shadow of their incestuous origins in the (folk-) etymology of their names, Moab, from-the-father, and Benei Ammon, sons-of-kin;[3] and perhaps we are encouraged to infer that in their historical destiny these peoples will be somehow trapped in their own inward circuit, a curse and not a blessing to the nations of the earth, in consonance with their first begetting.   (36)

But is this really the case? Alter's "perhaps" is a rather large one; we are not, in fact, encouraged to infer anything by the impassive narrator. No comment is made on the act of procreation, no curse pronounced upon the progeny. Even poor Matthew Henry, who clearly longs to denounce the events of Genesis 19:30–38 and to expound upon their horrible consequences, finds himself unable to do so in a straightforward manner:

> Note, Though prosperous births may attend incestuous con-
> ceptions, yet they are so far from justifying them that they
> rather perpetuate the reproach of them and entail infamy
> upon posterity; yet the tribe of Judah, of which our Lord
> sprang, descended from such a birth, and Ruth, a Moabitess,
> has a name in his genealogy, Matt. i. 3, 5.   (127)

The "though" and the repeated "yet" indicate Henry's inability to make an unqualified statement here. And it is likely more than the ethnicity of Ruth that gives him such trouble; if the Sodomites, the Moabites, and the Ammonites are to be cursed because of "abominations," what are we to make of the discovery in Genesis 20 that Abraham and Sarah are not only husband and wife, but also half-brother and sister (v. 12)? This type of union is also cited in Leviticus 18 as an "abomination" that will defile the land and create disorder (vv. 9, 11, 26, 27).

Matthew Henry, not surprisingly, declines to comment on this revelation, but the lack of commentary here gives us an insight into the earlier attribution of lust to the daughters of Lot; the idea of lust enables distinctions to be made. Through the concept of sinful lust, "abomination" can be disavowed in connection with the chosen nation, disavowed and displaced onto foreign enemies (Moabites, Ammonites) and godless perverts (Sodomites), justifying their exclusion and violent destruction and facilitating the construction of the opposition us/them.[4] This double process of disavowal and displacement, incipient in the originary narrative of Sodom in Genesis and consolidated in commentaries like Henry's, is fundamental to sodomitical practices in the Restoration and eighteenth century.

In the previous chapter we saw that in the last half of the seventeenth and first half of the eighteenth centuries the sodomite achieved a significant discursive prominence as a social type, a deviant "discovered" at the margins of society. Conceptualized as the embodiment of a disorder at once sexual, cultural, political, and religious, the sodomite represented an anarchic force that threatened to undermine the nation and against which the nation might define itself. In this chapter I suggest that the formation of the sodomite as a social type was to a considerable degree the product of a displacement of social crisis, anxiety, and disruption—a process that figures typically in the construction of the "unnatural" and "perverse." As we saw in Ned Ward's "Of the Mollies Club," for example, the construction of the sodomite as a "Woman-Hater" asks us to understand misogyny as an aberration for which the "unnatural" sodomite is responsible, as though it were not a violence manifested everywhere in the workings of "order"—not to mention in Ward's writing itself. As Jonathan Goldberg has pointed out, the effort to treat sodomy as antithetical to the nation can be belied by the "spectre of its complicity with the nation. In a society that was male-dominated, that regarded male-male relations as the privileged site not only for political but also for the most valued emotional ties, . . . the abjection of and stigmatization of male-male relations can never quite be separated from male privilege" (6 *Reclaiming*).

The potential congruence between the prescribed bonds of male privilege and the proscribed bonds of male desire is often (mis)recognized in satiric jabs against people in power and their relationships with their favorites, most notably, perhaps, in the number of anti-Williamite satires which claim that "Billy with Benting [Bentinck] does play the Italian" (*POAS* 5:221). William III's tendency to trust only a few *foreign* men, like Bentinck, with state matters provided his opponents with plenty of satiric fuel:

> For the case, Sir, is such,
> The people think much,
> That your love is Italian, your Government Dutch
> Ah! who could have thought that a Low-Country stallion
> And a Protestant Prince should prove an Italian? (*POAS* 5:38)

This satirist rather deftly manipulates the associations with sodomy outlined in the last chapter in order to suggest that William is a tyrannical ruler. William's selection of foreign ministers is linked in the third line with "foreign" desires conventionally associated with Italy. Sodomy and Italy together evoke the specter of Catholicism which, in turn, was typically associated with absolutism. The interconnected associations of sodomitical practices enable the paradox of the last line in which "Dutch" becomes "Italian." In other words, we thought William would be a liberator (Dutch/Protestant/"stallion"), but it turns out that he is a tyrant (Italian/Catholic/sodomite).

Of course, from a slightly different, nonsatiric perspective, it is clear that "sodomy" here designates what is simply the way in which a head of state might consolidate his power, the way that state power works. What poems such as this one against William acknowledge— if only satirically and, indeed, unwittingly—is that which is everywhere else disavowed: the disorder or crisis which is characterized as sodomitical often actually emerges from within "order" itself, from within those forces defined as the means for excluding disorder and keeping it at bay. The responsibility for such crisis is then typically displaced. I draw here on Jonathan Dollimore's formulation of the way in which disavowal and displacement function in the legitimation of social order (see Dollimore 111–12): when groups whose authority is sanctioned by the dominant term in the order/disorder binary actually produce disruption—say, by fighting among themselves (court vs. parliament, Whig vs. Tory)—such conflict threatens to delegitimate order by reproducing the binary within the dominant term itself. Authority maintains its legitimacy, however, and restabilizes the binary by identifying disruption with the demonized figures signified by the binary's subordinate term. To call disruption "sodomitical" is thus to enact a displacement of responsibility for it, making it appear as though it were a perversion of the institutions of "order" rather than their effect. As Dollimore elucidates, such displacements of crisis "on to the sexual deviant, be he or she actual, imagined, or constituted in and by the displacement, are made possible because other kinds of transgression . . . [as we saw in chapter 1] are not only loosely associated with the sexual deviant, but 'condensed' in the very definition of deviance" (237). This process of displacement is, naturally, most prevalent during periods of intensified social crisis.[5] The rest of this chapter examines the figuration of social crisis as sodomitical in two texts: *Sodom: or, The Quintessence of Debauchery* (c. 1672–73) and *Love Letters Between a certain late Nobleman and the famous Mr. Wilson* (1723).

In a way, these two texts could not be more dissimilar. One is an almost surreal pornographic reworking of Genesis 19; the other is a pseudo-realistic epistolary fiction. Both texts, however, have achieved some prominence in recent attempts to reconstruct a "gay past." Rictor Norton, for example, cites some lines from *Sodom* in order to illustrate the sexual positions favored by late seventeenth-century sodomites (108). And *Love Letters* was recently the focus of an entire issue of the *Journal of Homosexuality* (1990); the editor of this particular issue informs us that the novel "illuminates the underworld of male homosexuality" (Kimmel, "Greedy Kisses" 7). But to read these two texts as descriptive of an underworld of homosexuality is, I suggest, to misread them—though such misreadings are instructive of the way that displacement constituted the sodomite as a social type. For what *Sodom* and *Love Letters* have in common is that both texts were generated by social crisis and both texts account for that crisis by figuring it as sodomitical. In each case, too, the crisis was precipitated not by some marginal and deviant group, but by those at the very centers of power and "order."

Sodom: or, The Quintessence of Debauchery has been most commonly attributed to Rochester, though not without controversy. It has also been attributed to a very minor poet, Christopher Fishbourne. The work was certainly associated with Rochester from the beginning of its publication history: editions appeared in 1684 and in 1689 under Rochester's name. However, the denials of Rochester's authorship appear just as early. The printers of the 1689 edition, Benjamin Crayle and Joseph Streater, were prosecuted for publishing *Sodom* as Rochester's work, and both Anthony à Wood in 1692 and Charles Gildon in 1698 asserted that the work was incorrectly "fathered upon the Earl" (see Johnson 122–26). J. W. Johnson, in the most recent survey of external and internal evidence (1987), concludes that Rochester was indeed the author. However, Harold Weber suggests that "all ascriptions of authorship remain unprovable until further evidence presents itself" ("Carolinean Sexuality" 68).

In the following discussion, I have chosen to refer simply to the "poet." I use the term "poet" rather than "playwright" because, despite the appearance of the text on the page, *Sodom* is better understood as a verse satire than as a drama; that is, it is a work clearly meant to be read, not performed, for the simple reason that it would be physically impossible to perform it as a play: one scene, for example, calls for a *"grove of cypress trees"* in which *"men are discover'd playing on dulcimers with their Pricks, and women with jews Harps in their cunts"* (109). *Sodom* belongs to that genre of Restoration satirical writing which mixes sex and politics, poems such as Rochester's famous scepter/prick satire on Charles or Oldham's "Sardanapalus." For as Richard Elias—to whose work I am indebted—has shown, *Sodom* deals with the power struggle between court and parliament that followed Charles's second attempt to issue a Declaration of Indulgence in 1672.

We have already seen (in chapter 1 in relation to Louise de Kéroualle), a few examples of the way in which satirists linked Charles's sexual life with the nation's political life. Indeed, Harold Weber suggests that Rochester's lines equating Charles's prick and his scepter are, by the 1670s, a commonplace: "Once what we would today call Charles's media honeymoon ended, his sexual misbehavior became a convenient, even irresistible, target for satirists. Indeed, so visible and productive of anxiety were the king's sexual antics that considerations of sexual power became inextricably linked with matters of monarchical authority" ("Charles II" 196). The majority of these satires lament Charles's abdication of his manly—and hence kingly—authority in allowing himself to be ruled first by his prick and then by his mistresses as in these lines from "A Ballad Called The Haymarket Hectors" (1671):

Our good King Charles the Second
Too flippant of treasure and moisture,
Stoop'd from the Queen infecund
To a wench of orange and oyster.

> Consulting his cazzo, he found it expedient
> To engender Don Johns on Nell the comedian. (*POAS* 2:169)

This stanza seems at first more comic than condemning; however, it does begin to hint at the dangers of Charles's consulting only his "cazzo," or penis. The king's whoring, for instance, is what has made him "too flippant of treasure" and, in stooping to consort with the low-born Nell Gwynne, Charles demonstrates that his "cazzo" can eradicate social hierarchy. The implications of Charles's actions, hinted at here, are made clearer in the rest of the poem:

> And now all the Fears of the French
> And pressing need of navy
> Are dwindl'd into a salt wench
> And *amo, amas, amavi.*
> . . . .
> If the sister of Rose [Gwynne]
> Be a whore so annointed
> That the Parliament's nose
> Must for her be disjointed,
> Should you but name the prerogative whore,
> How the bullets would whistle, the canon would roar!
>   (*POAS* 1: 170–71)

By the end of the poem, the effects of the king's "cazzo" appear grave indeed. Charles has not only disregarded social hierarchy in stooping to take up with Nell Gwynne, but in giving himself up to his mistresses, Charles has inverted the power hierarchy of gender. Power now resides with Nell Gwynne who, rather than Charles, is the "annointed" one, and with the Duchess of Cleveland who controls the "prerogative." Having weakened himself in this way and upset the social order, Charles has rendered the nation vulnerable to both French invasions from without and civil broils within.

While poems such as "A Ballad Called The Haymarket Hectors" portray Charles as weak and negligent, they exist side by side with an increasing number of poems in the early 1670s that connect the king with absolutism. Unlike the other poems which fear that the nation may be enslaved through Charles's neglect, these poems portray the king as actively attempting to enslave his own subjects, and a number of them begin by invoking Magna Charta. In "The King's Vows" (1670), Charles declares,

> I will have a religion then all of my own,
> Where Papist from Protestant shall not be known,
> But if it grow troublesome, I will have none.
> I will have a fine Parliament always to friend
> That shall furnish me treasure as fast as I spend,
> But when they will not, they shall be at an end.
>
> (*POAS* 1:156–60)

These last lines may have come to seem prophetic; in the following year, 1671, Charles, having received grants from Louis XIV that made him financially independent, prorogued parliament successively until 1673. "Nostradamus' Prophecy" (1672) bluntly calls Charles a tyrant:

> When the English Prince shall Englishmen despise,
> And think French only loyal, Irish wise;
> Then wooden shoes shall be the English wear,
> And Magna Charta shall no more appear;
> Then th' English shall a greater tyrant know
> Than either Greek or Gallic stories show.   (*POAS* 1:188)

The poem ends with an allusion to Aesop's fable "Of Jupiter and the Frogs" implying that the English are now paying for the mistake of having recalled Charles to the throne in the first place: "Too late the frogs, grown weary of their crane,/ Shall beg of Jove to take him back again" (*POAS* 1:189).[6] It is within this context of fears about Charles's absolutist tendencies and the Restoration convention of mixing sex and politics that *Sodom: or, The Quintessence of Debauchery* can be understood.

When Charles issued his Declaration from Breda, just prior to his Restoration, he promised "liberty for tender consciences" to those whose religious opinions did not disturb the peace (see John Miller 96, and Harris 40–46). This promise was subject to the approval of parliament, and parliament, unfortunately, disapproved. Nevertheless, in 1662, Charles defended his proposal for religious toleration and requested that parliament help him "exercise, with a more general satisfaction, that power of dispensing which we conceive to be inherent in us" (in Witcombe 8). Parliament, however, denied that Charles had the prerogative of dispensing and argued that as the Act of Uniformity had already been passed, it could not be dispensed with except by another Act of Parliament. Gilbert Sheldon, the Archbishop of Canterbury, made the same argument against toleration in a letter to Charles: "this toleration . . . cannot be done without a parliament, unless your majesty will let your subjects see that you will take unto yourself the liberty to throw down the laws of the land at your pleasure" (in Western 164). Charles acquiesced and, instead of an Indulgence, issued a new proclamation against priests and Jesuits. In 1672, however, Charles again issued a Declaration of Indulgence and, again, was forced to withdraw it, this time after a much nastier struggle with parliament which ended in the passing of the First Test Act, a bill which, ultimately, precipitated the Exclusion Crisis. The Declaration of Indulgence was seen as a step toward absolutism. Not only did Charles make this declaration without consulting parliament, which he had prorogued, but it also coincided with the declaration of war against the Dutch in alliance with France, also made without consulting parliament. The Indulgence for religious toleration, the alliance with France, and the presence in England of troops raised to fight the Dutch created fears that a standing army was being established to support the growth of popery and arbitrary government. The King might speak of "liberty," but clearly this was a move toward tyranny. Parliament reacted vigorously and rejected the Indulgence on the same grounds as they had before: the King did not have the right to establish toleration by prerogative. Parliament then simply held up passing the bill for supply, which Charles needed for the Dutch war, until the Indulgence was withdrawn (Witcombe 130–35). Charles eventually did revoke the Indulgence, but in the meantime a bill was introduced in parliament that would become the First Test Act. Once again, Charles's attempt at toleration ended in a renewed proclamation against priests and Jesuits.

The *Sodom*-poet draws on the equation between "natural" and "unnatural" sexual relations and "natural" and "unnatural" political relations I referred to in the previous chapter in order to suggest that Charles's use of his prerogative is unnatural, that is, tyrannical and arbitrary.[7] *Sodom* begins in mock-heroic style, its opening lines parodying the opening lines of Dryden's *The Conquest of Granada, Part I* (1669). Boabdelin's "Thus, in the triumphs of soft peace, I reign;/ And, from my walls, defy the powers of Spain" (19) becomes, in the mouth of Bolloxinion, the King of Sodom, "Thus in the Zenith of my Lust I reign:/ I eat to swive and swive to eat again" (57). Though in the zenith of his lust, Bolloxinion has grown tired of women. He decides, therefore, with the "Councill" of his advisers, to make sodomy legal:

BOLLOXINION
Henceforth Borastus, set the Nation free,
Let conscience have its force of Liberty.
I do proclaim, that Buggery may be us'd
Thro' all the Land, so Cunt be not abus'd
That, the proviso, this shall be your Trust. . . .
BORASTUS
Straight these indulgences shall be issu'd forth,
From East to West and from the South to North.   (62–63)

Prince Pockenello (the Duke of York?) echoes Bolloxinion's language of liberty, telling him that he permits "the Nation to enjoy/ That freedom which a Tyrant would destroy" (58). The scene ends with Pockenello telling the King of a "Trespass" upon the "Sovereign Prerogative": Pine, a "Pimp of Honour," has been having an affair with one of the King's mistresses, Fuckadilla (64). "With crimes of this sort," Bolloxinion replies, "I shall now dispense;/ His arse shall

suffer for his Pricks offence" (64). As Elias points out, this opening
scene rehearses all of the key terms in the power struggle between
the court and the parliament (433): liberty of conscience, indulgence, prerogative, and the power to dispense with laws. We also see
that Bolloxinion's/Charles's declaration has more to do with his own
desires than with any concern about "tender consciences." That is,
Bolloxinion's turning to sodomy refigures Charles's suspected turning to Catholicism. *Sodom* figures Charles's Declaration of Indulgence—seen as a mere invitation to popery and arbitrary government—as a Declaration of Indulgence for sodomy— popery, arbitrary government, and sodomy all being equally "unnatural."
The rest of the satire demonstrates the horrible consequences of toleration. Despite the proviso Bolloxinion makes when he issues his
decree that women should not be abused—that is, that "heterosexual" relationships need not be abandoned just because sodomy is
allowed—as soon as the proclamation is made every man in the
nation instantly becomes a sodomite. In allusions to fears that a
standing army and the French alliance would support and encourage
the spread of popery, we discover that the entire army of Sodom has
sided with Bolloxinion and turned to sodomy and that Bolloxinion
now has a close relationship with his "Brother King," Tarsehole of
Gomorrah. Buggeranthos, the general of the army, tells the King

> great Sir, your soldiers
> In double duty to your favour bound,
> They own it all, and swar and tear the ground;
> Protest they'l die in drinking of your Health. . . .
> BOLLOXINION
> How are they pleas'd with what I did proclaim?
> BUGGERANTHOS
> They practice it in honour of your name;
> If lust present they want not woman's aid
> Each buggers with content his own comrade.   (94–95)

The image of soldiers inflamed with lust by one another would
seem to be a punning, satiric play on the idea of a "standing" army

ready to do the king's bidding. And, just as Louis was sending Charles grants to keep him independent of parliament, King Tarsehole sends forty "young striplings" in order to encourage Bolloxinion in his new resolve (100). As the practice of sodomy spreads throughout the nation under Bolloxinion's decree, sex between men and women is shown to be repeatedly frustrated and, ultimately, the women of Sodom are simply abandoned.

Unlike the men of Sodom who repeat Bolloxinion's talk of liberty—mostly, it should be added, to gain the King's favor—the Queen, Cuntigratia, and her Ladies in Waiting have no qualms about labeling Bolloxinion a tyrant as they become more and more sexually frustrated:

OFFICINA
The day of Marriage you may justly rue,
Since he will neither swive nor suffer you.
CUNTIGRATIA
That Tyranny doth much augment my grief,
I can command all but my cunt's relief;
. . . I am not jealous, but my Envy must
Declare to all my pleasures he's unjust.   (66–67)

Officina advises Cuntigratia that she would be justified in taking a lover: "Tho' he [Bolloxinion] a Tyrant to your Honour be/ Your Cunt may claim a subject's liberty" (68). The only man the Queen can find, however, proves to be impotent (91). As *Sodom* moves toward its apocalyptic conclusion, the assessment of the women is proven to be correct. Despite his intent to "set the Nation free," Bolloxinion, once he finds everyone following him, degenerates into a raging, maniacal tyrant: "Which of the Gods more than myself can do?" he asks, and then proclaims that he will invade heaven "and bugger all the Gods" in order to become immortal (110). Far from setting the nation free, Bolloxinion and his declaration have brought about the nation's ruin; "I have fuckt and bugger'd all the land," he declares (99), and, indeed, so he has. Flux, the Royal Physician, makes this clear near the end: not only has the Queen died, the Prince got the clap, and the Princess run mad, but

> The heavy symptoms have infected all,
> I now must call it epidemical.
> Men's pricks are eaten of the secret parts,
> Of women, wither'd and despairing hearts. . . .
> The young, who ne'er on nature did impose
> To rob her charter, or corrupt her laws
> Are taught to break all former vows,
> And do what love and nature disallows.   (111–12)

In the same language that Matthew Henry used in his commentary on Genesis 19, Flux here sums up the effect of Bolloxinion's decree: the nation has been pulled out of nature's course, nature has been perverted, and the perversion has become "epidemical." Given the political nature of the satire, however, we also see added to Henry's language a stress on the "charter," "laws," and "former vows." Like the physical bodies described by Flux, the body politic has become diseased. The solution to the nation's distress, of course, is simple: "To Love and nature all their rights restore — / Fuck women and let buggery be no more" (113). Again, fittingly, the solution is framed not just in terms of a return to male-female relations, but in terms of the restoration of rights that have been usurped. The words, however, are meaningless to Bolloxinion and, in the end, "the heavens all in a flame appear," fire and brimstone descend, and the nation is destroyed (116).[8]

While *Sodom: or, The Quintessence of Debauchery* places the sodomite front and center, and raises him to mock-heroic proportions, the satire is not actually about sodomy at all.[9] *Sodom* asks its readers to see in the presentation of the monstrous sodomite the twin nation-destroying evils of popery and arbitrary government. As Richard Elias, quoting Marvell, writes, *Sodom*

> presents a message that Restoration readers heard elsewhere: "There has now for divers years a design been carried on to

change the lawful Government of England into an absolute
Tyranny, and to convert the established Protestant Religion
into downright Popery; than both which nothing can be
more destructive." In prose and verse Marvell and others
thumped the same tub. The author of *Sodom* may not share
their moral seriousness, but his ridicule is as effective as
their rhetoric.   (438)

As astute and historically informed as Elias's reading of *Sodom*
is, however, it does need to be qualified; for Elias accepts sodomy
as a perfectly reasonable figure for "political aberration" (435). I do
not merely mean to suggest here that this unreflecting acceptance
make Elias's reading homophobic—though of course it does.
Rather, what I wish to point out is that because Elias so readily
accepts sodomy as the "unnatural" (or tyrannical) side of the political equation, the violence and tyranny inherent in the "natural"
side are occluded from his vision, violence and tyranny which are
actually made quite explicit through the satire's use of sex as a
metaphor for the social order. If to read *Sodom* as a "description"
of late seventeenth-century sodomites is simply to misunderstand
the satire, then Elias understands the satire only too well and re-
inscribes in his reading the displacement of social violence onto
the sodomite.

Because *Sodom* figures the sociopolitical order through sexual
relations, the satire can, in a way, be read as something of an extension of Genesis 19:8, where Lot attempts to restore order by flinging
his daughters out to the crowd. That is, the whole trajectory of the
satire is an argument to restore those "natural" relations which
Bolloxinion's declaration has disrupted. But the depiction of the
sodomite as an unnatural tyrant for having turned away from
women is belied by the satire's insistently and grotesquely misogynistic portrayal of women as sexually insatiable and available, from
the Prologue—"That Lady who shall act the best her part,/ Doth
hope at least to have a fucking for't" (51)—to the Epilogues, spoken
by the "Ladies in Waiting":

> The best of cunts is like a common shore,
> Come 7 or 8 at least, come half a score:
> I'll swive with all, till I can swive no more!   (122)

And within the satire itself, the women of Sodom are presented in an abject state of continual sexual frustration. Banished from the presence of the almighty "Prick," the women can find no pleasure or satisfaction. Similarly, although they have been permitted the use of dildoes by the King, Cuntigratia and her Ladies in Waiting, unlike the women in Rochester's "Signior Dildo," for example, find absolutely no pleasure in these simulacra; dismissing them as "weak and simple bauble[s]" (104), the women continue to pine for a "stately Tarse" (72). Buggeranthos even relates to Bolloxinion the story of one woman who is driven to attempt intercourse with a horse, claiming that her "cunt could spare/ Perhaps as much room as his Lady Mare" (97). When the horse refuses to cooperate, she gives herself up to despair in this "cunt starving land" (97). Impressed, Bolloxinion thinks such determination ought to be "rewarded":

> Such woman ought to live, pray find her out;
> She shall Pintle have, both stiff and stout,
> Bollocks shall hourly by her Cunt be suckt;
> She shall be daily by all Nations fuckt.   (97)

Bolloxinion's idea of "reward" here emphasizes the way in which the satire conceives of men, and men alone, as the only source of pleasure—and therefore of value—in the sexual economy.

Despite the variety of sexual activities presented, and despite the fact that Bolloxinion's declaration makes every man instantaneously turn to sodomy, *Sodom* is incapable of imagining the possibility that any satisfying erotic activity might take place between the women themselves. Indeed this *cannot* be imagined. For the desperate and constant availability of the women is necessary: the return to the "natural" order is dependent upon it, dependent upon, that is, the sexual submissiveness of women. Through its presentation of women, *Sodom* asserts that the return to the "natural" order will be just that—natural, free from any coercion or force. "Naked we lie to entertain your tarses," Cunticula says reassuringly in one of the Epilogues, and proclaims the prick, "the female's king" (117, 119). However, the fetishization of the prick that the satire enacts, and its insistence that the women long to enslave themselves to it, suggests that violence and tyranny are really on the side of "nature." But it is a violence that is disavowed in the satire through its displacement onto the "unnatural" and monstrous sodomite. In this respect, at least, the presentation of the sociopolitical order in *Sodom* is quite accurate. Violence is an aberration of social structures, the satire asks us to believe, not their effect.

The anonymous *Love Letters Between a certain late Nobleman and the famous Mr. Wilson* moves us into a very different milieu, literarily speaking, than that of *Sodom*. Instead of *Sodom's* crude and unrestrained pornography, *Love Letters* has the pseudo-aristocratic, slightly risqué air of the *chronique scandaleuse*, focusing on passion, intrigue, and, especially in this case, money. An epistolary fiction, *Love Letters* chronicles "the course of a fictional homosexual relationship in early-18th century England," as Michael Kimmel puts it ("Greedy Kisses" 1); David Greenberg adds that "it depicts homosexual life in greater detail than most documents of the period" ("Socio-Sexual Milieu" 93). However, just as *Sodom* was not really "about" sodomy, *Love Letters*, I suggest in what follows, is not really "about" a love relationship. Rather, like *Sodom*, *Love Letters* uses sodomy to figure social disruption. And whereas *Sodom* rewrote the narrative of Genesis 19 in order to figure a political crisis, *Love Letters* rewrites the "real-life," mysterious rags-to-riches story of Edward Wilson in order to figure economic crisis.

In the early 1690s, Edward Wilson—or Beau Wilson as he came to be known—captured the attention of London. Having arrived in the city almost penniless, he was soon leading a life of the most extravagant luxury—despite the fact that he had no known means of income. No one was able to discover the source of Wilson's seemingly limitless riches, and he himself would not reveal it; naturally, he became the talk of the town. The mystery of Wilson's life was then further heightened when he was killed in a duel on April 9, 1694, by one John Law. Two weeks after Wilson's death, John Evelyn made the following entry in his diary:

> A very young Gentleman named Wilson, the younger son of one that had not above 200 pounds per Annum: lived in the Garb & Equipage of the richest Noble man in the nation for House, Furniture, Coaches & 6 horses, & other saddle horses; Table & all things accordingly: . . . being challenged by one Laws [*sic*] a Scots-man, was now killed in Duel . . . Laws [*sic*] is taken & condemned for Murder:[10] But the Mysterie is, how this so young gentleman, a sober young person, & very inoffensive, & of good fame, did so live in so extraordinary Equipage; it not being discovered by any possible industry, by any his most intimate Friends, no, tho' they had endeavoured to make him reveale it being in drink: But they could never find it out: It did not appear he either was kept by Women or Play, or Coyning, Padding; or that he had any dealing in Chymistry, but that he would sometimes say, that if he should live to never so great an age, he had wherewith to maintain it in the same affluence. . . . All which was subject of much discourse and admiration. (175–76)

It would seem that Wilson remained the subject of discourse and admiration even after his death, for thirteen years later, in 1707, a highly romantic account of his life appeared in a work attributed to Delariviere Manley—*The Lady's Pacquet of Letters*. While obviously much more developed than a diary entry, Manley's account focuses on the same related facts about Wilson's life as did Evelyn's: his highly visible wealth, its darkly secret source, and the fact that this wealth allowed Wilson to live as if he were himself a nobleman when in fact he came from "mean Circumstances":

> You must remember, Madam, that some Years since, one Mr. W—l—n, (who was known about the Town by the Name Beau W—l—n) from very mean Circumstances and an obscure

Condition, set up an Equipage, and made a Figure beyond many of the Nobility. After blazing some few Years, (I can't tell exactly how long) he was kill'd by one Mr. L. going to fight a Duel with him; . . . His Coaches, Saddle, Hunting, Race Horses; Equipage, Dress and Table, were the admiration of the World, and continu'd such, when they saw him continue them, and that they could not assign any support to all this Glory. He never play'd, or but inconsiderably; Entertain'd with Profuseness all who visited him; Himself drank liberally; but in all Hours, as well sober as otherwise, he kept a strict guard upon his Words; tho' several were either employed by the Curiosity of others, or their own, to take him at his looser Moments, and persuade him to reveal his Secret. But he so inviolably preserv'd it, that even their Guesses were but at random, and without probability or foundation.   (522–23)

The novel of intrigue may love a dark secret to begin with, but it loathes to leave anything in the dark, and *The Lady's Pacquet of Letters* goes on to "reveal" that Wilson was kept by a rich and powerful woman, who although she is not named in the text, is clearly meant to be Elizabeth Villiers, the mistress of William III. Briefly, the narrative of *The Lady's Pacquet of Letters* is that Villiers, after seeing Wilson in a park, arranges a secret love affair with him in which her maid, who is the narrator of the story, acts as a go-between. In all their encounters, Villiers wears a veil in order to conceal her true identity. After Wilson is overcome with curiosity and tears the veil away, Villiers hires John Law to murder Wilson and then arranges for Law's escape.[11] The source of the "famous Mr. Wilson's" fame, then — what kept his story alive — was his fabulous but mysterious wealth and his sudden and violent death before that mystery could be solved.

Whatever else may have been speculated about the means by which Beau Wilson accomplished his rise to wealth and fame, in 1723 the anonymous "editor" of *Love Letters* informed his readers that these documents would set "the Matter quite upon another Bottom" (13). Beau Wilson's own as it turns out. Comprised of twenty letters framed by a Preface and a section of "Observations" on the letters, *Love Letters* "reveals" the secret of Wilson's life to have been a passionate love affair not with Elizabeth Villiers, nor with any other woman, but with another man. In language which is completely conventional for the time, but which has, I think, an added resonance for us, this text performs a kind of "outing" of Beau Wilson and the Nobleman: the letters, we are told, "were found in the Cabinet of the Deceas'd, which had Pass'd thro' some Hands, before the private Drawer, the Lodgment of this Scene of Guilt, was discover'd" (13). As a result, a "Piece of History which has lain so long in the Dark . . . is now . . . coming so fair and open" (13).

This language is so conventional as to be almost obligatory in the Preface of an early eighteenth-century novel. Among scholars who have discussed *Love Letters*, only Rictor Norton persists in treating the letters as genuine (35–43), not noticing, apparently, that the text never manages to get Wilson's first name correct (his letters are signed "W. Wilson" and the Nobleman calls him "Willy"). The question, then, is not whether the letters are real, whether we finally have the truth of Wilson's secret, but why the story of Wilson's mysterious wealth and sudden death should be revived almost thirty years later, and why this story of money and intrigue should be figured as sodomitical? I suggest that the answer lies in contemporary anxieties about economic instability.

After the 1690s, an important change in socioeconomic organization occurred in England. This was the rise of a money and credit economy which followed the establishment of the Bank of England in 1694, an economy that was based largely on the holding of joint-stocks (see Dickson and Schubert). The possibilities—and also dangers—of the credit economy reached their climax in the South Sea Bubble of 1720–21 (see Carswell, Garber, and Reading). The South Sea Company had been founded in 1711 for trade in South America. However, due to continuing diplomatic difficulties with the Spanish government, no such trade actually ever took place (Carswell 65–68, 75–76). Despite this apparent drawback, in 1719 parliament accepted a proposal for the South Sea Company to take over a substantial portion of the National Debt by converting government annuities to stock.

This was an attractive proposal for the government, for the Company agreed to fix the interest on this portion of the Debt at a lower rate than that which the government was presently paying the annuitants. In order to make the proposal attractive to the annuitants as well, however, the South Sea Company had to create a rising market. The Company did this by opening the stock to the public and promising large dividends, supporting these promises with elaborate descriptions of the vast treasure-house that was South America and assurances that native South Americans wanted nothing more than English wool. This triggered a spree of buying which inflated the value of the shares and, in subsequent subscriptions, people were allowed to buy shares with money borrowed against South Sea stock they already owned, thus inflating the value of the shares even more. Eager to cash in on the apparent fever for speculation, several other companies sprang into existence selling stock in a variety of projects, and by 1720, just before the bubble burst, the aggregate capital of all the projects then on the go in London was over £300,000,000—or more than the total amount of money then in circulation in Europe (Reading 96).

Not surprisingly, this could not last; indeed, John Carswell estimates that for the South Sea Company alone to be able to pay its promised dividend on the amount of stock it had created, it would require a yearly profit of £15,000,000—this though its trade was at a standstill. In the end, the collapse of several smaller ventures set off a run of selling South Sea shares, and the value of the stock fell rapidly from a high point of £1350 to about £150. Several people—especially those who had bought stock late at the outrageously inflated value—were ruined; others were lucky enough to sell out in time. Scandalously, however, the effects of speculation seem to have had no regard for class, and while peers lost fortunes, innkeepers made them.

It does not take a great leap of imagination to see the parallel between the course of the South Sea Bubble and the narrative of Wilson's rise to spectacular wealth from a dubious source and his subsequent violent death—especially when one recalls that Wilson was killed by John Law whose Mississippi Scheme for the conversion of the National Debt in France provided the direct model for the South Sea Scheme in England (Carswell 100). (While the Mississippi Scheme had a sounder economic grounding than the South Sea Scheme—i.e., actual trade was taking place—it also eventually collapsed.) As well, just after the collapse of the South Sea Bubble, and just before the publication of *Love Letters*, John Law, as Rousseau reminds us, had finally returned to England after twenty-seven years abroad ("An Introduction" 69). It may be less clear, perhaps, why Wilson's story should be figured as sodomitical. However, as we saw in chapter 1, there was already a correspondence between the discourse of sodomy and the discourse of economics, production, and sterility. In addition, as J. G. A. Pocock has shown, the burgeoning credit economy was understood in the eighteenth century to be a feminized economy, whimsical and unpredictable. "Economic man," he writes,

> as a masculine conquering hero is a fantasy of nineteenth-century industrialization. . . . His eighteenth-century predecessor was seen as on the whole a feminized, even an effeminate being,. . .still wrestling with his own passions and hysterias and with interior and exterior forces let loose by his fantasies and appetites, and symbolized by such archetypically female goddesses of disorder as Fortune, Luxury, and most recently Credit herself. (114)[12]

The problem with the speculative economy is that it "gave itself credit for attaining levels of wealth, power, and satisfaction which it had not yet achieved" (Pocock 99). Or, to put it differently, the problem with the credit economy is that it produced nothing; that is, what it did produce was always only imaginary, always to be realized—perhaps—at some future date. The connection between the rise of a credit economy and sodomy lies in the fears which were expressed about each of these phenomena. It was feared that both speculation and sodomy would result in a thwarting of the proper circulation of industry on the one hand and of desire on the other,

both of which, ideally, should end in production—either of more
English goods or of more English people.

A number of early satires on the sodomites, like "The Women's
Complaint to Venus," are written in the voice of a woman who
complains that she has been forsaken due to an alarming rise in
sodomitical activity:

> But now we are quite out of Fashion:
> Poor Whores may be Nuns
> Since Men turn their Guns
> And vent on each other their passion.   (167)

The poem concludes with a call for men to "henceforth do their
duty" (168). The nature of that "duty" is made clear by the author of
Plain Reasons for the Growth of Sodomy who, as I have already had
occasion to note, writes: "An old *Proverb* says, *There is no Harm done
where a good Child's got*. . . . It is the Action of a *Man* to beget a
Child, but it is the Act of a *Beast*, nay worse, to ____ I scorn to stain
my Paper with the Mention" (23). At the same time that horror is
expressed, however, there is a corollary fear that men may be easily
led into a sodomitical relationship. One "Philogynus," or "Woman-
Lover," writes in the *London Journal*: "If the Legislature had not
taken prudent Measures to suppress such base and irregular Actions,
Women would have been a Piece of useless Work in the Creation"
(in Norton 123).

These fears about the effects of sodomy find a parallel in the fears
expressed about the effects of speculation. Instead of the horrible
practice of sodomy, though, it is the "pernicious practice of stockjobbing" that will lead people out of the path of production, "divert-
ing the genius of the nation from trade and industry" by "decoying
the unwary to their ruin by a false prospect of gain" (in Reading 62).
Even the King spoke against the "unwarrantable Practices" of stockjobbing, claiming that it would lure many of his subjects "from
attending their lawful Imployments" and introduce "a General
Neglect of Trade and Commerce" (in Reading 99–100). An anonymous pamphleteer further warned that stockjobbing

not only depraves and debauches the Morals and Manners of Mankind, but turns them aside from pursuing their proper business and Callings, whereby they might . . . be the Means of bringing Treasure into the Kingdom, and encouraging the Manufactures of *Great-Britain*.   (in Hentzi 35)

Similarly, if sodomy had the potential to turn "all things Arsy Versy in the nation," as one satire puts it ("Jenny Cromwell's Complaint"), the uncertainties of speculation could likewise invert the social order so the "Beggars [might] on horse-back ride/ Whilst Princes walked on foot" ("The Bubbler's Medley").

In *Love Letters*, these two strains of thought converge; in the economic turmoil of the 1720s, the history of Beau Wilson is revived as a "parable" of the present economic crisis, and what is most troubling in his story—the dubious source of wealth which allowed Wilson to transgress class barriers—is figured as sodomitical. Again, as in *Sodom*, the effort to present disruption as sodomitical, as somehow outside the order of things, is belied by the fact that the economic crisis of the South Sea Bubble was caused by the government itself.

At first the representation of the sodomite in *Love Letters* seems as though it were going to be conventionally straightforward. When the "editor" speaks in the Preface of "an affair of the odious and criminal . . . Nature" and of the "Sin which is not familiar to our Northern Climate" (13–14), when he tells us that Wilson's and the Nobleman's schemes to evade detection excelled "the most Jesuitical Designs that ever were known" (36), one expects the familiar representation of the sodomite as an unnatural, foreign sinner to ensue. But *Love Letters* only evokes these associations with sodomy to then move beyond them. Instead of focusing specifically on the horrific unnaturalness of Wilson's affair with the Nobleman, *Love Letters* repeatedly returns to the economic fact of Wilson's "profuse Grandeur," characterizing him as a "Meteor of Mortality" and a "Meteor of Profuseness" while reminding us all the while that he started out in a lowly condition (13, 36). "Wilson became the Wonder of the whole Town," we are told, "who from being a private necessitous Dependent on Fortune, seem'd now to be the Ruler of her" (35). In this case, however, Fortune is distinctly a *him*.

The economic basis of this "worst Sort of Gallantry" (13) is made clear from the very first letter, from the Nobleman to Wilson, in which passion and money become almost interchangeable:

> Say, was it a cold Insensibility that caused you to shun a Challenge, where to give and receive excess of Pleasure, was to have been the only Combat between us; or conscious of your own matchless Charms, are you resolv'd with peevish coy Pride, to be won at the Expense of a thousand Inquietudes and restless fond Desires. . . .
>
> If you are of a Turn insensible to Pleasure, I know Gold has the greatest ascendant over you; for all covet it for what it purchases. This Bill may convince you, I have that in my Power: I can be Fortune to you.   (15)

The Nobleman then asks Wilson to meet him on the following evening. Letter II is Wilson's enthusiastic response — but he plainly thinks that it is a "fine Lady" who has been captivated by his charms and who has requested the meeting (16). What Wilson's initial reaction is at discovering that his "fine Lady" is actually a man is left in the dark. However, as the rest of the letters indicate, he and the Nobleman develop an intimate relationship, one in which money continues to play an important part. "I had not above a hundred Pieces by me when I receiv'd yours," begins Letter III from the Nobleman, "which made me send, swift as the Minutes, to the Bank to fetch this. I would have my Willy believe, I am never so delighted, as when I am doing that which may convince him, how very dear he is to his [own] Love" (17).

Significantly, then, Wilson is presented initially as being open to — even eager for — a relationship with a woman. Like the fears expressed about the corrupting dangers of speculation which would lure the king's subjects away from their "lawful Imployments," *Love Letters* presents Wilson as having been diverted from the "proper" path by the promise of wealth. Since Wilson was a "Stranger to his

Passion," his Lordship, the "editor" knowingly comments, naturally imagined that "a Cash-Note must be the only Bait to draw this cold Insensible" (35). Wilson, the "editor" implies, would have had no interest in a sodomitical relationship were it not for the lure of easy wealth. The "Cash-Note" has the desired effect and Wilson is raised, as the Nobleman will later remind him, "from a wretched necessitous Life, perplex'd with petty Duns . . . to be the Nation's Wonder" (29).

Throughout their affair, Wilson and the Nobleman are forced to carry out a number of "Plots" in order to keep their relationship secret, plots which "must, by all, be own'd to be the Masterpieces in their kind," the "editor" judges (36). The success of these plots is credited to the Nobleman rather than to Wilson and, indeed, the Nobleman takes a conspirator's glee in duping the Town: "They are all devilishly puzzled about you," he writes to Wilson in Letter V; "it is pleasant to see how the Ideot's [sic] Curiosities are raised . . . ; when the dull three Days are over, I'll fly to my Dearest . . . and there laugh at all their ridiculous Conjectures" (19). The aura of a secret conspiracy is reinforced by the "editor" who calls the Nobleman's schemes "Jesuitical" and observes that this narrative "may convince the World that his Lordship was no less a Politician in his private Affairs, than he was in the Publick" (36). It is clearly the Nobleman who is figured as the force of corruption in *Love Letters*, a figure of wealth and power who encourages the wrong sort of transactions.

Interestingly, two recent suggestion for the identity represented by the Nobleman are both men who were implicated in the scandal of the South Sea collapse: James Stanhope, First Earl of Stanhope, and Charles Spencer, Third Earl of Sunderland (suggested by Rousseau and Norton, respectively). While Stanhope's involvement in the scandal was slight, his name was dragged into the investigation because of his cousin, Charles Stanhope, the Treasury Secretary. Sunderland, however, as First Lord of the Treasury, was deeply implicated and investigated by the Secret Committee for receiving bribes from the Directors of the South Sea Company. Although Sunderland was acquitted, a strong enough case was made against him that he eventually resigned his post (see Carswell, ch. 12, "The End of the Ministry;" and Reading 130–55).

Those ministers felt to be responsible for the South Sea Bubble had already been castigated in 1721 in a political satire entitled *The Conspirators; or, the Case of Cataline*, attributed to Thomas Gordon. This work is, in fact, dedicated to "The Right Honourable, The Earl of S——D"; however, the terms of the dedication are sufficiently ambiguous to suggest that Sunderland is the target rather than simply the dedicatee: "As soon as I had collected the *Memoirs* of this horrid Conspiracy, I was not long deliberating with my self, to whom I should make bold to address them" (iii); or, "I don't know, but that our circumstances may be like those of old *Rome*, when this Plot of Cataline was set on Foot: But of this your Lordship is the *ablest Judge*" (iv). In *The Conspirators*, government ministers and South Sea directors are represented as Cataline and his corrupt followers, plotting the downfall of Rome. Most significant, however, is that the conspirators are characterized as a gang of sodomites:

> He [Cataline/Sunderland] married several times, but chiefly, as People suspected, for the Convenience of strengthening himself by *Alliances* with *Great Men*, rather than out of any Affection for the *Ladies*. For if we may believe some Authors, he had a most *unnatural* Tast [sic] in his *Gallantries*: And in those Hours when he gave a Loose to Love, the Women were wholly excluded from his Embraces. . . . There are some Vices, which give too gross Ideas, to be repeated by the Names that are affix'd to them. 'Tis certain, however odd and unnatural his Lewdness was, (yet it was a notorious Practise among some great Men of the Age) and some of his *Ganymedes* were pamper'd and supported at a high Rate of Expence. (24–25)

As Carswell has remarked, it would not be an exaggeration to say that anyone involved in stockjobbing "gradually replaced the jesuit as everyman's idea of a conspirator" (16).[13] It is not surprising, then, that the charge of sodomy, which had been linked for so long with papists in general and jesuits in particular, should come to be linked with those who dealt in stocks. This is clearly the case in *The Conspirators* and, I suggest, it is also the case in *Love Letters*, which retells the story of Wilson's mysteriously acquired wealth by casting him as a "Ganymede . . . supported at a high Rate" by the corrupt Nobleman.

The Nobleman's corrupting influence is figured not only in his drawing Wilson into a secret affair which, as the "editor" reminds us, ultimately proves fatal to Wilson, but also in his virulent misogyny, something which is made much of in the "Observations." In Letter X, Wilson writes a panicky note after hearing a beautiful young woman he has seen at the theatre spoken of as the Nobleman's mistress. "Did it fret and tease itself because I have got a Wench," the Nobleman writes back; "it's true, I had her dirty Maidenhead, . . . not so much to amuse the dull Time in thy tedious Absence . . . as to stop some good natur'd Reflections I found made on my Indifference that way" (25). The story of this woman—"the unfortunate Cloris"—is related by the "editor," and it takes up almost the last half of the "Observations."

Cloris has been sent from the country by her parents to stay with a relative of the Nobleman in town so that she might have the benefit of a more genteel education. After the Nobleman makes some "splenatick Reflections" on Cloris's "awkward Country Airs," Cloris resolves to let him see that he has outlived his own attractiveness and takes "an Opportunity before Company, to run Pins in his false Calves" (41). The Nobleman swears eternal revenge for this insult; and, seeing that he can exact his revenge and simultaneously silence the reflections on his lack of interest in women, he sets out to seduce Cloris, substituting his previously malicious remarks with ones of flattery and admiration. The Nobleman accomplishes his goal with surprising ease, and decides to "keep Cloris in so grand a Way, as might make the Loss of her Reputation the more remarkable" (42). By the time that Cloris has been set up, Wilson returns from a short absence from town and the Nobleman, having no more use for Cloris, pretends to discover that she has been unfaithful to him and he casts her off.

Thrown into a life of shame and destitution, Cloris attempts a reconciliation with the Nobleman, but he remains unyielding—even when she acquaints him with "her moving Condition of being pregnant" (43). In desperation, Cloris disguises herself as a handsome youth in order to gain the Nobleman's attention and to meet with him. Once they are alone, Cloris begins to upbraid the Nobleman and then draws a pistol against him. The Nobleman, however, easily gets the gun from her and, pretending *not* to see through her disguise, he knocks her to the ground with repeated blows and kicks and leaves her to die. Apparently unwilling to leave anything to speculation, the "editor" makes certain we comprehend the point of the story: "This barbarous Usage to a Woman, and with Child by himself, plainly shews what a Hatred he had to the *whole Sex*" (43; my emphasis). A passing soldier finds Cloris and takes her to her lodgings where, after "three or four Days" of agony, she gives birth to a dead child and then expires herself (44).

The text ends at this point with the death of Cloris and her child and does not, as one might expect, go on to make further observations about Wilson and the Nobleman. "Thus fell the unfortunate Cloris," reads the final sentence, "a Sacrifice to one who had not even the Excuse of once liking her; but work'd her Ruin, to gratify his own Pride, and mortify hers" (44). Leaving Wilson and the Nobleman in the background, the conclusion of *Love Letters* emphasizes instead the result of their relationship. The "proper"—that is, "heterosexual" and productive—economy of desire is brutally destroyed and the birth which that economy might have occasioned is thwarted. What is left in its place is the Nobleman's affair with Wilson, a "false" economy of desire—its mock-status figured in the Nobleman's request that Wilson wear women's clothing (17)—an economy which is not productive but in which the circulation of mere pleasure, like the unproductive circulation of mere paper called stock, creates a destructive potential for erasing social and economic boundaries. In its conjunction of money and desire, *Love Letters* asks us to recognize the cause of England's economic turmoil—the credit economy—as dangerous, unproductive, and unmanly—as sodomitical.

This attempt, however, to signify economic "deviance" through sexual "deviance" is, like *Sodom*, fraught with incoherences, incoherences that mark the way in which social crisis gets displaced from its source onto a despised figure. In order to characterize economic deviance as sodomitical, *Love Letters* relies on our perception of the relationship between Wilson and the Nobleman as horrifically unnatural and "other"—as the invasion of something "foreign to our Northern Climate"—and the Preface and "Observations," for the most part, ask us to read the letters in this light. It is worth pointing out that stockjobbing, too, was often described in terms of an impending foreign threat. Sir John Barnard in a speech to the House of Commons, for example, asserted that "there is a foreign evil attending the game of stock-jobbing, by which the nation may be plundered of great sums of money at once" (in Roseveare 101). By implication, then, *Love Letters* calls for a return to more steady, manly, *English* practices.

Yet, revealingly, presenting the sodomitical relationship as something distinctly "other" is precisely what *Love Letters* can hardly do. *Love Letters* is an epistolary fiction and, as such, the series of twenty letters constitute a relatively independent narrative which the book's editorial framework can only imperfectly contain. The letters themselves are highly conventional of the love-letter genre, taking us through a common trajectory of ecstatic first meeting, overpowering passion, bitter jealousies, and happy reunion. Filled with stock phrases about enfolding arms, melting ecstasies, and doting to madness, there is little in the letters to mark them off as radically different. In fact, at one curious point in the Preface, the "editor" himself suggests that if we find it too offensive to read these documents as letters between two men, then we need only imagine that one of the correspondents is a woman: "All the Weeds will then vanish," he says, "or be turn'd to Flowers" (14).

Without the "Observations" and their focus on the story of Cloris, *Love Letters*, in its conventionality, might actually be said to naturalize rather than demonize passion between men by situating it within a familiar and popular generic context: "Did I not strictly charge my dearest Boy, at parting, not to omit one Opportunity of acquainting me with his returning Health, by which alone my Joys can be restored," the Nobleman exclaims conventionally in Letter VIII; "It's Hell to love and doat to Madness, as I do on Thee" (22). "Command me to be well and live," comes the expected, if hyberbolic reply, "but not (for Oh! I cannot) live without you" (23). Even the story of Cloris, so clearly meant to mark out the sodomite from other men, would not be out of place in one of the popular seduction novels by the contemporaneous Eliza Haywood, and would there signify the "normal" state of male-female relations. Indeed, the misogyny attributed to the Nobleman as a defining characteristic of the sodomite seems rather to be a projection of the misogyny of the "editor" who tells us that Cloris succumbed to the Nobleman's addresses because of "the natural Failure of her Sex" (42). Thus, what is meant to be radically "other" in *Love Letters* repeatedly turns out to be the "same." (The disturbing familiarity with which the sodomite can appear is a subject I take up in the next chapter.) In order to characterize the cause of social crisis as sodomitical, *Love Letters* relies on the violent and enduring mythology of the sodomite, the mythology that it evokes in the Preface, but which it cannot itself quite manifest.

Of course, *Love Letters* probably did not *need* to manifest this mythology, any more than *Sodom* needed to entirely eradicate the violence of its "natural" order. Contemporary readers likely needed little convincing that the sodomite was a terrifying and unnatural figure bent on the destruction of the social order. As Jonathan Dollimore writes,

> The process of displacement/demonizing can never be assured of success, . . . [b]ut what stacks the odds in favour of displacement succeeding is the brute fact of the minority's relative powerlessness and probable disrepute. Also of course the struggle is usually . . . for representation, especially of *how* instability is represented, and those who control the means of representation have more than a head start.   (90)

In reading *Sodom: or, The Quintessence of Debauchery* and *Love Letters Between a certain late Nobleman and the famous Mr. Wilson* I have attempted to show not just that crisis and disruption integral to the social "order" get displaced (in an attempt to preserve that "order") onto the figure of the sodomite, but that the figure of the sodomite is to a considerable degree constituted through that very act of displacement. This second fact is one that is often ignored by those carrying out projects of historical reconstruction. Thus, Michael Kimmel writes that the calculated undoing of Cloris in *Love Letters* is a reminder that "male homosexuals, defined as effeminate and passive, could still conform to the norms of a misogynist masculinity in relation to women" ("Greedy Kisses" 8). By not taking into account the way in which, and the extent to which, sodomitical practices constitute what they purport to describe, even gay-affirmative criticism risks recycling stereotypes such as this one.

This chapter and the previous one have argued that sodomitical practices constituted a complex signifying economy in which the sodomite appears as a refigured representation of a variety of social concerns and anxieties. To read sodomitical practices as descriptive of a proto-modern "homosexual identity," then, is to misread them, and to embrace "identity" at the site of its rejection and dispersal. However, it is not my wish to entirely desexualize the sodomite, to evacuate a discourse of desire from the discourse of sodomy. As we have already begun to see, sodomitical practices do not constitute a stable, monolithic discourse. In the following two chapters, I turn to the instabilities and discursive ruptures in sodomitical inscription in an attempt to locate the place of desire within the language that would negate it. We should not, however, expect to find a coherent and integrated voice of sodomitical desire.

Chapter Three
Sodomitical Smollett

By this time we had dragged the criminal [i.e. the schoolmaster] to a post, to which Bowling tied him with a rope he had provided on purpose, after having fastened his hands behind his back, pulled down his breeches, and tucked up his garments and shirt, as far as they would go. –In this ludicrous posture he stood (to the no small entertainment of the boys, who crowded about him, and shouted with great exultation at the novelty of the sight). —*The Adventures of Roderick Random*

MY DISCUSSION of sodomitical practices has thus far paid little attention—purposely—to the place of erotic desire in the representation of the sodomite. Indeed, to the contrary, I have been attempting to stress the extent to which the figure of the sodomite was made to bear a meaning that was not "merely"—or even primarily—sexual. Rather, I have been suggesting that the sodomite figured a number of social concerns and anxieties—political, economic, religious, and ethnic. I have emphasized this aspect of sodomitical practices because, as I have indicated, it has been generally ignored. However, as implicated as the sodomite is in the structures of social ordering and control, his representation cannot be accounted for entirely in terms of power relations. Repeatedly represented as foreign, the sodomite is, through repeated representation, necessarily rendered a domestic phenomenon; repeatedly rejected as not fit for representation, the sodomite nevertheless repeatedly returns as the object of a fascinated representation. As Peter Stallybrass and Allon White have argued, that which is marked out as "low" and repulsive by dominant culture, and so rigorously excluded at the social level, frequently returns at the imaginative level as "the object of nostalgia, longing and fascination" (191):

It is for this reason that what is *socially* peripheral is so frequently *symbolically* central (like long hair in the 1960s). The low-Other is despised and denied at the level of political organization and social being whilst it is instrumentally constitutive of the shared imaginary repertoires of the dominant culture.   (5–6; original emphasis)

So, for example, while satires, fictions, and works like *Select Trials at the Old-Bailey* constructed the sodomite as a figure to be shunned with horror or brought to the punishment of the law, these same texts also reconstructed the sodomite and his actions for perusal in the privacy of one's own home. Accordingly, in this chapter and the next I trace the inscription of the sodomite as the object of "longing and fascination," primarily in works by Tobias Smollett and in John Cleland's *Memoirs of a Woman of Pleasure.* In other words, these final two chapters examine the ways in which sodomitical practices can become the discursive field in which sodomitical desire is actually articulated, even in the same terms that effect its denunciation.

That I begin my discussion of desire in this study under the title "Sodomitical Smollett" may be the cause of some consternation to traditional Smollett scholars.[1] Such critics seem never to tire of informing us that Smollett's works are "robust," "bawdy," "boisterous," "earthy," and "rumbustious," by which they appear to mean "manly" in the most conventional sense of that word. Paul-Gabriel Boucé's remarks in his introduction to the Oxford World's Classics edition of *The Adventures of Roderick Random* may be taken as typical:

> *Roderick Random* is very much of a man's book, written mostly with men in mind—but not exclusively so, as the love-interest was obviously meant to catch and hold the female reader's attention. But all the same, in *Roderick Random* the rough, but enjoyable give and take of the gunroom or wardroom, the barbed banter of the coffee-house, the playhouse, and gambling den are never far away. A man's world then, not unlike Kipling's at times, with its brief flashes of material glory.   (xxv)

"Obviously," in this "man's world," the romantic portion of Roderick's narrative can only be there for the delight of the female reader. For who else would care about it? Certainly not the "rough, but enjoyable" denizens of the gunroom, the coffee-house, the gambling den, and, one assumes, Smollett criticism. Indeed, that critic who is so remiss as to refuse to raise his voice in this paean to masculinity, who is perhaps so squeamish as to find Smollett's "manly" humor, say, coarse, is probably just not man enough to take it. Boucé wonders if such a critic might not "answer the barbed definition given by Goldsmith in Letter XIII of *The Citizen of the World* (1762):

> a set of men called answerers of books, who take upon themselves to watch the republic of letters, and distribute reputation by the sheet; they somewhat resemble the eunuchs in a seraglio, who are incapable of giving pleasure themselves, and hinder those that would.   (xxiv)

To own that one is a disliker of Smollett is practically to own that one is emasculated—incapable of participating in the rough but enjoyable man's world, and jealous of those who can.[2] Why should Smollett's work elicit such a strident assertion of manliness?

Of course, in a sense Boucé's remarks are quite accurate. *The Adventures of Roderick Random* and *The Adventures of Peregrine Pickle* do present us with what is almost entirely a man's world—what we would now call a homosocial world: the army, the navy, a group of men on the Tour—a world in which the primary relationships are those between men. In each novel the "love-interest" which Boucé refers to plays something even less than a secondary role (Boucé's hypothetical "female reader" must be easily pleased), and it remains unclear whether the successful completion of the love-plot in marriage is in fact a cause for unalloyed rejoicing: throughout these two novels Smollett generally presents marriage as a state of miserable oppression for men, as less satisfying, less tender, less emotionally expressive than male friendship. Further, the homosocial world provides not simply the setting for but also the thematics of these works. *Roderick Random, Peregrine Pickle,* as well as Smollett's two early satires *Advice* and *Reproof*, are concerned with how one makes one's way, and takes one's place, within the homosocial world, and with the difficulties involved in this process. "I have attempted to represent modest merit struggling with every difficulty to which a friendless orphan is exposed," writes Smollett in the Preface to *Roderick Random* (xxxv), hoping that his narrative will animate the reader with a "generous indignation . . . against the sordid and vicious disposition of the world" (xxxv).

Boucé's effusions notwithstanding, Smollett's attitude to the homosocial world is actually marked by a strange ambivalence. On the one hand, the world of men is a carefree world of pranks, merry incidents, and relative freedom; on the other hand, it is a "sordid and vicious" world in which "modest merit" languishes unrecognized. And while the world of "modest merit" and merry pranks is represented by Smollett's heroes, the "sordid and vicious disposition of the world" is represented by Smollett most forcefully by the sodomite, a figure to which Smollett turns in three of the four works examined in this chapter.

Smollett's depiction of the sodomite, as we shall see, partakes of the conventional representational structures that we have already identified. The sodomite is an "unmanly" figure, the site of a disorder and corruption that undermines the values of the homosocial world and, hence, the nation. More particularly, Smollett depicts the sodomite as corrupting relationships between men at precisely those junctures where homosocial alliance should be, in theory, strongest, even purest. Military leaders who should be able to command the respect of their men turn out to be enervated fops with a repulsive taste for sodomy; powerful men of position who should be the advocates and patrons of merit instead encourage immoral mediocrity in order to indulge their base appetites. Smollett's poetic personae and novelistic heroes, of course, entertain "a just detestation for all such abominable practices" (*Peregrine* 242). As Robert D. Spector writes, "Dealing with male behaviour on the public scene Smollett displayed a strong distaste for anything that suggested less than heroic and manly conduct. . . . The novels, indeed, everywhere display Smollett's desire to show his truly masculine views of his world"

(*Smollett's Women* 13). And elsewhere, Spector has suggested that "Smollett, like Fielding, is a strongly masculine novelist; and sexual deviance arouses his wrath" (*Tobias* 8). Steven Bruhm agrees, and states that "Smollett's *oeuvre* . . . clearly condemns" the sodomite (407). In Smollett's "truly masculine" view, the sodomite appears as the complete opposite, the absolute "other" to the idealized homosocial world, perverting and debasing those relationships between men that Smollett otherwise celebrates.[3]

However, as his preoccupation with the figure might suggest, Smollett's representation of the sodomite is less stable, less straightforward, than the above statements can account for. While in the verse satires *Advice* and *Reproof*—where the sodomite literally is a figure, a static, satiric metaphor—Smollett is able to maintain a rel- -atively stable discourse of the sodomite as "other," in his novelistic narratives the sodomite occupies a more complex position. In turning from verse satire to the novel, however, Smollett appears to operate under the assumption that his satire will become keener, clearer, and more effective, as he explains in the Preface to his first novel *Roderick Random*:

> Of all kinds of satire, there is none so entertaining, and universally improving, as that which is introduced, as it were, occasionally, in the course of an interesting story, which brings every incident home to life; and by representing familiar scenes in an uncommon and amusing point of view, invests them with all the graces of novelty, while nature is appealed to in every particular.
>
> The reader gratifies his curiosity, in pursuing the adventures of a person in whose favour he is prepossessed; he espouses his cause, he sympathizes with him in distress, his indignation is heated against the authors of his calamity; the humane passions are inflamed; the contrast between dejected virtue, and insulting vice, appears with greater aggravation, and every impression having a double force on the imagination, the memory retains the circumstance, and the heart improves by the example. The attention is not tired with a bare Catalogue of charac-

ters, but agreeably diverted with all the variety of invention; and the vicissitudes of life appear in their particular circumstances, opening an ample field for wit and humour.   (xxxiii)

In this account, the movement from the "bare Catalogue of characters" one encounters in verse satire to "all the variety of invention" and "the vicissitudes of life" made available by the broader scope of the novelistic form is said to generate a greater clarity and force of satiric meaning. Through the reader's identification with, and emotional investment in the hero whose adventures he or she is pursuing, the binary opposition of "dejected virtue" and "insulting vice" is disclosed in stark relief and the lessons of the novel will remain in the reader's memory longer. Yet, as we shall see, the movement from verse satire to the greater structural complexity of the novel, from satiric *characters* to satiric *scenes*, does not necessarily guarantee the corresponding movement to a greater transparency of meaning that Smollett suggests. Indeed, the case is quite the opposite. As Tilottoma Rajan points out,

[s]cenes are more complex than figural moments, both in what they express and in their effect on a reader. A scene arises from a surplus of meaning that cannot be reduced to a conceptual statement. We narrate fundamental problems because our attempt to state them logically does not fully explain them. Moreover, narratives are situational and provisional: a particular episode occurs in a context of events that allows us to imagine that the story might be different in altered circumstances. . . . The point is that the substitution of characters and circumstances for tropes encourages the reader to elaborate the scene in a variety of ways.   (10–11)

In other words, while Smollett insists that narrative has "a double force on the imagination" which reduces meaning to a singular clarity, the complexity of the novel form actually opens up meaning, enabling the reader to contextualize and recontextualize scenes by situating them in relation to other scenes in the novel. This is par-

ticularly the case with the sodomitical scenes in *Roderick Random*
and *Peregrine Pickle* since the novels deal so insistently with relationships between men. And, as Smollett continues to use the language of sodomite as "other," we are actually encouraged to compare
these "bad" characters with his heroes.

In the context of the other male relationships depicted by Smollett, the sodomitical scenes can certainly seem from one point of
view—say, the avowed, respectable one—to be a distortion and perversion, a corrupt parody even, of true masculine friendship—the
homosocial world's "other." And yet, with only a slight shift in perspective, the sodomitical scenes seem simply to be the homosocial
world's *other side*, the direct enactment of desires more evasively fulfilled elsewhere in the novels. Parody, after all, depends upon similarity as much as upon difference. As Dollimore has noted, what is
often ignored or elided in abstract constructions of the "other" is the
significance of the *proximate*:

> that which is (1) adjacent and *there-by* related . . . or (2) that
> which is approaching . . . and thus (3) the opposite of *remote* or
> *ultimate*. . . . [T]he proximate is often constructed as the other,
> . . . [b]ut the proximate is also what enables a tracking-back of
> the "other" into the "same."   (33; original emphasis)

Or, to put it in Eve Sedgwick's more pithy formulation, "to be a man's
man is separated only by an invisible, carefully blurred, always-
already-crossed line from being 'interested in men' " (*Between* 89).

In the previous chapter we saw that the demonized figure of the
sodomite was constituted to a considerable degree through a process
of displacement, a process facilitated by the occlusion of the place of
the "proximate" in the construction of the "other." We also saw in
chapter 2, in relation to *Love Letters*, an example of what Dollimore
calls the "tracking-back of the 'other' into the 'same.' " In that text,
the sodomitical epistolary narrative of Wilson and the Nobleman,
characterized in the Preface as "odious and criminal" and "not familiar to our Northern Climate" (13–14), turns out to be quite familiar
and conventional: that is, the culturally defined "other" is in fact

encountered as "proximate"—something that the "editor" of *Love Letters* simultaneously acknowledges, exploits, and suppresses in the Preface via some rhetorical gymnastics:

> There is still behind another Objection to the Publication, which we will not dissemble, and that is, the Scandal of the Vice here described thro the Course of these Papers. The dead Languages are full enough of luscious Pictures of this Kind, and we don't find the Moderne Scruple to translate them, in order, as we may suppose, to raise a greater Abhorrence of the Sin which is not familiar to our Northern Climate. It is easy enough to take away all Offence of this Kind, by applying the Passion of the Letters to distinct Sexes, which we desire the Reader to do, and then he'll be a better Judge of the Spirit of the Writer. All the Weeds will then vanish, or be turn'd to Flowers, and in that View let them be seen. (14)

The "editor" here first assures us that the sodomitical narrative is indeed "other" ("not familiar"). He then tells us, however, that it can easily be assimilated to what it supposedly opposes ("It is easy enough to take away all Offence"); that is, the "editor" momentarily reveals the "proximate" within the "other." The existence of the "proximate," though, is immediately suppressed and is once more reconfigured as "other" when the "editor" asks us to apply "the Passion of the Letters to distinct Sexes": the "editor" thus accounts for the fact that the narrative of sodomitical passion can be *the same* by desiring us to read it as though it were *other than what it is*.

Most striking is that this mystification of the place of the "proximate" effects a total reversal in the justification and purpose of sodomitical representation: whereas at the start of the passage the point of "luscious Pictures of this Kind" is to provoke "a greater Abhorrence" in the reader, by the end of the passage the point is to give the reader delight, to enable the reader to enter into the "Spirit of the Writer." These manipulations by which the "other" is transformed into *its other*, by which the "proximate" is mobilized without relinquishing the concept of the "other," enable one to enjoy and invest desire in "the Passion of the Letters" without having to acknowledge what precisely is holding one's fascinated attention. Or to put it differently, by constructing a rhetorical lens of "distinct Sexes" through which to view the narrative of sodomitical desire, *Love Letters* can have its "other" and like him too.

Roderick Random and *Peregrine Pickle* enact a similar confusion of the place of the "proximate," but without the rhetorical interposition of "distinct Sexes." These two novels reveal—and then reconceal—the "other" as "proximate" in narratives of homosocial bonding. On the one hand the texts assert categorically that the sodomite is distinctly and obviously "other"; on the other hand, such assertions are called into question through a variety of narrative moments that reiterate the sodomitical scenes in a homosocial context. If *Love Letters* has its "other" and likes him too, *Roderick Random* and *Peregrine Pickle* have their "other" and *are* him too. In what follows, I shall first look briefly at Smollett's early satires. There the sodomite is constructed relatively straightforwardly as the embodiment of corruption and confusion; in other words, these satires participate in sodomitical practices as we have seen them thus far. I shall then turn to *Roderick Random* and *Peregrine Pickle* in order to argue that while these two narratives repeat a similar construction of the sodomite, they do so in such a way that seems to render the sodomite at once an overt locus of disgust and a covert locus of desire.

ADVICE AND REPROOF

Advice: A Satire (1746) and *Reproof: A Satire. The Sequel to Advice* (1747) are among Smollett's earliest publications, and they indicate that his fascination with the sodomite exists from the start of his career. *Advice* and *Reproof*, like Pope's *The First Satire of the Second Book of Horace Imitated*, take the form of dialogues between the Poet and a Friend, though in tone the satires are decidedly Juvenalian. In particular, Smollett draws upon Juvenal's Second Satire—which depicts the streets of Rome as full of sodomites who speak hypocritically of morality, who "having held forth about manly virtue,/ wriggle their rumps" (ll. 20–21), and the Ninth Satire—which deals with the subject of patronage by focusing on Naevolus, a man who is kept by both men and women. The persona that Smollett assumes in these two satires is that of the outraged and incorruptible—and therefore impoverished—poet disgusted at the vice he sees around him. The Friend is the voice of prudence and compromise who advises the Poet on how to get ahead in the world: "Let prudence more propitious arts inspire:/ The lower still you crawl, you'll climb the higher" (ll. 63–64). Of course, the more the Friend urges the Poet to reconcile himself to the ways of the world, the more the Poet resolves to stand alone and speak the truth:

> P. Two things I dread, my conscience and the law.
> . . . .
> Fr. Too coy to flatter, and too proud to serve,
> Thine be the joyless dignity to starve.
> P. No; —thanks to discord, war shall be my friend;
> And moral rage, heroic courage lend
> To pierce the gleaming squadron of the foe,
> And win renown by some distinguished blow.
>
> (ll. 219, 235–40)

The Poet adamantly maintains his moral high-ground which he conceives of, as the above lines show, in terms of manly, martial "heroic courage," qualities—especially manliness—he feels are lacking in society at large.

Smollett also aligns himself with Pope's persona in *Epistle to Dr. Arbuthnot* (1735), a poem which *Advice* and *Reproof* frequently echo. In Pope's *Epistle*, the perversion of values he is attacking finds its most complete expression in the sexual "perversion" of Sporus/Lord Hervey:

> Yet let me flap this Bug with gilded wings,
> This painted Child of Dirt that stinks and stings;
> . . . .
> His Wit all see-saw between *that* and *this*,
> Now high, now low, now Master up, now Miss,
> And he himself one vile Antithesis.

Amphibious Thing! that acting either Part,
The trifling Head, or the corrupted Heart!
Fop at the Toilet, Flatt'rer at the Board,
Now trips a Lady, and now struts a Lord.
Eve's Tempter thus the Rabbins have exprest,
A Cherub's face, a Reptile all the rest;
Beauty that shocks you, Parts that none will trust,
Wit that can creep, and Pride that licks the dust.

(ll. 309–10, 323–33)

Sporus/Hervey embodies the confusion which, as we have seen, is associated with the sodomite: he is an "Amphibious Thing," neither that nor this, Master nor Miss, Lady nor Lord. And, as the last two lines quoted show, sodomitical confusion inverts the order of things, turning virtues, qualities, and talents into their opposites. In contradistinction to Sporus, the poet is (self-)characterized by a determined steadiness.[4] The poet is not "Fortune's Worshipper, nor Fashion's Fool,/ Not Lucre's Madman, nor Ambition's Tool" (ll. 335–36); nor does he wander long in "Fancy's Maze" (l. 340). True to himself, the poet is, above all, "manly": "Not proud, nor servile, be one Poet's praise/ That, if he pleas'd, he pleas'd by manly ways" (ll. 336–37). Smollett uses this same binary of sodomitical vice vs. manly integrity, and he even acknowledges his debt to Pope when he refers to one of his satiric targets as a "child of dirt (to use a great author's expression)" (note to l. 88).

Advice begins with the Friend advising the Poet to exert his talents: he would not be poor if he chose to write panegyrics upon the great instead of satires, and the Friend then lists a number of noblemen as possible objects of flattery. The Poet ironically answers that the advice is good; he wonders, however, if "These names and virtues ever dwelt together" (l. 24). He also thinks that it is unlikely that he will be able to capture the "ingag'd attention of the Great" who are probably all busy, amused with "C[ope]'s prolific bum" (ll. 28–29). Sir John Cope was the commander in chief in Scotland whose troops had been defeated at Prestonpans by Prince Charles Edward Stuart in 1745. Cope was accused of cowardice and of fleeing the battle, and his actions were the subject of a military board review. Cope thus represents the opposite of the "heroic courage" that the Poet claims for himself at the end of *Advice*, and Smollett implies that the only way someone like Cope could have become a commander in chief would have been by being a pathic to the great. Smollett expands upon this idea in a bizarre footnote to the line about Cope's bum:

> This alludes to a phaenomenon, not more strange than true. The person here meant, having actually laid upwards of forty eggs, as several physicians and fellows of the R—y—l S—ci—ty can attest; one of whom (we hear) has undertaken the incubation, and will (no doubt) favour the world with an account of his success. Some virtuosi affirm, that such productions must be the effect of a certain intercourse of organs, not fit to be named.

The annotator of the modern edition of *Advice* writes that the "phenomenon mentioned in Smollett's footnote remains unidentified" (441), but it seems likely that by "eggs" Smollett is referring to the "piles," the result of Cope's "prolific" intercourse "not fit to be named." Indeed, the poem's epigraph from Juvenal suggests as much: "*Sed podice levi/ Caeduntur tumidae medico ridente Mariscae* [but your anus is smooth, as the surgeon/ notes with a grin when he takes a knife to your swollen piles] (ll. 11–12). And, of course, to represent the piles as eggs is also to figure Cope hermaphroditically, as a kind of backwards woman, or man-woman, whose "eggs" are located in the anus rather than the womb.

To become pathic to the great is precisely the advice that is being offered by the Friend, the advice that gives the poem its name. Exasperated by the Poet's intractable nature, the Friend lays out for him the sure road to success. "Go then, with ev'ry supple virtue stor'd," he tells him, "And thrive, the favour'd valet of my Lord":

> Th' ascent is easy, and the prospect clear,
> From the smirch'd scullion to th' embroider'd Peer.

Th' ambitious drudge preferr'd, postilion rides,
Advanc'd again, the chair benighted guides;
. . . .
But if exempted from th' *Herculean* toil,
A fairer field awaits him, rich with spoil;
There shall he shine, with mingling honours bright,
His master's pathic, pimp, and parasite.

(ll. 65–66, 71–74, 77–80)

Naturally, the Poet rejects this method of rising in the world as base
and, interestingly, as un-British:

Eternal infamy his name surround,
Who planted first that vice on *British* ground!
A vice that 'spite of sense and nature reigns,
And poisons genial love, and manhood stains!   (ll. 91–94)

Thus, although the Poet apparently sees sodomy everywhere he
turns (following these lines the Poet describes the various "unnatural tastes" of a number of noblemen), he persists in characterizing
it as foreign. Such a characterization of sodomy is, of course, necessary; the sodomite is the "other" to the unpoisoned genial love and
unstained manhood of the *true* British man represented by the Poet.
The ideas of poisoning and staining further mark sodomy as something *external* which infects or disfigures an otherwise pure and
complete masculinity. The sodomite, despite appearances, must be
foreign in order for the idealized homosocial world of manly
integrity and heroic courage to be recuperable.

   In *Reproof*, the Friend upbraids the Poet for having published
the advice he gave him; that counsel, he says, was meant to have
been kept "private" (l. 20). *Reproof* does not deal with sodomy as
does *Advice*; however, Smollett does return to the subject of Sir
John Cope. In between the publication of *Advice* and the publication of *Reproof*, the military board that was reviewing Cope's actions
cleared him of any misbehavior, something which clearly outraged
Smollett. The Poet relates Cope's behavior at Prestonpans and the

conduct of the board of inquiry in the form of a beast fable (ll. 43–94). Cope appears as a "courtier ape" who can out-run the enemy but who cannot out-run "report." "Sir Ape," however, has "interest enough at court" to be pardoned. Since *Reproof* is meant to be read in the context of *Advice*, Smollett implies here that Cope obtained his pardon by the same means that he was first promoted to general: his "prolific bum."

In presenting the figure of the sodomite as "other" in his verse satire then, Smollett draws upon the conventions of sodomitical practices—disorder, corruption, effeminacy, un-Britishness—and is able to use these conventions in a more or less stable fashion. As Byron Gassman notes, "the homosexuality attacked in *Advice* . . . is for Smollett a metonymic construct for the whole social ethos the satirist is attacking" (13). Smollett can position the sodomite as a "metonymic construct" for the world of vice he opposes because in the "bare Catalogue of characters," to use his own terms from the Preface to *Roderick Random*, the sodomite remains distinctly "other" because the satirist keeps asserting that he is so, because, that is, the sodomite is the object of the satiric fury, representing that which is to be eliminated.

That said, however, we can recognize even here in the satires that strange dynamic described by Stallybrass and White by which what is marked out in the social sphere as repulsive and to be eliminated comes to occupy the imaginative sphere as the object of "longing and fascination" (191)—a dynamic that becomes more apparent in the novels. The graphic epigraph from Juvenal and the detailed foot-note on Cope's "prolific bum"—both of which are not unconnected to the anal/excremental "humour" that fills the novels—the variety of sodomitical behaviors attributed to the social world, as well as Smollett's continual return to the figure of the sodomite across his works, suggest an interest that cannot be accounted for entirely in satiric terms. They suggest, instead, what Stallybrass and White call "phobic enchantment" (124), the combination of disgust and fascination in which "a *political* imperative to reject and eliminate the debasing 'low' conflicts powerfully and unpredictably with a desire for this Other" (5). Stallybrass and White understand "phobic en-

chantment" as the result of a process not unlike what Dollimore
called the "tracking-back of the 'other' into the 'same' " via the "proximate." If Smollett's world of manly integrity is defined by its rejection of the detested sodomite, then this rejection is in fact constitutive of that manly world which defines itself as not "other." In other
words, the homosocial world idealized and desired by Smollett actually *includes* the sodomite "internalized under the sign of negation
and disgust" (Stallybrass and White 191). "Phobic enchantment,"
like the "proximate," indicates an "interconnectedness whereby the
antithetical inheres within, and is partly produced by, what it
opposes" (Dollimore 33).

RODERICK RANDOM AND PEREGRINE PICKLE

In turning to Roderick's and Peregrine's encounters with the sodomitical "other," it will be helpful, I think, to set Smollett's sodomitical
practices against a larger, though connected, image pattern that one
finds in his novels. I draw here on my own observations of *Advice,
Reproof, Roderick Random,* and *Peregrine Pickle,* but also on Robert
Adams Day's study of Smollett's oeuvre, "Sex, Scatology, Smollett."
Among the most frequently recurring images in Smollett's work are
the "arse" and, relatedly, what comes out of it or goes into it. In
Roderick Random, to take only a few examples, Mr. Potion is accused
of "kissing the arse of every body" (26); Strap's bowels are frequently
"disordered"—particularly when he and Roderick share a bed—and
the disorder forces Strap "to go backward" (51, 60); Captain Weazel
"befoul[s]" himself (59); Roderick returns to London as a man of
fashion and becomes acquainted with a "Dr. Wagtail" (269); and Mr.
Ranter has the point of a sword "applied" to his "posteriors" (277).

   In *Peregrine Pickle,* Peregrine puts a number of large pins in his
schoolmaster's breeches "which when he sat down . . . penetrated the
skin of his posteriors" (59); Peregrine also puts a purgative in Mrs.
Trunnion's drink which affects her bowels in church and she sus-
tains an "excess of evacuation" (66–67); when Gamaliel Pickle is
challenged to a duel, his bowels undergo "such violent agitation on
the spot, that one would have thought the operation proceeded from
a severe joke of the apothecary" (174); and Tom Pipes has his poste

riors "saluted" with a bayonet, which "incommode[s]" him much (247). In addition, a vast number of unsuspecting people in both novels have either chamber pots or close stools emptied upon them. And if this perhaps seems simply a product of Smollett's youthfulness, Eric Rothstein has argued that in *Humphrey Clinker* (1771) bare buttocks are an important organizing image for the novel (see "Scotophilia and *Humphrey Clinker*), and Robert Adams Day, examining *The History and Adventures of an Atom* (1769), claims that the "characterization 'obsessive' is hardly too strong" to describe that text's extensive references to the buttocks (229):

> The Emperor of Japan (George II of England) turns his rump on people as a snub . . . and constantly kicks his ministers in the breech. His prime minister (the Duke of Newcastle) soothes himself after these encounters by having his arse kissed by bishops, whose beards produce exquisite (in fact, orgasmic) pleasure. . . . [T]here are learned digressions on haemorrhoids, kicking, [and] breeches. (229)

Of course, as Day himself is aware, the focus on the "arse" in *Atom* is part of its satirical method of operation,[5] and the anal eroticism, a comment on the "immorality" of the Duke of Newcastle. As Day also points out, though, the difference between Smollett's savage satire and his spirited comedy is primarily one of tone than of predominate image (230). Further, I would add to this observation that, just as he does in his scathing satire, Smollett not only frequently depicts the "arse" in his comic novels, but depicts it as a charged locus of contact between men, suggesting a refiguration of an eroticism that is elsewhere condemned.

For example, in the scene which forms the epigraph to this chapter, Roderick, with the help of his schoolmates and his Uncle Bowling, takes revenge on a schoolmaster whom he feels has mistreated him. At a prearranged signal Roderick and two other boys wrestle the schoolmaster to the ground. Uncle Bowling—acting on Roderick's behalf—then ties the man to a post, pulls down his breeches, tucks up his shirt, and proceeds to flagellate his "withered posteriors" with a cat-o'-nine-tails (18). This operation gives the schoolmaster "exquisite pain" and sends a gust of exultation through the boys who are delighted with the "novelty of the sight" (18). In this scene of revenge, the schoolmaster's buttocks become the site of his shame and of Roderick's triumph, the site at which the drama of homosocial rivalry (and bonding) is played out—"shout, boys, shout," cheers Uncle Bowling when the flogging is over (18). But this scene of revenge and bonding cannot be entirely divested of an erotic suggestiveness.

In a parallel scene of schoolmaster humiliation in *Peregrine Pickle*, Peregrine is assisted by Tom Pipes in bringing his tutor, Mr. Jolter, to "utter shame and confusion" (81). Having discovered that Mr. Jolter has conceived a passion for a chambermaid, Peregrine convinces her to seem to yield and bless Mr. Jolter "with a declaration, that her chamber-door should be left open at midnight" (82):

> True to the assignation, [Jolter] rose at the hour appointed, and full of the most vigorous expectation, in his shirt, darkling explored his way to the place of rendezvous. His heart throbbed with joy when he found immediate admittance; he saw the cap of his Dulcinea, who seemed to be asleep; he sprung into bed, and clasped in his arms—oh heavens! no other than the traitor Pipes, who, by his master's direction, personated the maid; and returned the embrace with such muscular contraction, that the unfortunate lover felt the disappointment, and the impossibility of disengaging himself, at the same time.   (82)

Peregrine, a friend, and the maid rush into the room and discover Mr. Jolter in "disgrace," thus destroying "all the remains of authority which he had hitherto preserved over Peregrine" (82). The power struggle of male rivalry is emblematized in these two episodes by images of mastery and enslavement, freedom and restraint. Not only do Peregrine and Roderick have men to do their bidding—Peregrine is actually called a "master"—but while they stand freely, exultingly, their opponents are immobilized: Mr. Jolter is unable to disengage himself from Pipes "muscular contraction" and Roderick's teacher, of course, is tied to a post. The episode in *Peregrine Pickle*, however, makes explicit what the flagellation scene only suggests: ultimately, the hero's triumph over another male is dependent on his establishing a *sexual* authority over the latter. These two scenes return us, then, to the instability in the constitution of Smollett's manly world: the project of establishing one's masculine superiority seems inevitably to produce an eroticized image of the rival male, and in Smollett, that eroticism tends to focus on the "arse."

In this context, we might place the scene from *Roderick Random* beside another parallel scene—this one not by Smollett, but from a novel published not long after *Roderick Random*:

> I unbutton'd his breeches, and rolling his shirt up rather above his waist, tuck'd it in securely there; . . . I led him then to the bench, [and] . . . tied him slightly hand and foot, to the legs of it; which done, his shirt remaining truss'd up over the small of his back, I drew his breeches quite down to his knees; and now he lay, in all the fairest, broadest display of that part of the back-view, in which a pair of chubby, smooth-cheek'd, and passing white posteriours rose cushioning upwards from two stout, fleshful thighs, and ending their cleft, or separation, by a union at the small of the back, presented a bold mark, that swell'd, as it were, to meet the scourge.   (Cleland 146)

This scene is from John Cleland's *Memoirs of a Woman of Pleasure* (1748–49). As Peter Wagner has demonstrated, flagellation was a common *topos* in eighteenth-century pornography (see *Eros Revived*, esp. 21–24). Cleland's scene is, clearly, more luxuriant in its language than is Smollett's, more decidedly marked as erotic (after all, Mr. Barvile *is* paying Fanny to do this). Yet the similarity, that the scene of masculine revenge and triumph should take a similar form to a familiar scene of pornographic indulgence, points to the fine line that separates that manly world of competition from a world of eroticism that the former would strenuously disavow, offering us another example of the "other" turning out to be the "proximate." If Roderick and Peregrine wrest their triumph from the sexual humili-

ation of their schoolmasters it is not because they just happen to
stumble across them with their breeches down or locked in the
embraces of another man—another man, it must be added, who
merely enacts the hero's will; rather, Roderick and Peregrine themselves generate these scenes. In other words, the sexual humiliation
of the rival—a humiliation metonymically linked to sodomy through
the focus on the "arse" and the male-male embrace—is achieved
only by the hero actively assuming a sexualized position vis-à-vis the
other man.

The sexualized nature of male competition is most explicitly figured in yet another scene in which Roderick takes vengeance upon
a rival. Finding himself alone in France with no money, Roderick
joins the French army as a means of survival. Conversing one day
with a fellow soldier, an old Gascon, Roderick rather unwisely (and
rudely) makes a number of disparaging remarks about the French
king; the situation ends in a duel. Roderick begins confidently—
especially as his opponent is "a poor, little, shivering creature
decrepid with age, and blind of one eye" (247). Much to his surprise,
however, when the fighting starts, Roderick finds himself not only
wounded, but disarmed; that is, Roderick is unmanned, castrated
one might even say, as with a slice to his sword hand the old Gascon
deprives Roderick of his weapon. Never one to let matters rest,
Roderick practices his swordmanship and eagerly awaits an opportunity to renew the confrontation. That opportunity comes after the
battle of Dettingen when Roderick—despite being on the French
side—expounds on the "valour of the English" and the "pusilanim-
ity of the French" (249). The old Gascon, angered, reminds Roderick
that he has already been bested once in duel, a statement to which
Roderick makes "no reply but by a kick on the breech, which over-
turned him in an instant" (249). Reminded of his previous defeat,
Roderick now overturns that situation and asserts his own superiority.
Again, the buttocks become the site at which the scene of conflict is
staged. In the ensuing duel, Roderick is, of course, victorious and, in
order to "mortify [the Gascon's] vanity, . . . I thrust his sword up to
the hilt in something (it was not a tansy) that lay smoking on the
plain, and joined the rest of the soldiers with an air of tranquility and

indifference" (250). Roderick's recuperation of his manhood, then, begins with the Gascon being turned over and ends with a "mortifying" penetration. Day writes of this scene that Roderick humiliates the Gascon

> by thrusting his sword into a "smoaking" (therefore fresh) turd and "with an air" of (therefore pretended) "tranquility and indifference" rejoins his comrades: . . . a male, humiliated by a male . . . by means of a symbolic phallus, acquires a powerful phallus himself, defeats his rival, figuratively sodomises him without contaminating his own virility symbol, and departs, concealing his relief and triumph. (239)

I agree with Day that this is clearly a scene of displaced sodomy; but, of course, it is impossible for Roderick to remain "uncontaminated"—or, let us say "unimplicated"—as, indeed, his *air* of indifference indicates. If, to use Mark Simpson's terms for the sublimated erotics of masculine competition, the old Gascon is "fucked," then Roderick is the "fucker" (see *Male Impersonators* 69–93). But these positions are only tenable if framed in terms of violence and a struggle for dominance. Combat and rivalry are undoubtedly part of the robust, manly world celebrated by Smollett and his more traditional critics. Nevertheless, Smollett's continual use of anal and excremental imagery, particularly in scenes of passionate contact (albeit "manly" passion) between men, represents, I suggest, a libidinal subtext disavowed by the novel's more overt sodomitical practices to which I now turn.

I want to begin by considering an encounter with the "other" in *The Adventures of Peregrine Pickle* (1751), which I take to be paradigmatic of Smollett's sodomitical practices. Following a dinner in "the Manner of the Ancients" during which "all the guests forgot their chagrin, and paid their respects . . . piously to the bottle" (241), Pallet, a companion of Peregrine, is left alone in a room with an Italian count and a German baron. Pallet, a painter, has been speaking to the Italian count about art "with wonderful volubility" when, suddenly, the count, tired with the eternal babble of the painter, reeled towards the sleeping baron, whom he viewed with rapture, repeating from the *Il Pastor Fido* of Guarini,

Come assetato infermo
Che bramò lungamenté
Il vietato licor—
—Tal' Io! gran tempo infermo,
E d'amorosa sete arso, e consunte.

[Like the thirsty sick man, who long desired the forbidden liquor, such am I, a long time ill, burning and consumed with amorous thirst.][6]
  Then boldly ravished a kiss, and began to tickle him under the ribs, with such expressions of tenderness, as scandalized the virtuous painter.   (242)

Alarmed, Pallet "stagger[s] in great hurry and discomposure" from the room and puts himself "under the protection" of Peregrine, "to whom he impart[s] his suspicion of the count's morals, by describing the indecency of his deportment" (242). Confronted with the "other," then, Pallet immediately removes himself "into the next room," thus asserting and confirming his distance from such a spectacle, which he frames in terms of its moral indecency. However, what causes Pallet to stagger from the room is not the shock, revulsion, or incomprehension occasioned by the sight of what is alien and remote. Rather, Pallet is moved to flee the room by the sudden, discomposing "conscious[ness] of *his own attractions*" (242; my emphasis). In other words, instead of seeing the sodomitical scene as that which has absolutely nothing to do with him, Pallet's immediate reaction is to imagine himself as a potential participant in that scene, as the possible object of desire. What *composes* Pallet—his position as not-"other"—is thus *discomposed* at the sight of that "other," and Pallet must struggle to regain a stable position as he "stagger[s]" (to "walk or stand unsteadily, totter; hesitate, waver in purpose" [*OED*]) from the room.

Peregrine is "incensed" by the information he receives from Pallet and, going to the door of the room Pallet has just left, he sees, "with his own eyes enough to convince him, that Pallet's complaint was not without foundation, and that the baron was not averse to the addresses of the count" (242). Having "a just detestation for all such abominable practices," Peregrine's first impulse is to "rush in, and take immediate vengeance on the offenders" (242). However, Peregrine checks himself and decides not to rush in for reasons not unlike those which caused Pallet to rush out:

> but, considering that such a precipitate step might be attended with troublesome consequences to himself, he resisted the impulse of his wrath, and tasked his invention with some method of inflicting upon them a disgrace suited to the grossness of their ideas. (242)

Afraid of "troublesome consequences to himself," Peregrine resists asserting his position as not-"other." As Lee Edelman points out, Peregrine's fear of consequences to himself indicates that he fears that he cannot intervene in the sodomitical scene without becoming somehow implicated in it, a fear which Edelman asserts already implicates Peregrine in the scene since it represents a challenge to his "sexual authority," effectively unmanning him (187). The sight of the "other" thus causes Peregrine, like Pallet, to stagger as he hesitates between wrath and fear, action and passivity. In the end, Peregrine sends the landlady into the room with a pretended message. She is "so much offended and enraged" at the sight of the baron's and the count's "mutual endearments" that she drives them from the house, and the two men find themselves "obliged to make a very disorderly retreat . . . in a most disgraceful condition" (243). The banishment of the sodomites fills Peregrine with delight and he "embrace[s] the mistress of the hotel with transport," thus re-establishing his shaken manliness, and, being rendered "frolicksome" with the adventure, he proposes that he and Pallet should go to a masquerade (243). Pallet agrees and they soon set out, Peregrine dressed in a Spanish costume with Pallet on his arm—*dressed*

entirely as a woman! Peregrine foresees "abundance of diversion in
the execution of this project" (243). With the horrible sodomites out
of the way, the boys go out for some good, honest fun, having borrowed the landlady's clothes.

This short scene is representative of the instabilities of sodomitical
practices as they operate in *Peregrine Pickle* and *Roderick Random*.
The representation of the sodomite is framed by terms which mark
the sodomite and sodomitical desire as distinctly "other"—"abominable," "scandalous," "not fit to be named," "Italian"—as that to
which Smollett's protagonists stand in opposition. Demonizing
rhetoric aside, however, the actual encounter with the sodomite and
his transgressive passion effects a destabilization of the certainties by
which the self is distinguished from the "other," revealing, if only
momentarily, the "proximate" within the "other." Confronted with
the sodomitical scene, Peregrine and Pallet suddenly become aware
of their own "attractions"—a suitably ambiguous word, signifying
alternately those attractions one might possess, but also those one
might feel—and they become aware that the encounter with the
"other" could have consequences for one's *self*. In this way, the representation of the sodomite as "other" ends up undermining precisely
that very representation, as self and "other" collapse momentarily
into each other, a situation Dollimore would call "intrinsically perverse: deviance emerges from the terms of its exclusion, eventually
undermining that of which it was initially an effect, and which
depended upon its exclusion" (244). The stability of self and "other"
is seemingly restored, then, through the banishment of the sodomite
from the narrative scene; his transgressive desire, however, is not as
easily banished as is his transgressing person. Indeed, the thwarted
desire of the sodomitical scene seems to linger in the text, deflected
though into the type of homosocial activity that Smollett celebrates—
here, the merry prank of the masquerade, or, elsewhere, scenes of
combat, rivalry, or "chaste" affection. Thus in *Roderick Random* and
Peregrine Pickle, sodomitical practices are ultimately generative of the
very desire they seek to police and negate.

To celebrate the routing of the sodomites, Peregrine and Pallet
attend a masquerade. As Terry Castle has amply demonstrated, mas-

querade functioned symbolically in the eighteenth century as a locus of almost unlimited sexual license: [t]he exchange of garments was also an exchange of desires. The result was a flight from the 'natural' . . . into new realms of voluptuous disorder" (161). We have already seen that transvestism was associated, at least discursively, with sodomy—the preeminent "flight from the 'natural' " and prime example of "voluptuous disorder"—particularly in Ned Ward's *History* and in Jonathan Wild's *Answer to a late Insolent Libel.* In *Memoirs of a Woman of Pleasure,* as well, Cleland links disguise with sodomy; Emily attends a masquerade dressed as a boy and is picked up by a man who thinks she really is a boy and who attempts to sodomize her (154–56). Smollett himself elsewhere connects the masquerade with the excitation of transgressive passion: it is after attending a masquerade at the Haymarket that Peregrine attempts to rape Emilia (405–09). On the one hand Smollett seems to erase the shock of the sodomitical scene by returning to the familiar *topos* of the merry prank; on the other hand, though, he sets his characters in a milieu notorious for illicit passion—where the "exchange of garments" was an "exchange of desires"—with one of them in drag. As Castle has also suggested, the masquerade could function as a "symbolic mechanism through which suppressed forms of behaviour found representation" (173), and here, the frame of the prank and of the masquerade enable Peregrine and Pallet to act out what, two pages earlier, they could scarcely look at.

Appearing together arm in arm, Peregrine and Pallet stroll about the ball-room as a couple "to the astonishment of the whole company" (244). The company are astonished because they take Pallet to be really a woman, but his large, awkward figure makes him a monstrous woman and, together, he and Peregrine form a monstrous, unnatural couple. More remarkable than any of the "remarkable masques," the two are gazed at "as a preternatural phaenomenon" (244). In other words, Peregrine and Pallet now embody the type of unnatural spectacle that had before so disconcerted them; rather than banishing the offending desire of the Italian count and the German baron, this scene seems to replay it in a more "acceptable" (because disguised) fashion—though still with a resulting destabilization of position. When a French nobleman begins "to be very free" with Pallet in an "indelicate" manner, Pallet, in a moment reminiscent of the earlier scene, again puts himself under Peregrine's "protection" (245). This time, however, far from hesitating, Peregrine interposes and asserts "his pretensions to the insulted lady" (245). Whereas the prank started out with Pallet as a "supposititious female" and a "supposed lady," he/she is now simply a "lady," and one to whom Peregrine has "pretensions." The episode ends with Peregrine and Pallet being surrounded when they leave the masquerade, ostensibly because they have insulted the nobleman. As if to suggest that this is the real scene of transgression, the hero and his companion, unlike the baron and the count who escape the crowds that gather at the door to the inn, are seized and thrown in jail.

With Peregrine and Pallet in jail, that narrative turns less humorous than cruel, perhaps reflecting some unease on Smollett's part and suggesting the need to reassert the kind of triumphing masculinity that Peregrine had earlier enjoyed in his humiliation of Mr. Jolter. Concealing from Pallet that they have actually obtained their release, Peregrine tells the painter that the authorities have decided to castrate him:

> the French court was of the opinion that the delinquent should for ever forfeit the privileges and characteristic of a man, which he had so shamefully deposited, or in other words, be deprived of his virility.   (252)

Though directed at Pallet, this pronouncement really encompasses both the painter and Peregrine, for both felt the threat of being unmanned in the encounter with the sodomitical "other." Both, if only momentarily, "shamefully deposited" their position as not-"other." With this cruel trick, Peregrine regains the "privileges and characteristic of a man" as he triumphantly "reap[s] some diversion from [Pallet's] distress" (251). Indeed, even Pallet now exerts himself and, as they speed from the jail in a coach (Pallet thinks that they are escaping), he sounds the battle cry of their restabilized masculinity:

Drive, damn ye drive! to the gates of Jericho and ends of the earth! Drive you raggamuffin, you rapscallion, you hell-hound! drive us to the pit of hell, rather than we should be taken, and lose the treasures of virility.   (255)

However, he makes this exhortation while still in drag.

This pattern, which unfolds remarkably compactly in *Peregrine Pickle*, is more diffuse in *The Adventures of Roderick Random* (1748), spread out over more of the narrative. The instant confusion between self and "other" that Pallet and Peregrine experience upon encountering the Italian count and the German baron in their "mutual endearments" occurs for Roderick over two separate encounters. Further, Roderick is frequently unaware himself that any such confusion is taking place, and his assertions of distinction happen retrospectively. Similarly, the residual desire of the sodomitical scenes is redeployed less immediately in *Roderick Random*, appearing in the form of narrative echoes, perhaps the most significant of which happens in a climactic scene in which Roderick discovers his long-lost father and so, presumably, his true place in the homosocial world.

Roderick's first encounter with an "actual" sodomite happens when the ship he is serving on as a surgeon's mate receives a new commander: Captain Whiffle. Whiffle takes up his duties in high style, arriving in "a ten-oar'd barge, overshadowed with a vast umbrella" meant to "preserve his complexion from the injuries of sun and weather" (194). What is most striking about Capt. Whiffle, however, is his spectacular mode of dress, described to us by Roderick in equally spectacular detail:

a white hat garnished with a red feather, adorned his head, from whence his hair flowed down upon his shoulders, in ringlets tied behind with a ribbon.—His coat, consisting of pink-coloured silk, lined with white, by the elegance of the cut retired backward, as it were, to discover a white sattin waistcoat embroidered with gold, unbuttoned at the upper part, to display a broch set with garnets, that glittered in the breast of his shirt, which was of the finest cambrick, edged with right

mechlin. The knees of his crimson velvet breeches scarce
descended so low as to meet his silk stockings, which rose
without spot or wrinkle on his meagre legs, from shoes of blue
Meroquin, studded with diamond buckles, that flamed forth
rivals to the sun! A steel-hilted sword, inlaid with figures of
gold, and decked with a knot of ribbon which fell down in a
rich tossle, equipped his side; and an amber-headed cane
hung dangling from his wrist:—But the most remarkable parts
of his furniture were, a mask on his face, and white gloves on
his hands, which did not seem to be put on with an intention
to be pulled off occasionally, but were fixed with a ring set
with a ruby on the little finger of one hand, and by one set with
a topaz on that of the other.—In this garb, captain Whiffle, for
that was his name, took possession of the ship.   (194–95)

The only other physical description of Whiffle that Roderick provides is, by contrast, exceedingly vague: he is "a tall, thin, man"
(194). There would seem to be nothing to Whiffle but his clothes.
Covered by an umbrella, a hat, a mask, and gloves, Whiffle seems
unwilling to expose any part of himself to nature or to let any part of
himself appear "natural." He is designed for display rather than for
purpose: his gloves are "fixed;" his cane dangles. Whiffle is nothing
but a surface sparkle, a glittering artifice. Even his adornments are
themselves adorned. In fact, the only signs of animation about
Whiffle are also provided by his clothing—his coat retires, his
breeches descend, his stockings rise, his buckles flame forth.

Indeed, divested of his finery, Whiffle immediately collapses, life-
less, in a swoon. What could be more different from the active,
manly hero? Further, simultaneously adorned and eclipsed by his
numerous accoutrements including lace from Mechlin and leather
from Morocco ("Meroquin"), Whiffle is characterized by the kind of
commodification that Laura Brown has argued was typically associated with *women* in the eighteenth century (See *Ends of Empire*
103–34). Whiffle is thus effete and effeminate. Robert Spector calls
this description a "stereotypical portrait of homosexuality" (*Smollett's
Women* 14); G. S. Rousseau claims that this passage is the "first

authentic description of the enduring male homosexual stereotype
in modern culture" ("Pursuit" 147); and Steven Bruhm, more simply,
states that what we have here is "the modern gay man" (401)—passive and feminized. In other words, Whiffle's clothes function seemingly as unequivocal signifiers. Thus, when we are informed a few
pages later that Whiffle's personal surgeon, Mr. Simper, is given a
cabin "contiguous to the state-room, where Whiffle slept," we hardly
need the added information that the two are thought to maintain "a
correspondence . . . not fit to be named" (199).

Roderick and his shipmates can encounter Whiffle—and his
attendants, "all of whom, in their different degrees, seemed to be of
their patron's disposition" (195)—with a relatively uncomplicated
disdain because everything about him so clearly screams "other,"
from his ridiculous clothing to his *valet de chambre* Vergette (Boucé
notes in his annotations that this name is French for "brush" but
also means "small penis" [460]). "[H]e is disguised and transfigured,
and transmographied with affectation and whimsies," cries Morgan,
Roderick's mess-mate; "he is more like a [baboon] than one of the
human race" (196). Bruhm points out that Morgan is "somewhat
vague here about the exact form of his disdain":

> he either objects that Whiffle is *too* artificial—"transfigured,
> and transmographied with affectation and whimsies"—or
> that Whiffle is not artificial enough—he is more like a beast
> than a gentleman.   (401)

But, of course, in terms of sodomitical practices, this is not a vague
description at all; confusion is precisely what marks Whiffle as the
sodomitical "other." Like Sporus/Lord Hervey, Whiffle is a "painted
Child of Dirt," an "Amphibious Thing." Like Sir John Cope in
Smollett's *Reproof*, he is a "courtier ape appointed general." And
Whiffle's interest in clothes as a sign of sodomy can be traced as far
back, within the bounds of this study, as *Almonds for Parrots* or
Mundus Foppensis in which we saw that extravagant dress was figured as a perversion of "nature" by "art" equivalent to, and therefore
indicative of, sodomy: thus Whiffle is "transmographied," and

Simper, Roderick notices, "was obliged to art for the clearness of his complexion" (198). While Whiffle and his men unnaturally impregnate the air with so much perfume "that one may venture to affirm the clime of Arabia Foelix was not half so sweet-scented" (195), Roderick and the crew are simply natural (i.e., dirty and smelly): "I have no smells about me, but such as a christian ought to have," Morgan proclaims (196).

The entire episode with Captain Whiffle is marked by a comfortable certainty and stability, unenjoyed by Peregrine and Pallet, but here shared by the characters and the critics alike. Whiffle is an open book in which one can plainly read the assurance that one is not-"other" and that the "other" is clearly marked and, so, easily avoided (cf. Edelman 4–10). Here is the "other" as it is meant to operate, the mirror that confirms what one *is* by reflecting back what one *is not.* Whiffle's efforts to make over the crew in his own image meet only with a resistance that confirms difference. He orders that no lieutenant should appear on deck without a wig, sword, and ruffles, and that no midshipman or petty officer should be seen with a check shirt or dirty linen: "[t]hese singular regulations did not prepossess the ship's company in his favour; but on the contrary, gave scandal an opportunity to be very busy with his character" (199). It is at this point that "scandal" pronounces that Whiffle and Simper are maintaining a correspondence "not fit to be named"; the attempt to blur the line of difference causes it to be drawn all the more fiercely. Yet the certainty about the self and the "other" that characterizes this episode will prove to be ill-founded, the open book in which otherness is written, a mere fiction. For Roderick's encounter with the novel's other sodomite, Earl Strutwell, unfolds in an entirely different manner, one which calls into question the distinctions so strongly maintained in the above scene. Before Roderick meets Earl Strutwell, however, two events occur which seem almost to prepare us for the collapse of self and "other" into the "proximate."

The first of these two events is Roderick's duel with the old Gascon, an episode, as I have already indicated, that I read as a displaced scene of sodomy. This scene is perhaps the novel's most explicit acknowledgment of the erotics which underwrite the "manly" world to which we are presumably meant to assume Whiffle and his entourage so clearly do not belong. That said, one still might argue that the duel does in fact shore up Roderick's manliness. After all, Roderick manages to emerge from the second duel as a "fucker" and not as a "fucked," and as we saw in chapter 1, the act of penetration alone can establish one's position in the (rhetorical) gender hierarchy; that is, the distinction between penetrator and penetrated might be said to maintain a difference which would otherwise seem to be collapsing. However, the second event I would draw attention to here is what happens to Roderick immediately following the displaced scene of sodomy. Right after the duel with the Gascon, Roderick is reunited with his old friend, Strap who has been left a legacy by a nobleman for whom he worked. Through Strap's generosity, Roderick shares in this good fortune and is transformed—*into Captain Whiffle*:

> My wardrobe consisted of five fashionable coats full-mounted, two of which were plain, one of cut velvet, one trim[m]ed with gold, and another with silver-lace; two frocks, one of white drab with large plate buttons, the other of blue, with gold binding; one waistcoat of gold brocard; one of blue sattin, embroidered with silver; one of green silk, trimmed with broad figured gold lace; one of black silk, with figures; one of white sattin; one of black cloth, and one of scarlet; six pair of cloth breeches; one pair of crimson, and another of black velvet.   (256)

And on, and on; Roderick enumerates stockings (silk and cotton), hats, ruffled shirts, neckcloths, handkerchiefs, diamond rings, swords, buckles (for the knees *and* shoes), a gold-headed cane, and a tortoise-shell snuff-box. Paul-Gabriel Boucé reads this episode as symbolic of Roderick's pride, indicating that he has not yet achieved "the moral maturity which will enable him to confront both good and bad fortune successfully" (*Novels* 118), an assessment with which Susan Bourgeois agrees (43). Yet, given that this episode occurs not long after the Whiffle scene, one cannot but read it in that context; Roderick himself, however (like Boucé and Bourgeois), makes no connection (410). Indeed, Roderick is determined to act out the behavior he so recently condemned, to "put on the gentleman of figure" and return to London "in hopes of obtaining the character of a pretty fellow" (257), with Strap supplying the place of *valet de chambre*.

Upon his appearance in the *beau monde*, Roderick informs us—with some retrospective regret—that he had "vanity enough to make [him] believe that [he] was observed with an uncommon degree of attention and applause" and that he performed "a thousand ridiculous coquetries" (257). Like Whiffle, Roderick becomes an object of display:

> I got up and sat down, covered and uncovered my head twenty times between the acts; pulled out my watch, clapped it to my ear, wound it up, set it, gave it the hearing again;— displayed my snuff-box, affected to take snuff, that I might have an opportunity of shewing my brilliant, . . . dangled my cane, and adjusted my sword-knot. . . .   (257)

The description that Morgan had earlier applied to Whiffle, now applies perfectly to Roderick: he is "disguised and transfigured, and transmographied with affectation and whimsies" (196). In other words, Roderick now embodies himself all of those signs which before supposedly so clearly signified "other." Like Pallet, Roderick has become aware of "his own attractions"—indeed, he plans to use them to get ahead in the world. What Roderick is not yet aware of, though, are the "troublesome consequences to himself" that will ensue.

It is in his manifestation as a "pretty fellow" that Roderick encounters Earl Strutwell, an man represented to him as being "hand and glove with a certain person who ruled the roast [*sic*]" (307). Roderick's plan is to rise in the world through the Earl's patronage. After their first, brief meeting, Roderick is "charmed with [his] reception," discovering much "sweetness of temper and candour in this Earl's countenance" (307). At their second meeting, Roderick receives even more encouraging signs from the Earl. Strutwell squeezes Roderick's hand frequently, looks at him "with a singular complacency," and finally asks him if he would like to be secretary to an embassy (308). Roderick is overcome with gratitude:

> I could not even help shedding tears, at the goodness of this noble lord, who no sooner perceived them, than he caught me in his arms, hugged and kissed me with a seemingly paternal affection. (309)

Roderick is a little confused at this "uncommon instance of fondness" (309), but he remains full of hope. At their third and final meeting the Earl "absolutely promise[s]" Roderick that he has found him a place (309). The Earl is too well-bred, however, to force Roderick into making numerous expressions of gratitude, and so he politely changes the topic. "Among other topicks of discourse," Strutwell introduces a discussion of literature, in general, and of Petronius Arbiter, in particular. Conceding that many have condemned that author's "taste in love," Strutwell goes on to give an *apologia* for sodomy, concluding that the most powerful reason for cultivating "this inclination" is "the exquisite pleasure attending its success" (309–10). This conversation, not surprisingly, makes Roderick apprehensive; what is surprising, however, is what Roderick becomes apprehensive about: "I began to be apprehensive that his lordship finding I had travelled, was afraid I might have been infected with this spurious and sordid desire abroad, and took this method of sounding my sentiments on the subject" (310). Roderick fears that Strutwell thinks that *he* is a sodomite.

This episode completely undermines the certainties about the self and the "other" which structured the Whiffle scene, and it does so in two different ways. First, Roderick obviously cannot "read" Strutwell in the same way that he "read" Whiffle. While everything about Whiffle was "remarkable" or "singular," this is not the case with Strutwell and Roderick simply fails to recognize him as "other." Indeed, as Roderick has now "put on the gentleman of figure," it is likely that there are no differences for him to read. Second, and more interestingly, Roderick cannot be certain that he does not appear as "other" himself. Like Peregrine and Pallet, Roderick staggers as he finds himself in a position of uncertainty. Roderick, who should, presumably, be identifying the "other" in the person of Strutwell, instead fears that it has been identified in him, a reversal, it should be pointed out, that even as it renders the position of the "other" self-defeatingly mobile, manages to retain it as an at least abstract concept. Roderick, in fact, immediately attempts to reconstitute a stable vision of the "other" in its most conventional form, connecting it with an infectious desire only contracted abroad and arguing against it as an "appetite unnatural, absurd, and of pernicious consequence" (310). Roderick caps his argument by quoting, of all things, Smollett's own satire, *Advice*:

> [I] declared my utter detestation and abhorrence of it in
>   these lines of the satyrist:
> 'Eternal infamy the wretch confound
> Who planted first, this vice on British ground!
> A vice! that 'spite of sense and nature reigns,
> And poisons genial love, and manhood stains!'   (310–11)

However, as stable as the "other" may be in the abstract, the concept has become uselessly unanchored, and Roderick is unable to tell whether it applies—or is thought to apply—to anyone in the room. In addition, Smollett's quoting himself here only serves to emphasize the ambiguities of the scene: Smollett invokes himself as the voice of anti-sodomitical authority to condemn the scene that he himself has imaginatively generated.

After Roderick quotes the lines from *Advice*, Strutwell merely smiles and tells Roderick that he is "glad to find [his] opinion of the matter so conformable to his own, and that what he had advanced was only to provoke [Roderick] to an answer" (311). Steven Bruhm has intriguingly argued that this moment announces "the birth of the closet" (405)—though as we find out on the next page that the Earl is "notorious," it would seem to be something of a still-birth. It is true that Strutwell prevaricates, but what I would point to here is not the closet, but the occluded place of the "proximate" in the construction of the "other." That is, unarmed with the prior knowledge that the Earl is "notorious," Roderick does not encounter him as "other" at all, and he leaves Strutwell's house happily dreaming of his eventual promotion to prime minister. It is only after he has been informed by his friend Banter that Strutwell is "notorious for a passion for his own sex" (312) that Roderick can retrospectively reconstruct events making the Earl appear as distinctly "other":

> upon recollection, I found every circumstance of Strutwell's behaviour, exactly tallying with the character [Banter] had described: His hugs, embraces, squeezes and eager looks, were now no longer a mystery; no more than his defence of Petronius, and the jealous frown of his *valet de chambre*, who, it seems, was at present the favourite pathic of his lord. (313)

Thus Roderick suddenly sees Strutwell as occupying the same unequivocal status that earlier characterized Whiffle: "every circumstance" of the Earl's behaviour becomes evidence of his "notorious" position, "exactly tallying with the character" of the "other." Roderick recaptures the certainty that the whole episode had so disturbingly undermined.

Of course, Roderick's reconstruction of events is something of a sham—not only because it posits a certainty that never actually existed, but because what Roderick leaves out of the account is his own behavior. But just as Roderick unselfconsciously transforms into a replica of Captain Whiffle, he also never seems to notice that his own actions replicate the very behavior he comes to claim unlocks the mystery of Strutwell's character. For example, Roderick's rise to the status of "pretty fellow" prefigures the Strutwell scene in a number of ways. Strap, at the sight of Roderick, leaps upon him, hangs about his neck, and kisses him from ear to ear. He makes a number of promises, including using his "interest" with a nobleman on Roderick's behalf, for which Roderick hugs him in return. And, finally, he decks Roderick out in the finery described earlier (252–56). Returning to London as a man of fashion, Roderick's first plan is to captivate an heiress with his dazzling appearance, but finding himself "baffled" in "matrimonial schemes," he turns his attention to men instead, and begins to court "men of interest" in a way not unlike the manner in which Strutwell will court him (306). He cultivates a friendship with Straddle and Swillpot—who eventually introduce him to the Earl—and finds these men "as open to [his] advances as [he] could desire" (306). We might well ask whether it is Roderick, and not the Earl, who prevaricates: the irony in Roderick's emphatic quotation from *Advice* is that he makes it within the context of courting the "great" in the very manner that that poem denounces.

Once Roderick has been told the truth about Strutwell, however, he can safely reposition him as "other," and the Earl and his notorious passion then disappear from the narrative—or seem to. In fact, the thwarted sodomitical scene reappears near the conclusion of *Roderick Random* in a refigured form, one which allows everyone's desires to be fulfilled. Once more the surgeon of a ship, Roderick travels to South America. There, in Buenos Aires, Roderick is introduced to an "English signor," Don Rodriguez. Don Rodriguez treats everyone in the party "very complaisantly," but "fixing his eyes attentively" on Roderick, he utters a deep sigh (411). Roderick cannot help himself: he sympathizes involuntarily, and sighs in return. During the course of the visit, Don Rodriguez continues to eye Roderick "with uncommon attachment;" Roderick, in turn, feels "a surprizing attraction towards him" (412). He is filled with "affection and awe; and in short, the emotions of [his] soul, in the presence of this stranger, were strong and unaccountable" (412). That night, Roderick is unable to get to sleep; he is "seized with an irresistible desire" concerning this man and is pleased when a message comes the next day from Don Rodriguez desiring him to return. Don Rodriguez continues to show " a particular regard" for Roderick and, as a token of affection, presents him with "a ring set with a beautiful amethyst" (412). Of course, Don Rodriguez turns out to be Roderick's long-lost father. (Whew!) The language of romantic infatuation which characterizes this episode can be indulged because of, and is cleansed by, the discovery of consanguinity. Whereas Earl Strutwell caught Roderick in his arms and kissed him with only a "*seemingly* paternal affection"—offering a perversion of this most sacred of homosocial relationships—Don

Rodriguez can offer the real thing, clasping Roderick in his arms and crying "my son! my son!" (413) And Don Rodriguez can also perform what the Earl could not: as it just so happens that Roderick's new-found father has become immensely wealthy, he can recognize his son's "modest merit" and raise him to a station in the world befitting his birth.

This conclusion—meant, I would maintain, to be read in opposition to the Strutwell episode—represents the achievement of the homosocial ideal, a pure bond between men, cleansed of the "sordid and vicious disposition" that characterized other relationships in the novel. That it is a father-son bond only emphasizes its utter purity. But the comparison between the scenes can move in both directions, and this ecstasy of homosocial bonding contains within it the suggestion of an evasive fulfillment of the more libidinal bonding denounced earlier in the novel. Embracing Roderick with "unutterable fondness" and transported with "unspeakable joy," Don Rodriguez is brought at last to an "ejaculation" (413)—albeit a verbal one. For his part, Roderick is "affected with the tumults of passion" bodily—particularly in his "lower extremities" (414). He is taken to bed, Don Rodriguez never leaving his side, and after a relieving emission of bodily fluid ("a critical sweat"), Roderick achieves a kind of post-coital "agreeable lassitude" (414). Unutterable. Unspeakable. Unnamable? Manly passion in this scene finds its (non)articulation in the same terms regularly applied to the sodomite; the ideal and the transgressive collapse into similar representational structures. The thinly veiled erotic nature of this reunion, and the language of infatuation that preceded it, demonstrate again how in Smollett's sodomitical practices a disturbing sameness inheres within difference and the reviled "other" turns out to be "proximate." As such, this climactic scene in *Roderick Random*, in which Roderick's happiness is "compleated," seems finally to repudiate and finally to fulfill simultaneously the notorious passion associated with Whiffle and with Strutwell.

Although Smollett tends not to stray from the conventions of sodomitical practices as we saw them in chapters 1 and 2, in his works the depiction of the sodomite becomes the locus of a strange conjunction of satire, disgust, fear, fascination, and desire. Represented as the complete antithesis of Smollett's manly world and banished from the narrative scene as such, the sodomite nevertheless makes a disturbing return within and across Smollett's writing. In *Roderick Random* and *Peregrine Pickle,* sodomitical practices seem to become the focus of sodomitical desire even as it is repudiated; this topic is further explored in the next chapter.

Chapter Four
The Sodomitical Spectacle

IN THIS final chapter I turn to the possibility that sodomitical practices could become the means for the expression of erotic fantasy. The two texts I have chosen to focus upon—the anonymous *Account of the PROCEEDINGS Against CAPT. EDWARD RIGBY* (1698) and John Cleland's *Memoirs of a Woman of Pleasure* (1748–49)—are, in a way, obvious choices for the examination of such a possibility. For both texts offer us, with a degree of explicitness we have not yet encountered, the spectacle of the sodomite in action. In short, if explicitness of representation is taken as the criterion, both of these texts are pornographic. Yet it is not their degree of explicitness alone that leads me to suggest that these texts are expressive of desire. The *Account* roundly condemns the scene that it so graphically displays, characterizing sodomy as an "Abominable SIN." And it is after all a trial account: Rigby does go to jail. Similarly, sodomy is the one sexual act that Cleland's novel appears to reject without qualification, the only act not included when the procuress Mrs. Cole describes sexual pleasure as the "universal port of destination, and every wind that blew thither a good one, provided it blew nobody any harm" (144). Fanny, the novel's narrator and heroine, calls sodomy a "taste, not only universally odious, but absurd" (156). The *Account* and *Memoirs* both set their sodomitical spectacles squarely within the condemnatory conventions of sodomitical practices, repeating those representational structures with which we are by now familiar. However, as we shall see, it is a repetition with a difference, a reconfiguration and recontextualization of sodomitical practices that constitutes what Jonathan Dollimore would call a "transgressive reinscription" or "transgressive mimesis."

Dollimore defines "transgressive reinscription" as "a mode of transgression which finds expression through the inversion and perversion of . . . pre-existing categories and structures . . . , a mode of transgression which seeks not an escape from existing structures but rather a subversive reinscription within them, and in the process their dislocation" (285).[1] In my Introduction, I distinguished "transgressive reinscription" from what Foucault would call a "reverse discourse," that process by which the subjects of an exclusionary discourse find their voices and demand their acceptance by appropriating to themselves the very vocabulary used initially to exclude them (see *History* 100–102). As I pointed out there, we do not find such an open appropriation of sodomitical practices by the self-proclaimed sodomite during this period. Neither the *Account* nor *Memoirs* is written in the voice of the sodomite; neither relinquishes the language of condemnation. However, what we do find in each of these texts is a blurring of the distinction between the representer and the represented, the observer and the observed, the condemning and the condemned. If we do not have the voice of the sodomite, we have a voice which threatens to collapse into what it is not; if the language of condemnation cannot be relinquished, we find that it can be suspended while the sodomitical scene plays itself out. The *Account* and *Memoirs* transform sodomitical practices even as they mimic them, reproducing sodomitical fantasy in the same terms that would reject it, and, in the process, offer to their readers a position from which to indulge in the erotics of the sodomitical spectacle. In what follows, I shall first consider the *Account of the PROCEEDINGS Against CAPT. EDWARD RIGBY*, using that broadside as a point of reference for a discussion of prohibition, fantasy, and erotic spectatorship. I shall then turn to *Memoirs of a Woman of Pleasure* and, reading the novel through its sodomitical scene, argue for its status as sodomitical fantasy by showing how it exercises (and then exorcises) the reader's sodomitical gaze.

In 1698, perusers of broadsides could, in order to edify their sense of justice, read *An Account of the PROCEEDINGS Against CAPT. EDWARD RIGBY, . . . for intending to Commit the Abominable SIN of SODOMY, on the Body of one William Minton.* In emphatic, if somewhat overdetermined, language, the broadside announces at the start the contriving, scheming nature of Rigby's guilt as well as the distanced, passive nature of Minton's innocence. Rigby, it seems,

> did Solicite, Incite, and as well by words as otherways, endeavour to perswade one *William Minton* (of about the Age of Nineteen Years) to suffer him the said *Rigby*, to commit the Crime of *Sodomy* with him the said *Minton*. And the said *Rigby* did also Endeavour and Attempt, to Commit the Crime of *Sodomy* with him the said *Minton*; and did also do and perpetrate divers other Enormities and abominable things, with an intent to Commit the Crime of *Sodomy* with the said *Minton*.

Here is the language of official, jurisprudential condemnation— the repeated "said *Rigby*" and "said *Minton*" giving the passage an appropriate, legal-sounding air—a context which would seem to permit the naming of the unnamable as the phrase "to Commit the Crime of *Sodomy*" appears almost like an incantation. The legal condemnation, of course, also draws force from the more traditional religious and moral prohibitions concerning sodomy: "divers . . . Enormities and abominable things" cannot be said to fall within the bounds of the strictly legal, and the "crime" is called a "sin" in the title. Having abundantly pronounced Rigby's guilt at the start, the *Account* concludes with the "Exemplary Judgment against him," a judgment which, exemplary as it is, "could not be Adequate to his Crime." Rigby was sentenced to stand in the pillory on three occasions, to pay a fine of £1000, to go to prison for one year, and before being discharged from prison, to provide "Sureties for his good Behaviour for Seven Years." *An Account of the PROCEEDINGS Against CAPT. EDWARD RIGBY* is an exemplary tale of crime and punishment, of enormities performed and their enormous consequences.

However, between this frame of crime announced and judgment meted out, the *Account* seems calculated to edify quite another sense than that of justice. For immediately following the passage quoted above, and in contrast to the legalese that characterizes it, the *Account* quickly becomes a narrative of intrigue, plotting, and double-crossing, remarkable in its explicit sexual detail:

> [O]n *Saturday* the Fifth of *November* last, *Minton* standing in St. *James's Park* to see the Fireworks, *Rigby* stood by him, and took him by the hand, and squeez'd it; put his Privy Member Erected into *Mintons* Hand; kist him, and put his Tongue into *Mintons* Mouth, who being much astonish'd at these Actions went from him; but *Rigby* pursued him and accosted him again.

Rigby then asks Minton to meet him at a tavern on the following Monday. Conferring with some friends the next day, Minton is convinced to keep the appointment in order to "detect and punish the Villany designed by *Rigby*." Accordingly, Minton goes to the tavern on the Monday evening accompanied by a constable and his assistant who conceal themselves in an adjoining room. Their plan is that if Rigby should offer Minton "any Violence," Minton will cry out "*Westminster*" and the constable and his assistant will spring into the room and apprehend Rigby.

> *Rigby* seemed much pleased upon *Mintons* coming, and drank to him in a glass of Wine and kist him, took him by the Hand, put his Tongue into *Mintons* Mouth, and thrust *Mintons* hand into his (*Rigby*) Breeches, saying, *He had raised his Lust to the highest degree, Minton* thereupon askt, *How can it be, a Woman was only fit for that, Rigby* answered, DAM'EM, THEY ARE ALL POXT, I'LL HAVE NOTHING TO DO WITH THEM. Then *Rigby* sitting on *Mintons* Lap, kist him several times, putting his Tongue into his Mouth, askt him, *if*

> *he should F — — — him,* how can that be askt *Minton, I'le show*
> *you* answered *Rigby.* . . . Then *Rigby* kist *Minton* several times,
> putting his Tongue in his Mouth, and taking *Minton* in his
> Arms, wisht he might lye with him all night, and that his Lust
> was provoked to that degree, he had — — — in his Breeches,
> but notwithstanding he could F — — — him; *Minton* there-
> upon said, *sure you cannot do it here,* yes, answered *Rigby,* I
> can, and took *Minton* to a corner of the Room, and put his
> Hands into *Mintons* Breeches, desiring him to pull them
> down, who answered he would not, but he (*Rigby*) *might*
> *do what he pleased;* thereupon *Rigby* pulled down *Mintons*
> Breeches, turn'd away his shirt, put his Finger to *Mintons*
> Fundament, and applyed his Body close to *Mintons,* who feel-
> ing something warm touch his Skin, put his hand behind him,
> and took hold of *Rigbys* Privy Member.

Minton, whose powers of deduction were apparently not all that
they might have been, then cries out: "*I have now discovered your*
base Inclinations, I will expose you to the World, to put a stop to these
Crimes. . ." Minton shouts "*Westminster*" and the constable and his
assistant rush in and seize Rigby.

Gregory Bredbeck, looking at this broadside, has commented that
it is difficult to tell whether it is "more interested in condemning
Rigby's 'abominable' behavior or displaying it" (8). The question
seems just: if sodomy was not even supposed to be named, what justification can there be for such a detailed description of sodomitical
behavior? Why not just say that Rigby made a sodomitical attempt
upon Minton and let the specific acts rest under the shroud of "divers
. . . Enormities and abominable things"? And, in what is frankly an
explicit scene, why continue the pretense of concealment by gutting
"F — — —" and "he had — — — in his Breeches"? In other words, to
borrow Linda Williams's terms, why bring "on/scene" what is so
resolutely meant to be "off/scene (ob/scene)" (see "Pornographies
On/scene")?

Of course, to ask whether the *Account* is intent on condemning
Rigby's behavior or on displaying it is to answer the question: it does

both. Indeed, Bredbeck's condemn/display dichotomy may be something of a false one. For one might sensibly argue that the display of Rigby's behavior is part of the condemnation: "*I will expose you to the World*," cries Minton. We are also told that, in court, Rigby would not plead "not guilty" because he was "sensible of his Guilt, and unwilling the same should be disclosed to the World."[2] Exposure is similarly the (earthly) punishment that the "Minister of the Church of England" threatens in *The Sodomites Shame and Doom* (discussed in chapter 1), despite his claim that the act of sodomy is too hateful to be even reproved in sermons and books: "many of your *Names* and *Places* of Abode are known: and tho' they are at present concealed, to see whether you will reform; some way may be taken to publish you to the World" (2).

To be "published" to the world is what happens to Rigby in the *Account*. The various machinery of power—here the court of law and the press—combine to condemn Rigby precisely by making a spectacle out of him, recreating in a brief narrative both the enormity of his crime and the swift and magnificent workings of justice. *An Account of the PROCEEDINGS Against CAPT. EDWARD RIGBY*, "Printed by Order of the Court," puts the criminal and his punishment on display and thus functions as a more widely circulating, longer-lasting, verbal counterpart to the sentence to stand in the pillory.

Yet the reservations mentioned above remain. Surely simply to publish Rigby to the world as a sodomite, without the explicit recounting of his actions, would render him spectacle enough. If, on the one hand, Rigby is rendered an abject spectacle by the condemning gaze of authority, comprised of the court, the press, and right-minded readers of broadsides—as indeed he surely is—on the other hand the spectacle here seems to take on some life of its own. In its representational excess, the spectacle of Rigby's criminal attempt upon Minton appears to overwhelm—or at least suspend—the disciplinary regime that creates it and the exemplary account of crime and punishment is eclipsed by the text of pornographic display.[3]

As Foucault has noted, describing the "spectacle of the scaffold" in *Discipline and Punish*, the disciplinary spectacle can rarely be contained entirely within the regime of the controlling gaze (32–69). During the successful public execution, Foucault states, the creator of the spectacle, the sovereign, certainly manifested the extent and totality of his or her power by rendering the condemned person a spectacle of restraint, humiliation, and, ultimately, lifelessness. Spectators, too, could appropriate to themselves the power of the sovereign, and frequently did, hurling insults at the condemned person, and occasionally even attacking him or her. At the same time, however, Foucault notes that the spectacle itself was also meant to manifest the power of the sovereign in a manner that would overwhelm the spectators through a "policy of terror" that made "everyone aware, through the body of the criminal, of the unrestrained presence of the sovereign" (49).

Conversely, the spectacle was also capable of manifesting a power over the spectators that countered the sovereign's: the criminal could be regarded as a popular hero, and be cheered rather than jeered by the spectators.[4] In such cases, the crowds occasionally rejected the punitive power of the sovereign and prevented the execution from taking place. Even if the criminal did not escape execution, the power of the sovereign could be temporarily suspended in a "momentary saturnalia, when nothing remained to prohibit or punish. Under the protection of imminent death, the criminal could say everything and the crowd cheered" (60). In the spectacle of the scaffold, then, Foucault suggests that power can be surprisingly and unexpectedly mobile, and the event of the disciplinary spectacle can proceed according to a contradictory inner logic which suspends, or even negates, the project of voyeuristic mastery.[5]

Perhaps most interesting for our purposes is Foucault's observation that, in the pseudo-festival atmosphere that attended the execution, crime tended to flourish, that the crush of spectators could become an ideal venue for crime—for even the same crime that the people had gathered to see punished. In other words, in the public spectacle of the scaffold we have a system of control that, in part, generated the opportunity for its own transgression.

We may posit a similarly intimate connection—or, perhaps, an even more intimate connection—between prohibition and transgression in the *Account of the PROCEEDINGS Against CAPT. EDWARD RIGBY*. For the bulk of the *Account* delivers to its readers, in pornographic detail, precisely that erotic spectacle its legal frame would restrain, condemn, and abject. Indeed, by (re)producing the scene it ostensibly wishes to eradicate, the *Account* offers us a striking instance of the paradoxical process described by Judith Butler in which "prohibitions of the erotic are always at the same time, and despite themselves, *the eroticization of prohibition*" ("Force of Fantasy" 111; my emphasis).Discussing antipornography calls for censorship, Butler maintains that such efforts to enforce a limit on erotic fantasy can only always fail because limits are "what fantasy loves most, what it incessantly thematizes and subordinates to its own aims" (111). Prohibition is what gives fantasy its delightful *frisson*. A similar point is made by Elizabeth Cowie in her discussion of desire and pornographic fantasy: desire, she writes, "is defined by what it is not—namely, socially organized sexuality. . . . Desire . . . is most truly itself when it is most 'other' to social norms, when it transgresses the limits and exceeds the 'proper' " (134).

Moving one step farther, Butler argues that the scene of pornographic fantasy is actually structured by those prohibitions "that appear to arrive only after the fantasy has started to play itself out" (115); in fact, she asserts, "prohibition depends on transgressive fantasies" and actively reproduces them (111). But so, too, does fantasy depend on prohibition. For Butler, erotic fantasy does not constitute an essential evasion of a prohibitive law; rather, it occurs as a temporary suspension of the prohibitive law which brackets it, first producing the scene as that which ought not to happen, and then reappearing to condemn the scene as that which ought not to have happened. Prohibition, that is, provides the occasion for fantasy. We can see, then, that Butler conceives of erotic fantasy as a kind of "transgressive reinscription," always operating within prohibition, but simultaneously overturning that prohibition and producing a knowledge beyond it.[6]

It may seem that a discussion of fantasy is somewhat beside the point in relation to what, after all, purports to be the description of an actual event; however, I suggest the *Account* enacts precisely the process of pornographic fantasy that Judith Butler describes, both structurally and thematically.

We can understand (the figure of) Minton as the "author" of this sodomitical spectacle in—at least initially—the strictly disciplinary sense. First, Minton is the "injured party," the one who seeks redress. Second, within the narrative itself, Minton stands as the representative of outraged innocence, with whom readers might identify, from whose point of view the narrative is told, and on whose behalf the *Account* is disseminated. And last, the *Account* itself exists as the culmination of Minton's authorial cry "*I will expose you to the World,*" following which he invokes the seat of government ("*Westminster*") and sets the spectacle-making process in motion.

But this shout that ultimately generates the text marks not the emergence of a prohibitive law which forecloses on the erotic scene, but rather a *re*emergence of those prohibitive and disciplinary forces which produced the scene in the first place. For before Minton even steps into the tavern where Rigby is waiting, the sodomitical spectacle already exists fantasmatically in Minton's mind and in the minds of his friends; it is the imaginary scene around which they form their plan of action, the wished-for event that gives meaning to their exertions. Significantly, though, the prohibitive force is (must be) suspended on Minton's part when he enters into the erotic scene. Minton's curiously blockish innocence is what enables and even encourages the unfolding of the scene—as, for example, when he refuses to lower his breeches, but tells Rigby that he might do what he pleases. If Minton authors the sodomitical spectacle as a condemnatory punishment, it is only because he first authors/authorizes that spectacle to be played out on his remarkably passive body. In fact, Minton seems almost to succumb to, to be seduced by, the spectacle that he himself has created. And at this moment, the *Account* begins to blur the distinction between the text of erotic condemnation and the text of pornographic indulgence, the connection between the two provided by the ambiguous position of Minton.

While it is no longer the critical commonplace it once was, the dynamic described by Laura Mulvey in which the author/spectator enjoys a voyeuristic mastery over the passive "to-be-looked-atness" of the spectacle still exerts a considerable authority over discussions of the erotic scene, i.e., pornography (see "Visual Pleasures"). In other words, there is a tendency to place the pornographic spectacle within the same regime of the controlling gaze said to govern the disciplinary spectacle.[7] But like the disciplinary spectacle, the pornographic spectacle is subject to reversals and suspensions (if only temporary ones) of the powerful spectator/passive spectacle dynamic. In fact, they would seem to be fundamental to the workings of pornography. At some point—presumably the point at which the spectator, like Minton, enters into the erotic scene—the spectator, however briefly, succumbs to the spectacle, and the spectacle exerts an at least physiological power over the spectator. This, in fact, would seem to be the point of pornography; when it works, pornography disrupts any project of voyeuristic mastery by seducing its spectator.

Consider, for example, the following lines from one of the, perhaps spurious, prologues to *Sodom; or, The Quintessence of Debauchery*, written in the voice of the poet:

> Our scenes are drawn to th' Life in every shape
> They'll make all pricks to stand and cunts to gape
> . . . .
>
> The author's prick was so unruly grown
> Whilst writing this, he could not keep it down
> *But thinking on the postures of the play*
> *Was forc'd at last to take his strength away*
> And make him sick, by frigging till he spews,
> A sweet revenge, cause he disturbs his Muse.
>
> (50—my emphasis)

The poet emphasizes his own mastery as the creator of erotic "scenes." But he does so by drawing attention to his and all other spectators' *loss* of mastery before the spectacles he creates which prove their power upon the body. Seduced by the spectacle, the poet no longer controls the scene, but is controlled by it.

Turning from the spectacle in order to masturbate, the poet's original position vis-à-vis the spectacle is reversed as he now recreates in himself what he once observed. Of course, this feeds circularly back into his sense of mastery ("see what a good poet I am," "see how sexually powerful I am"),[8] but the brief suspension of mastery, the loss of "strength," signals the moment when the erotic spectacle takes over. Likewise, the similar suspension of mastery in the *Account*, the point at which Minton becomes enthralled by what he has come to see and condemn and is passively manipulated by it, while ostensibly part of the "plan," marks the moment when the erotic spectacle suspends its condemnatory frame.

The extent to which the *Account* replicates the text of pornographic indulgence within its disciplinary frame will become clear if we compare it with a more conventional scene of forbidden erotic pleasures. This is a typical episode from one of Eliza Haywood's popular seduction novels, *The Unequal Conflict; or, Nature Triumphant* (1725). Fillamour and Philenia, who cannot marry because their parents forbid it, have sworn themselves to a "Platonick passion" (57). Their passion being, in a sense, unlawful, Fillamour and Philenia can only imagine it, and, indeed, the prohibition against it inspires endless imaginings. After spending an afternoon "in conversation on the tender theme" of their forbidden love, the two end up succumbing to their own imaginations:

> Spite even of himself, [Fillamour] must transgress—His roving hands without design, took liberties treasonable to Platonick laws—His words no more maintain'd their cool reserve—His glowing cheeks and sparking eyes avow'd wild, and irresistible desire— . . . Philenia, frighted and asham'd, yet all dissolv'd and melting too, felt the destructive softness spread from the overflowing heart thro' every little vein, and thrilling fibre— Faintly she chid, but much more faintly struggled—Soon she lost all the breath to form denials; nor was the will, amidst that sweet confusion, capable of inspiring any—While he more

actuated by his passion, and growing still more bold, took in his
arms her, now, but half reluctant body, and threw her with
himself upon the bed.   (58)

Haywood, using dashes and semicolons, eschews full stops in
order to capture the breathless excitement of the scene, a technique,
we might note, also used by the writer of the *Account*. The similari-
ties between the two scenes are quite clear. In both cases, the scene
of erotic fantasy is occasioned by the very law that prohibits it.
Further, if Rigby, like Fillamour, is actuated by his passion, Minton,
like Philenia, seems to dissolve and melt as he allows Rigby to sit on
his lap, clasp him in his arms, and kiss and fondle his "but half reluctant body." Also like Philenia, Minton only faintly chides Rigby:
"sure you cannot do it here" is not the most unequivocal of refusals.
And in both texts, the erotic scene is ultimately interrupted at the
brink of consummation by a sudden return of the prohibitive law: in
The Unequal Conflict it arrives in the shape of Philenia's father.

But the difference between the scenes is also clear and significant. For while Haywood maintains the transgressive and the prohibitive as two distinct positions, the *Account* collapses these positions into one. Minton figures as both the representative of the prohibitive law (*"Westminster"*) *and* as a participant in the erotic scene
(*"he . . . might do what he pleased"*) — as both the indignant and condemning spectator and the "but half reluctant" spectacle. The sudden (re)appearance of Minton's authoritative voice not only comes
at what seems a rather late point in the scene, but also highlights his
earlier bewildered innocence as something of a pose. It is useful to
recall that when the seat of British government is so gloriously
invoked and assistance rushes in, Rigby is not the only one caught
with his pants down. Moreover, the *Account* offers to its reader a
position as ambiguous as Minton's — and not only because, as Anne
McClintock points out, the "pornographic imagination shifts libidi-
nously: I am the watcher/the watched; I am the pleasurer/the plea-
sured" (125). Because of the way this text merges spectator and spectacle, the condemning and the condemned, even the reader who
comes to the *Account* ready and willing to condemn its subject will

find himself (I use the pronoun consciously) insinuated into the sodomitical spectacle, and dwelling on "abominable things" until they are abruptly—and belatedly—halted. The *Account* turns sodomitical practices back upon themselves, using them to name the unnamable, show the unshowable, and articulate the space of fantasy within prohibition.

Before I turn to the much more developed articulation of fantasy within prohibition that we find in *Memoirs of a Woman of Pleasure,* there are two final points worth making. First, in reading the *Account,* it has not been my intention to trivialize either the seriousness of sodomitical assault or the severity of Rigby's treatment. That is, my intention has not been to capitalize on Rigby's and Minton's misfortunes in order to benefit my own theoretical narrative. Rather, my point has been that the *representation* of this event seems to exceed its purpose in a way that transforms sodomitical practices as we have seen them so far. We ought not to forget that this event likely ruined Rigby's life, but to remember that is also to remember that the only discursive space available during this period for the articulation of sodomitical desire was the space of its negation. Second, given this, is not what I am labeling "transgressive reinscription" simply always an instance of transgression contained? The *Account of the PROCEEDINGS Against CAPT. EDWARD RIGBY* concludes with the law in ascendancy, but this really cannot be said to constitute a containment that eradicates everything that precedes it. The *Account* displays, among other things, the way that prohibition and transgression are intimately connected, that prohibition can actually produce in part the transgression it opposes. But this does not mean that transgression is merely a ruse of prohibition. For if the prohibitive law produces transgression initially as a ruse (i.e., in order to apprehend Rigby), the *Account* reproduces it in the form of knowledge—knowledge of "enormities, that ought never to be supposed to exist" (Louis Simonds, cited in Edelman 173), and with that, knowledge that, as Dollimore puts it, the "path we thought we were on naturally, or by choice, we are in fact on by arrangement, and in straying we discover alternative ways to alternative futures" (106).

Near the end of John Cleland's *Memoirs of a Woman of Pleasure*, the narrator and heroine Fanny Hill is forced to take refuge in a public house while the carriage in which she has been traveling undergoes repair. Fanny hires a room in which to wait and, "prompted by a spirit of curiosity far from sudden," she decides to spy on the people whom she can hear in the next room (157). Looking about, Fanny finds a paper patch in the partition that separates her room from the next, and piercing it with a needle, she forms a peep-hole through which she can observe "two young sparks romping, and pulling one another about, entirely to [her] imagination, in frolic, and innocent play" (157). However, matters quickly take another turn, and the two young men embark on a "project of preposterous pleasure," proceeding to "such lengths as soon satisfied [Fanny], what they were" (157–58). Fanny then witnesses a scene of male-male sodomy—a spectacle which so shocks her, so fills her with "rage, and indignation," that, in her haste to alert the authorities, she falls to the floor and knocks herself "senseless" (159). As in the *Account*, the scene that Fanny witnesses is described for us in explicit detail, the whole episode taking up almost three pages. And also as in the *Account*, this "so criminal a scene" (159) is framed by the language of condemnation and disgust. Fanny, for example, regrets that she must deal with "so disagreeable a subject," one which is "universally odious" (156). And Mrs. Cole, having been informed of what Fanny has seen, "very sensibly observ[es] . . . that there was no doubt of due vengeance one time or another overtaking these miscreants"; she then goes on to make a declaration "extorted from her by pure regard to truth":

> whatever the effect this infamous passion had in other ages, and other countries, it seem'd a peculiar blessing on our air and climate, that there was a plague-spot visibly imprinted on all that are tainted with it, in this nation at least; for that among numbers of that stamp whom she had known, or at least were universally under the scandalous suspicion of it, she could not name an exception hardly of one of them, whose character was not in all other respects the most worth-

less and dispicable that could be, stript of all the manly virtues
of their own sex, and fill'd up with only the very worst vices
and follies of ours: that, in fine, they were scarce less exe-
crable than ridiculous in their monstrous inconsistency, of
loathing and contemning women, and all at the same time
apeing their manners, airs, lisp, skuttle, and, in general, all
their little modes of affectations, which become them at least
better, than they do these unsex'd male-misses.   (159–60)

Mrs. Cole deftly manages to touch upon all the fundamental
points of sodomitical practices, starting with the most basic: the
sodomites will undoubtedly bring down vengeance upon themselves. The sodomites are also connected indirectly with foreign
countries by virtue of their being such anomalies in Britain that they
are marked by a "plague-spot." Further, Mrs. Cole sees sodomites as
being hermaphroditic "male-misses" who have relinquished all
"manly virtues" and who, having gathered to themselves all manner
of vice, typify sodomitical confusion in their "monstrous inconsistency." In short, this passage is practically a primer of sodomitical
practices. There is, however, one slight prevarication: to the number of this "stamp" that Mrs. Cole has encountered, she claims that
she "could not name an exception hardly of one of them" whose
character was not "worthless and dispicable." She "could not name
an exception hardly of one of them": does this ambiguous phrase
not seem to imply that there are exceptions?

Critics have not been slow to take these sodomitical practices at
face value. Peter Sabor writes that throughout the novel Fanny "condemns what she considers unnatural practices, including lesbian-
ism, masturbation, sodomy, . . . and, most intransigently, male
homosexuality" (xxv). Similarly, Madeleine Kahn states that Fanny
is presented as being so enamored of active, male "heterosexuality,"
that "the only men who inspire any critical words from her at all are
two homosexuals. . . . Her scorn is particularly directed at the
younger the more passive of the two men" (158). [9] Recent gay criticism, though, has begun to look at the sodomitical scene in a new
light. Kevin Kopelson, for example, suggests that the sodomitical

spectacle transgresses the novel's representational structures to the extent that it constitutes a Barthesian release from meaning. Lee Edelman has similarly—though more complexly and less utopically—argued that the scene confounds "the stability or determinacy of linguistic or erotic positioning" (184). And Donald H. Mengay views it as part of the novel's critique of "the code of bourgeois heterosexuality" (196).

Although I am primarily in agreement with these last three critics, I do have some reservations about their arguments, not the least of which is that I see the sodomitical scene as being meaning*ful* rather than constituting simply a release from, or destabilization of, meaning. If *Memoirs of a Woman of Pleasure* transgresses, it is as a "transgressive reinscription." That is, it is not just an disarticualtion of old meaning, but an articulation of new meaning through old structures. *Memoirs of a Woman of Pleasure* is a sodomitical fantasy and, as such, the sodomitical scene does not so much confound the novel's representational structures as lay them bare. As in the *Account of the PROCEEDINGS Against CAPT. EDWARD RIGBY*, *Memoirs'* status as a "transgressive reinscription" becomes apparent through the ambiguous position of the sodomitical spectacle's author/spectator: Fanny Hill.

As Nancy K. Miller has pointed out in an influential article, Fanny as a narrator, is really an "I in drag," a female impersonation (see " 'I's' in Drag"). Miller argues that, because of this, the narrative of *Memoirs of a Woman of Pleasure* is fundamentally homoerotic: "the founding contract of the novel as it functions in the phallocentric (heterosexual) economics of representation is homoerotic: 'woman' is the legal fiction, the present absence that allows the male bond of privilege and authority to constitute itself within the laws of proper circulation" (49). By homoeroticism, however, Miller is not referring to an expression of sexual desire between men, but rather to the "narcissistic gain implicitly achieved by occupying the space of the desired object in the syntax of the Other" (57). That is, the male author impersonates a female narrator "the better to be admired by and for himself" (49). In Miller's account, homoeroticism functions entirely within a "heterosexual" economy of desire; it is an expression of male, "heterosexual" fantasy in which a man impersonates a woman in order to represent the effect he desires to have upon her, "a wish-fulfillment," Miller writes, "that ultimately translates into structures of masculine dominance and authority" (54). Anne Robinson Taylor similarly argues that Cleland's pose as a woman is betrayed by "a strong undercurrent of dislike for women" (93), and Madeleine Kahn agrees that "Fanny is an uncomplicated misogynist" (156). These arguments stand in sharp contrast to Leo Braudy's assertion in 1970 that "Cleland through Fanny is transmuted into the first feminist" (37)! One recent critic, however, has attempted to recuperate Cleland's "drag act" positively. Roy Roussel argues that *Memoirs of a Woman of Pleasure* "moves toward a certain idea of androgyny in which the equality between masculine and feminine triumphs over the difference between the sexes and allows the man and the woman to converse freely across this difference" (41). Roussel's argument is not at all convincing, but I cite him here to show that, even in an attempt to recuperate Fanny as an "I in drag," Roussel, like Braudy, Kahn, Taylor, and Miller, is unable to conceive that via this "drag act," the novel might exceed a "heterosexual" paradigm and inscribe homoerotic fantasy within the terms of its exclusion.

Miller's argument has been justly influential, and it is not my intention to dispense completely with her formulation; clearly, even the briefest perusal of the novel's criticism indicates that *Memoirs of a Woman of Pleasure* has elicited—and continues to elicit—male, "heterosexual" pleasure. Neither do I wish to detract from her insight into the way that authorial female impersonation marginalizes or, in fact, effaces female pleasures and desires while seeming to give voice to them. But I do think that we can complicate Miller's argument to show how the novel invites quite another reading. For Fanny is not simply an "I in drag," she is also an "eye in drag," a frequent voyeur whose desiring gaze is repeatedly riveted upon the specularized male body and its "wonderful machine." Unlike the *Account*, Cleland's novel is overtly intent on providing material for erotic fantasy; but as the *Account* clearly shows, there was no discursive space for *homo*erotic fantasy outside of its condemnation.

Through Fanny, however, the reader is provided with a point of interpolation into the eroticized spectacle of another man. As a spectator, Fanny functions less as a fantasized projection of the presumed male reader, I suggest, than as a surrogate for him, mirroring in the masturbatory pleasures of her erotic viewing the masturbatory pleasures of erotic reading. Like the peeping Fanny, the reader of erotic fiction is meant to be "inflamed" and, ultimately, "melted by the sight" (32). Central to this connection between Fanny and the reader is the way in which Cleland's novel begins by constructing Fanny's initiation into sexual desire through a number of erotic spectacles. When she arrives at Mrs. Brown's in London, Fanny is, in her own words, an "unpractised simpleton who was perfectly new to life" (9); however, it is not long before she is educated out of this state of ignorance: "sight," she says, "gave the last dying blow to my native innocence" (25). In *Memoirs of a Woman of Pleasure*, desire is discovered by means of erotic spectatorship.

In the first of these scenes, Fanny becomes a spectator quite by chance and witnesses an encounter between Mrs. Brown and a young grenadier. This spectacle thrills Fanny to her very soul and makes "every vein in [her] body circulate liquid fires" (25). Fanny is seduced into desire by sight and then takes action "guided by nature only":

> Whilst they were in the heat of the action, guided by nature only, I stole my hand up my petty-coat, and with fingers all on fire, seized, and yet more inflamed that center of all my senses; my heart palpitated, as if it would force its way through my bosom: I breathed with pain: I twisted my thighs, squeez'd, and compress'd the lips of that virgin-slit, and . . . brought on at last the critical exstasy, the melting flow, into which nature, spent with excess of pleasure, dissolves and dies away.   (25)

This scene asserts a "natural" relationship between vision, desire, and masturbation. Like the poet in the prologue to *Sodom*, Fanny here emphasizes not the mastery involved in erotic spectatorship, but the loss of mastery. Fanny feels no temptation to join the scene she witnesses; rather, vision provides a pleasure of its own, like the transports of "luscious dreams" which, Fanny tells us, "are scarce inferior to those of waking, real action" (13; cf. Roussel 48).

Indeed, the novel emphasizes throughout the pleasures of erotic viewing: Phoebe, Fanny's "tutor," insists that her "sight must be feasted" (12); Fanny watches Mr. H—— in action with her maid Hannah (68); Harriet watches a man swim naked in a river (101–2); Fanny, Harriet, Louisa, Emily, and their "gallants" take turns watching each other (112–24); and Mrs. Cole, of course, has several spyholes from which she watches the goings-on in her house. As with the scene quoted above, these episodes of spectatorship stress the spectator's loss of power when confronted with the erotic spectacle: people melt, dissolve, are spent. Shortly after the meeting of Mrs. Brown and the grenadier, Phoebe arranges for Fanny to witness another scene. This is the meeting between Polly and the Genoese merchant. Again, Fanny describes the whole scene and then her reaction. And again, Fanny is "melted by the sight" and "overcome" (32). Even Phoebe, "the hackney'd thorough-bred *Phoebe*, to whom all modes and devices of pleasure were known," could not "be unmov'd by so warm a scene" (12, 32). This time, Fanny is relieved by Phoebe's "busy fingers" (32).

As Roy Roussel has written, because readers see events only through Fanny's eyes, "their reactions will be, in some way, a function of hers" (45). Like Fanny—and through Fanny—the reader is offered a similar voyeuristic position and is presented with a number of erotic spectacles whose intent is clearly to arouse and seduce. "In this context," Roussel continues, "these early incidents, with their emphasis on spectacle and masturbation, seem almost to function as a set of instructions . . . [for] . . . the use of pornographic texts" (49). The pornographic text works if the reader, like Fanny, is engrossed in, and excited by, the spectacle; and the pornographic text is successful if the spectacle leads to the *reader's* orgasm as well as Fanny's. The opening of Cleland's novel, then, instructs, and constructs, the reader and Fanny alike, and it is precisely because the novel invites the reader to share Fanny's perspective that *Memoirs of a Woman of Pleasure* exceeds the "heterosexual" boundaries that Roussel, Miller, and the critics mentioned above would place on it. For through the supposedly "female" eyes of Fanny, the reader—whom all critics agree is presumed to be male—is invited again and again to gaze upon men's bodies as objects of desire. "I soon had my eyes called off by a more striking object, that entirely engross'd them," Fanny tells us when recounting the scene between Mrs. Brown and the grenadier:

> Her sturdy stallion had now unbutton'd, and produced naked, stiff, and erect, that wonderful machine, which I had never seen before, and which . . . I star'd at with all the eyes I had. . . . [T]he flaming red head as it stood uncapt, the whiteness of the shaft, and the shrub-growth of curling hair that embrowned the roots of it, the roundish bag that dangled down from it, all exacted my eager attention, and renewed my flame.   (25–26)

This is just the first of many scenes in which the reader is provided, through Fanny (or Harriet, or Louisa, or Emily), with a detailed, lingering, and fascinated description of the male body that focuses on the genitalia. Indeed, the male genitalia figure much more prominently, and are described much more elaborately, in Cleland's novel than the female (see Mengay 189).

In an important article, "Masculinity as Spectacle," Steve Neale has suggested that "in a heterosexual and patriarchal society, the male body cannot be marked explicitly as the erotic object of another male look: that look must be motivated in some other way, its erotic component repressed" (14). Certainly, the male reader's "look" at the young grenadier in the scene quoted above is mediated by the presence of Fanny's "eyes" which designate the look as "natural." The spectacle of the naked, aroused grenadier is also further qualified by the man's position in a scene of "heterosexual" action with Mrs. Brown. But one cannot really say in this case that the reader's "look" is motivated by anything other than the scene's "erotic component." Nor can one say that Mrs. Brown constitutes the focal point of the erotic gaze: "her fat brawny thighs hung down and the whole greasy landskip lay fairly open to my view: a wide open-mouth'd gap, overshaded with a grizzly bush, seemed held out like a beggar's wallet for its provision" (24). It is clearly the grenadier who is the object of desire.

In chapter 1 we saw that sodomitical practices frequently involve the interposition of a rhetorical hermaphrodism in the scene of male-male desire in order to maintain a rigidified gender hierarchy: the "unnatural" is assimilated to the "natural" in a way that shores up the "natural" and effaces any challenge to it. Cleland's "I/eye in drag" would seem to turn this practice on its head. For in *Memoirs of a Woman of Pleasure* Fanny's "natural" look is what provides the reader with access to a spectacle otherwise prohibited. Cleland's rhetorical hermaphrodism, in other words, assimilates the "natural" to the "unnatural."

Significantly, these first two erotic spectacles—of Mrs. Brown and the grenadier, and of Polly and the Genoese merchant— which instruct and invite us to look and to desire with Fanny are immediately followed by a third in which the male body is not simply a participant, but *is* the erotic spectacle itself. In this scene, Charles lays naked and asleep, his body displayed to be looked at, admired, desired, while we, through Fanny's eyes, "devour" his "naked charms":

> I hung over him enamour'd indeed! and devour'd all his naked charms with only two eyes, when I could have wish'd them at least a hundred for the fuller enjoyment of the gaze.
>
> Oh! could I paint his figure as I see it now still present to my transported imagination! a whole length of an all-perfect manly beauty in full view. Think of a face without a fault, glowing with all the opening bloom, and vernal freshness of an age, in which beauty is of either sex. (44)

Thus begins a *blazon* of Charles's beauties that goes on for nearly two pages, cataloguing the "ruby pout of his lips," "the smoothness of his skin," "his snow-white bosom," the "simmetry of his limbs," and, of course, that "column of the whitest ivory, beautifully streaked with blue veins, and carrying, fully uncapt, a head of the liveliest vermillion" (44–46). This is the longest description of any body in the

novel—more than twice as long as the description of Fanny herself
(14–15)—marking Charles's body as the narrative's supreme object of
desire. In this scene, too, there is a commensurability between
spectator and spectacle: Charles's body shares in the rhetorical hermaphrodism of the spectatorial position. His beauty is at once
"manly" and appropriate to "either sex." Like Fanny, the reader is
here allowed to linger over Charles "for the fuller enjoyment of the
gaze." We shall be asked to gaze in a similarly lingering fashion at
Will (71–73), at Harriet's man in the country (101–2),[10] and at the
appropriately named "*Good-natur'd Dick*" (162). Again, the presence
of Fanny as the "I" of the narration and as our "eye" into the textual
world maintains and guarantees the look as "natural" even as it
simultaneously enables the solicitation of the homoerotic gaze.

As a vehicle for sodomitical fantasy, Cleland's novel builds
incrementally to its sodomitical scene, beginning with episodes in
which the spectacle of the male body is situated in a "heterosexual" setting, then offering the spectacle of the male body alone
(Charles, Harriet's country man), and finally, just before the
sodomitical scene proper, a pseudo-sodomitical scene in which
Emily attends a masquerade dressed as a shepherd and captures
the attentions of a man who thinks she really is a boy. It is worth
pausing to look at this pseudo-sodomitical scene, for in it Cleland
appears to hint at how one might read his novel as a "transgressive
reinscription." Describing Emily in her costume, Fanny tells us, in
language that suggests some "unnaturalness" to come, that "*nothing
in nature* could represent a prettier boy" than did Emily (154; my
emphasis). Sure enough, at the masquerade Emily is accosted by a
gentleman who begins "to make violent love to her . . . all in a style
of courtship dash'd with a certain oddity" (154). Fanny explains the
cause of this oddity:

> He took her really for what she appear'd to be, a smock-fac'd
> boy, and she forgetting her dress, and of course ranging quite
> wide of his ideas, took all those addresses to be paid to herself
> as a woman, which she precisely ow'd to his not thinking her
> one: however, this double error was pushed to such a height

on both sides, that *Emily* . . . suffered herself to be perswaded
to go to a bagnio with him.   (154)

What Fanny refers to in this passage as a "double error" is, in fact, a
kind of double reading, exactly the sort of double reading that
Memoirs of a Woman of Pleasure invites. The novel, like the situation at the masquerade, can be read either "straight" or sodomitically; and the sodomitical reading, in this scene as in the novel as a
whole, is facilitated by the figure in "drag." At the bagnio, of course,
the gentleman discovers the "truth" about Emily ("By heavens a
woman!"), but the two proceed nonetheless to have sex. This barely
constitutes a return to "nature" however:

> he was so fiercely set on a mis-direction, as to give the girl no
> small alarms for fear of losing a maiden-head she had not
> dreamt of; however her complaints and a resistance gentle,
> but firm, check'd, and brought him to himself again; so that
> turning his steed's head, he drove him at length in the right
> road, *in which his imagination having probably made the most
> of those resemblances that flatter'd his taste,* he got . . . to his
> journey's end.   (155–56; my emphasis)

With this episode at the masquerade, Cleland informs his readers of how to read his "drag act" as a "transgressive reinscription."
For not only does Emily's drag act inspire a sodomitical reading of
the situation, but this double reading persists after the supposed
return to "the right road," and the ostensibly heteroerotic scene is
subsumed into homoerotic fantasy. On the one hand the gentleman
is returned "to himself again" and to "nature"; on the other hand he
continues imaginatively to read the scene sodomitically. Within this
system of representation that elicits homoerotic desire in a heteroerotic guise, the actual spectacle of sodomy that immediately follows gains an importance that makes it more than just another
episode in what is primarily an episodic narrative. The spectacle
of sodomy functions as the culmination of the text's embedded
sodomitical desire — culmination in the sense of the most complete

expression of it, apparently realizing what the text has been flirting with all along in its lingering descriptions of the male body and in the pseudo-sodomitical scene at the masquerade; as we shall see, however, the scene is also a culmination in the sense of a termination of, and foreclosure upon, any avowal of such desire.

The scene of sodomy is *Memoirs of a Woman of Pleasure*'s most forceful articulation of the text's homoerotic dynamics—not simply because it gives the reader access to a spectacle of anal intercourse between two men, which is obvious—but because it is the scene that comes closest to revealing Fanny's status as an "eye in drag," a surrogate male in the erotics of vision. This revelation is surely related to Kevin Kopelson's observation that this is the novel's only scene of voyeurism "in which the voyeur is stationed in a position of instability or insecurity" (175). Finally, and significantly, since Fanny so forcefully rejects sodomy from her sexual world, this is also the only scene in which a secret voyeur is discovered and, therefore, implicated in the erotic spectacle.

The scene begins with Fanny gaining visual access to the room. At first she is unable to discover any means by which she might spy on the two men, but

> at length I observ'd a paper-patch of the same colour as the wainscot, which I took to conceal some flaw, but then it was so high, that I was oblig'd to stand on a chair to reach it, . . . and with the point of a bodkin soon pierc'd it, and open'd myself espial-room sufficient: and now applying my eye close, I commanded the room perfectly.   (157)

While the disavowal of the text's homoeroticism depends on our undoubting acceptance of Fanny as a *woman* of pleasure—that is, on our being taken in by her "drag act"—and while the rejection of sodomy depends on Fanny, not to mention the reader, remaining a detached, disgusted observer, this scene begins by emphasizing Fanny's masculinized and eroticized position as spectator. Not only does Fanny assume what she at least considers the power of the gaze ("I commanded the room perfectly"), but Cleland sexualizes her

achievement of this power in a decidedly masculine way by figuring
it as an act of penetration: in order to satisfy her longing, Fanny
pierces the "paper-patch" and thus establishes, in Lee Edelman's
phrase, "intercourse between the two rooms" (186). Fanny's penetration into the scene of sodomy constitutes an interesting variant
on what Kaja Silverman has called "sodomitical identification," "an
identification which permits the fantasizing subject to look through
. . . [another's] eyes and to participate in his sexuality by going
'behind' him . . . , to penetrate by identifying with the one-who-pen-
etrates" (173, 179).[11]

Further, in noting Fanny's sexualized position in relation to the
sodomites, it is worth pointing out that they are all actually *in the
same room*: "[t]he partition of our rooms," Fanny relates, "was one
of those moveable ones that when taken down, serv'd occasionally
to lay them into one" (157). Despite initial appearances, Fanny and
the sodomites occupy the same space. The staging of this scene,
then, suggests from the start Fanny's involvement in, rather than
detachment from, the erotics of the sodomitical spectacle, an involvement that threatens to undermine her pose as a "female"; pre-
cariously balanced on a chair, Fanny is "oblig'd" by the spectacle of
sodomy to move onto shaky ground.

Fanny observes the elder lad begin to fondle the younger, "all
receiv'd by the boy without other opposition, than certain wayward
coynesses, ten times more alluring than repulsive," she assures
us (158). The elder boy then produces his "engine" and the scene
continues:

> Slipping then aside the young lad's shirt, and tucking it up
> under his cloaths behind, he shew'd to the open air, those
> globular, fleshy eminences that compose the mount-pleas-
> ants of *Rome*, and which now, with all the narrow vale that
> intersects them, stood display'd. . . . [A]t length, the first
> streights of entrance being pretty well got through, every
> thing seem'd to move, and go pretty currently on . . . : and
> now passing one hand round his minion's hips, he [the elder
> boy] got hold of his [the younger boy's] red-topt ivory toy,

that stood perfectly stiff, and shewed, that if he was like his
mother behind, he was like his father before; . . . after which,
renewing his driving, and thus continuing to harass his rear,
the height of the fit came on with its usual symptoms, and
dimiss'd the action.   (158–59)

Fanny assures us that she has only had the patience to witness this
scene to the end in order to gather more facts and, thus, by supplying evidence, bring the sodomites to their proper punishment; she is
shocked, appalled, burning with rage and indignation. But, clearly,
Fanny is fascinated too, as her detailed description shows. In addition, rather than maintaining a detached distance, Fanny is involved
enough in the erotic and emotional dynamic of the scene to note that
the younger boy's coyness is "ten times more alluring than repulsive."
It is also worth noting, given Cleland's penchant for adapting his language to each particular episode (for example, when Fanny has sex
with a sailor, the scene is described in nautical terms), that he should
here, in what ought to be the most unconventional episode, resort to
words like "driving," " harassing," and the "streights of entrance" that
form the most conventional "Artillery of Love" *topos*.

However, aside from the explicitness of the description of the sexual act itself, we can recognize in this depiction of the sodomites the
hallmarks of sodomitical practices. Yet, in the context of *Memoirs of
a Woman of Pleasure*, even the most conventional of images seem to
take on an added resonance and double meaning that further implicates Fanny in the sodomitical spectacle. For example, when Fanny
describes the younger boy's buttocks as the "mount-pleasants of
Rome," she relocates the *mons Veneris* and evokes the familiar association of sodomy with Italy in general, and with papists in particular. This familiar method of constructing sodomy as something
distant and foreign is reinforced by Mrs. Cole when she mentions
the "peculiar blessing" on British air and climate that renders the
sodomite an anomaly. But the Rome reference only makes up part
of this phrase. What are we to make of the relocatable "mount-pleasant"?[12] For if the "mount-pleasant" can be the site of sodomical
action, or, to put it differently, if the "mount-pleasant" is the

sodomite's rear, what then is a *Fanny Hill?* In addition, when Fanny says that the boy's erection shows "that if he was like his mother behind, he was like his father before," she conventionally delineates the sodomite as hermaphroditic. Again, this is a line of thinking reinforced by Mrs. Cole when she expounds upon the disgusting effeminacy of sodomites and dismisses them as "monstrous" "male-misses." But if the hermaphroditic term "male-miss" is what distinguishes the sodomites, distinguishes, that is, those who enact their sodomitical desire, it is also the term which most aptly characterizes the desiring "I/eye in drag" of the narrative, as well as the narrative's paragon of desirability, Charles, whose beauty is "of either sex." Thus these typical rhetorical moves to render male-male desire distant and outcast seem only to center it back in the text itself. Indeed, all the expressions of moral outrage that place sodomy outside of Fanny's and Mrs. Cole's sexual world are what in fact "justify" its representation within Cleland's textual world. Fanny asserts that "all young men" should view this scene so that "their innocence may not be betrayed into such snares, for want of knowing the extent of their danger, for nothing is more certain than, that ignorance of a vice, is by no means a guard against it" (158).

It is, in fact, in assuming a moral stance that the text, metaphorically, and Fanny, literally, lose their footing. Determined that the sodomites should meet with "instant justice," Fanny jumps down from her chair "in order raise the house upon them,

> with such an unlucky impetuosity, that some nail or ruggedness in the floor caught my foot, and flung me on my face with such violence, that I fell senseless on the ground. (159)

For Kevin Kopelson, Fanny's being flung senseless on the ground signifies the moment of the Barthesian release from meaning (180). Lee Edelman here sees Fanny as embodying "the instability of positioning that radiates out from the sodomitical scene" (186). Again, I am not essentially in disagreement with these critics, but we might more "meaningfully" look at how this event is related to Fanny's status as an "I/eye in drag." For here Fanny's cries for justice pull the rug out from under her, as it were, and the narrative action thwarts the moral imperative of sodomitical practices. The sound of Fanny's head hitting the floor alerts the two young men to their danger and gives them "more than the necessary time to make a safe retreat" (159); their would-be persecutor is transformed, then, into their unwitting savior. Unlike the debauched Mr. Norbert who is made to die of a high fever in Bath, the sodomites, for all the narrative bluster, are not punished in any way for their sexual pleasures.[13]

Of course, like the "Exemplary Judgment" at the end of the *Account*, the condemnatory language of sodomitical practices in *Memoirs of a Woman of Pleasure* cannot be, and should not be, entirely ignored. If the spectacle of sodomy constitutes the text's most forceful articulation of male-male desire, it also enables the text's most forceful *dis*articulation of it. For the open representation of male-male sexual relations affords the opportunity for an open disavowal and denunciation of the homoeroticism that has operated in an oblique manner throughout the text. After all, it is this scene which allows John Illo to write, "Fanny . . . is introduced to sexuality by a Sapphic encounter, not normal, perhaps, but not ugly, like male homosexuality, which is the only reprehended sexual behaviour in the book" (21); and it is this scene which enables Robert Markley to argue that while "[l]esbianism is discouraged," "male homosexuality is positively abominated" (351).

In a very real sense, this scene, paradoxically, functions to exorcise the specter of sodomitical desire from the text, enabling the reader to deny that what has held his rapt attention throughout has been the male body far more frequently than the female body. "But here washing my hands of them [the sodomites]," Fanny says, "I replunge into the stream of my history" (160), clearly indicating that we are meant to see this episode as lying outside that history. Indeed, in only a few more pages Fanny is reunited with Charles and the "stream of [her] history" concludes in the unending and transporting bliss of heterosexual domesticity. Well, not quite; one final image. Summing up this "happiest of matches," Fanny declares, [t]hus, at length, I got snug into port" (187), an image which, as Donald Mengay points out, establishes Fanny as the penetrator and

Charles as the receiver (191); I would add that it also recalls the sailor who, when stopped by Fanny on the brink of sodomizing her, replies, "Pooh . . . my dear, any port in a storm" (141). Because the spectacle of sodomy in John Cleland's *Memoirs of a Woman of Pleasure*—and in the *Account of the PROCEEDINGS Against CAPT. EDWARD RIGBY*—both actively does and does not invite sodomitical identification, it figures the way in which Cleland's novel as a whole turns sodomitical practices back upon themselves in a "transgressive reinscription," expressing desire in precisely those terms that would deny it: it is *Fanny* who looks, *Fanny* who is inflamed. In this context, the sodomitical spectacle serves ostensibly to demarcate acceptable desires from unacceptable desires: the representation of men desiring men is meant to indicate that *that* is something shocking, horrible, absurd—or, at any rate, something vastly different from what goes on in the rest of the novel. Of course, this segregation is impossible to maintain. In *Memoirs of a Woman of Pleasure* and the *Account of the PROCEEDINGS Against CAPT. EDWARD RIGBY*, spectator and spectacle, prohibition and pornography merge, articulating desire where desire ought not to be. Fanny and the sodomites may seem to be in different rooms, but that partition is movable.

Conclusion

. . . prior to the distorting effects of the intervening years of persecution, there existed a gay subculture characterized by camaraderie, solidarity, resistance to oppression, and positive self-identity. With the aid of historical research, we can look back through the veil of repression, and discover a gay heritage worth celebrating.   —Rictor Norton, *Mother Clap's Molly House*

Experience of suffering in the present may turn us towards the past, maybe to discover something forgotten. . . . But it is exactly then, when the past is potentially most informative in relation to a present vulnerability, that our relation to it runs the risk of becoming most conservative: we find in the past an explanation of the present which is also a comforting deception. Often it comes in the form of "tradition," wherein we rediscover the eternal verities, and fatalistically accept the recurrence of the past as the only kind of future, possibly the best kind of future.

—Jonathan Dollimore, *Sexual Dissidence*

THESE QUOTATIONS offer us two different approaches to historical gay studies—or, perhaps more precisely, one approach and one reservation concerning that approach. The opposition encapsulated in the above passages is one that I encountered before I could have even articulated it. At a very early stage in my research, I arranged a meeting between myself and an academic who works in gay studies, hoping that I might get some advice on how to proceed. Asked to describe my proposed project, I said that I was interested in examining representations of the sodomite in the Restoration and early eighteenth century. "Oh," he sighed, his eyes glazing over, "representations." He fell silent, and no advice appeared to be forthcoming. I too fell silent, aware that I seemed to have said something wrong, but also aware that I lacked a critical language with which to explain myself more completely. When our conversation resumed, it was clear that all that could be said about my project had been said, summed up in that despairing "Oh, representations."

Throughout the research and writing of this study, that early conversation has weighed heavily on my mind, more heavily than I would have expected, and more heavily than is probably apparent in the result. Was the study of representational practices a kind of evasion of the project of gay studies? As Jim Ellis has noted, it seems "obvious that anyone who is self-identified as gay has at least an emotional or imaginary investment in essentialism, whatever their intellectual project. . . . By extension, gay studies depends to a certain extent on an investment in essentialism and identity politics for its very existence, both actual and intellectual" (175). Why was I not recuperating eighteenth-century accounts of the sodomite into a progressive "gay history"? Or, if I really thought such accounts unrecuperable, should I not simply label them the products of a benighted past that slowly, but surely, was being overcome?

Yet, I could not get over the sense that to write such a progressive narrative would be somehow complacent and strangely disempowering, forcing me to treat any instance of homophobia in the present as merely a residue of the benighted past that had not quite yet withered away and died. In the end, two recent and remarkable examples of sodomitical practices *redux* convinced me of the necessity of learning to read sodomitical inscription within a larger representational economy and within a larger context of discursive process. For they have taught me that Foucault's conception of "reverse discourse" and Dollimore's conception of "transgressive reinscription" become more compelling—though less comforting—when we realize that they work in more than one direction, that the discourse that makes itself available for appropriation remains available for reappropriation, even in its supposedly reconfigured form.

Quentin Tarantino's recent and much talked-about film *Pulp Fiction* (1994) provides us with a striking example of what we might call, adapting Dollimore's term, a "regressive reinscription." Using a frame of hip, ironic, pop-cultural knowingness, *Pulp Fiction* does not so much reflect upon as revitalize essentially conservative narrative structures, making them palatable once more to a hip and knowing audience. In each of the film's loosely connected sections, the protagonist with whom we are asked to identify (invariably male) is confronted with some obstacle to overcome (usually female, but in one significant variation, sodomitical). A hit man is saddled with the responsibility of entertaining his boss's weird wife; a boxer is involved in life-threatening trouble when his dippy girlfriend forgets to do the one thing he asked her to do; a group of slick, and not-so-slick, gangsters must dispose of a bloody corpse before one of their wives, who just won't understand, gets home; the robbery of a diner is almost botched when the female partner appears to lose her nerve and get confused. In each case, a woman either causes or simply *is* the problem with which the man must deal. And, of course, along the way the bullet-riddled bodies pile up. Narratives that, in the usual Hollywood context, might have been greeted with critical scorn, were in this case cheered and celebrated: they were so ironically self-reflexive, so cool. *Pulp Fiction* draws attention to the contrived and parodic nature of its representations, appearing to acknowledge the exhaustion of their cultural currency; in precisely the same gesture, however, the film engages viewers by offering "knowingness" as the position from which these representations can be re-enjoyed. Significantly, this "regressive reinscription" is enabled and guaranteed by the film's sodomitical scene.

At the "ironic" center of *Pulp Fiction* is the story of a boxer who double-crosses a powerful crime-boss named Marsellus Wallace by winning a fight that he has been paid to throw. He not only wins the fight, he also kills his opponent. The boxer is forced to postpone his planned getaway, however, when he discovers that his girlfriend has forgotten to pack his most prized possession, his dead father's watch. In a flashback scene, we have seen the boxer as a child receiving this watch from his father's old army buddy. The boy is told how, languishing in a POW camp, his father preserved the watch for him by hiding it up his ass; when the father died, the friend assumed responsibility for the watch and, in turn, hid it up *his* ass. This flashback scene—a send-up of the Hollywood narrative staple of the overinvested patriarchal legacy—is marked by the kind of parodic excess in which Tarantino appears to delight. Yet, however "ironically" this scene is played, the rest of the narrative graphically shows—with a progressive loss of irony—that the maintaining of the patriarchal legacy in fact depends precisely on the ability to keep one's butt-cheeks tightly clenched. For while reclaiming the patriarchal token—from female neglect—the boxer assumes the position of his father (a warrior) and with a very large sword vanquishes two evil sodomites. The sacred locus of the paternal signifier remains inviolable.[1]

Through a series of plot twists, the boxer and Wallace end up together, at the mercy of a redneck pawnshop owner and his equally redneck friend. These two take Wallace and the boxer down into a dungeonlike basement, and, there, they release their "Gimp," a figure clad and hooded in black leather, who is brought up from *beneath* the basement. It then becomes clear that the boxer and Wallace are going to be sodomized. We can recognize here some of the conventions of sodomitical practices: the pit of the basement and the figure of the "Gimp," for example, place the sodomites within a context of "demonic" imagery. As well, their status as rednecks indicates that the sodomites are "foreign" to the obsessively urban character of the film. Importantly, though, in contrast to the witty banter of the hit men, the incongruous small talk of the corpse-disposing gangsters, and the cuddly billing and cooing of the armed robbers, there is little about the sodomites that marks their representation as "ironic": they are nothing but their act, an act not recuperable within the film's "ironic" frame. Positioned outside of that frame, the sodomites in fact enable it.

The response to this scene in the theater was striking. The audience that had cheered and laughed as a number of bodies were blown to bits, suddenly fell deathly, uncomfortably, silent. Here, they seemed instinctively to realize, was real evil indeed, compared with which murderers, mobsters, and armed robbers were nothing. After all, these other characters were funny. Though couched in more "sophisticated" discussions of "tone," this audience response was replicated in the critical response. Andy Pawelczak, for example, writing in *Films in Review*, appreciates Tarantino's "joking-on-the-edge-of-the-void insouciance" (56), but he regrets the sodomitical scene which "momentarily throws you out of the movie" (57). However, he assures readers that "Tarantino regains control of the picture's tone in the third episode in which Jules and Vincent have to dispose of a bloody corpse" (57), this being, apparently, an intrinsically more entertaining event. What Pawelczak fails to realize is the extent to which that "insouciant" tone is ensured by the presentation, and then eradication, of the sodomites. In its sodomitical scene, *Pulp Fiction* mobilizes a homophobia which, by displacing "real" violence onto the figures of the sodomites, enables the central characters to remain the site of viewer pleasure.

In the end, the boxer manages to free himself and runs upstairs to the shop. Instead of escaping, though, he grabs a sword off one of the shelves and returns to rescue his arch-enemy Wallace by dispatching the sodomites (cheers from the audience). Even in the context of hip knowingness, protagonist, antagonist, and audience unite when confronted with the sodomite.

The second recent and striking example of sodomitical practices that came to my attention was an article in William D. Gairdner's Alberta-based publication *Speaking Out.*[2] Titled "Economics, Keynes, and the Gay Ethic," this article draws attention to the "persuasive parallel between the economic theories of John Maynard Keynes, and the homosexual worldview" (7) as an explanation for Canada's so-called deficit crisis. Like most of the fear-mongering that has surrounded the deficit in this country—particularly in Alberta and, now, also in Ontario—*Speaking Out* uses the deficit as a vehicle for an ultra-right-wing agenda. The economic theory of the "entire Western world," Gairdner tells us, has been predominantly Keynesian since the publication of his *General Theory of Employment, Interest, and Money* in 1936. Before this, economic thinkers favored the "postponement of personal gratification" for this would lead to "savings" forming "capital pools" (7). These capital pools could then be lent out, "stimulating productivity in free markets" (7). In contrast to these staid and prudent measures, however, Keynes advocated "massive government spending and borrowing" which sanctioned "government-induced self-indulgence"; he advocated, that is, "credit formation" (7). In the same way that *Love*

Letters seemed to figure the National Debt and the South Sea Bubble as sodomitical, "Economics, Keynes, and the Gay Ethic" represents Canada's deficit as sodomitical, and casts John Maynard Keynes as the corrupt Nobleman who has thwarted the productive economy and instigated social disarray. Keynes, it seems, "intensely hated Victorian society, and the Christianity on which it was based" (7). More than this, he was a member of the "notoriously amoral" Bloomsbury Group who "indulged in homosexual liaisons" (7). Gairdner argues that Keynes was simply incapable of imagining an economic theory based on production instead of consumption, on future instead of present gratification, because he was homosexual.

Citing the views of Ken S. Ewart, Gairdner writes that a "life of homosexuality is, by its very nature, an extremely present-oriented and selfish choice . . . , a decision to live for oneself rather than for others" (7). Of course, just how interested Gairdner is in the welfare of others is graphically displayed in the article on the facing page— "Quebec Conundrum"—in which he laments the equalizing maneuvers of social democracy since "only a minority of any society are ever successful enough to accumulate significant property" and wealth; "a system of 'majority rule' . . . soon becomes a licence for the majority to plunder the successful minority" (6). Nevertheless, "Economics, Keynes, and the Gay Ethic" concludes by denouncing Keynesian economics as "a fundamentally anti-Christian economic philosophy, an echo of its expression in homosexuality. The first leads to economic, and the second to moral, bankruptcy" (7).

These two examples of sodomitical practices in the present alert us to the difficulty of turning to the past to discover a progressive "gay history" that lies outside of its representations, or whose only relationship to the issue of representation is the project of replacing old, "distorted" images with new, "pure" ones. For what such an approach cannot comprehend it the way that these later representations can themselves be reconstituted into new forms of repression. For if *Pulp Fiction* and *Speaking Out* set homophobic representational structures in motion—and I believe that they do—it is not because they are throwbacks to an earlier time, stubborn holdouts against the march of progress; rather, these two texts do something quite new. *Pulp Fiction*, for example, sets its sodomitical depiction within hyper-contemporary representational forms. In fact, in its determinedly ironic and parodic stance, *Pulp Fiction* succeeds in articulating homophobia through the kind of representational play closely associated with "queer theory." In contrast, *Speaking Out* appears to be more sincerely nostalgic for a golden past. But the homophobic idealization of the past in *Speaking Out* is not—and cannot be—thwarted by a progressive gay narrative. For *Speaking Out* has already appropriated that progressive narrative and incorporated it into its homophobic expression by re-presenting it as something else—degeneration, or even the loss of civil liberties: "The 1960s saw hordes of leftists, . . . feminazis, [and] homosexual activists . . . commandeer the instruments of power" (1). We are returned to Foucault's assertion that we should not imagine a world "divided between accepted discourse and excluded discourse" (*History* 100), though, perhaps in a less optimistic light than that in which we first encountered it. What these above examples suggest is that it is just as imperative for the project of gay studies that we learn how to *read* as it is that we learn how to *speak*.

I have intended the preceding chapters to form a critical rather than a necessarily chronological sequence. We have seen that in the Restoration and the first half of the eighteenth century, sodomitical practices formed a complex and flexible signifying system. On the one hand, sodomitical practices were capable of condensing a variety of transgressions into the figure of the sexual deviant. Paradoxically, or perversely, this very act that rejected the sodomite from the social scene also established him at the center of that scene, constituting the sodomite as a "social type." The constitution of the sodomite as a social type, however, did not necessarily entail the establishment of a distinct and stable sodomitical identity. As the works by Smollett and Cleland show, the attempt to partition off types of people is makeshift at best: walls of separation are movable or easily pierced; characters disappear and reappear occupying each other's positions. On the other hand, we have seen that sodomitical practices could become the means for the expression of desire; however, within the terms of sodomitical practices it is a desire always expressed at the scene of its negation. And yet, as I have attempted to show, there is a sense in which desire can, even within sodomitical practices, disrupt or suspend that negation and produce a knowledge beyond it.

Notes

Introduction

1. It will be noticed that I have moved from the word *buggery* to the word *sodomy*, treating them as interchangeable. This usage perhaps requires some explanation. Examining the usage of *buggery* and *sodomy* in seventeenth-century New England, Robert F. Oaks has written that the Puritan colonies usually "used the term sodomy to refer to homosexuality and buggery to refer to bestiality" (268). One can find such distinctions in English works of the period. In John Dunton's "The HE-STRUMPETS" (1710), for example, a number of terms are used to refer to sexual contact between men but "B——ry" is reserved to refer to bestiality (96). For the most part, however, *buggery* and *sodomy* are both used to refer to male-male sexual contact, as they are in *The Secret History of Clubs* (1709) without any attending confusion. And in *Sodom: or, The Quintessence of Debauchery* (c. 1672–73), set in the Kingdom of Sodom, the word *sodomy* is not used at all. My usage of both terms, then, is based upon the texts that I will be examining.

2. Jonathan Goldberg and Janet E. Halley, however, have shown how sodomy can still be mobilized as an "utterly confused category" today—at least in the United States—usually with disastrous legal consequences for gays and lesbians. See Goldberg's *Sodometries: Renaissance Texts, Modern Sexualities*, 1–26; Janet E. Halley, "*Bowers v. Hardwick* in the Renaissance," and "Misreading Sodomy: A Critique of the Classification of 'Homosexuals' in Federal Equal Protection Law."

3. For a complete discussion of the debate and its terms, see the essays collected in *Forms of Desire: Sexual Orientation and the Social Constructionist Controversy*, ed., Edward Stein; and Diana Fuss's *Essentially Speaking: Feminism, Nature and Difference*.

4. We would do well to remember, however, before we too smugly shout "naïve," the conditions in which these studies were produced. It is telling that both "Noel I. Garde" and "W. H. Kayy" are pseudonyms.

5. Of course, we might note how Boswell is forced to change the "essence" of "gay essence" (consciousness/unconsciousness) in order to maintain it.

6. There is, of course, a similar disparity between the "heterosexual role" and people who would identify themselves, or are identified, as "heterosexual."

7. Studies of legal prosecutions in England include Caroline Bingham, "Seventeenth-Century Attitudes Towards Deviant Sex"; Edward J. Bristow, *Vice and Vigilance: Purity Movements in Britain since 1700*; B. R. Burg, "Ho Hum, Another Work of the Devil: Buggery and Sodomy in Early Stuart England"; Arthur N. Gilbert, "Buggery and the British Navy, 1700–1861," "Sexual Deviance and Disaster During the Napoleonic Wars," "Sodomy and the Law in Eighteenth- and Early Nineteenth-Century Britain;" A. D. Harvey, "Prosecutions for Sodomy in England at the Beginning of the Nineteenth Century"; Polly Morris, "Sodomy and Male Honour: The Case of Somerset, 1740–1850."

For important studies of legal prosecutions in other countries, see L. J. Boon, "Those Damned Sodomites: Public Images of Sodomites in Eighteenth-Century Netherlands"; Arend H. Huussen, Jr., "Prosecutions of Sodomy in Eighteenth-Century Frisia, Netherlands"; E. William Monter, "Sodomy and Heresy in Early Modern Switzerland"; Dirk Jaap Noordam, "Sodomy in the Dutch Republic, 1600–1725"; Michel Rey, "Parisian Homosexuals Create a Lifestyle, 1700–1750: The Police Archives," "Police and Sodomy in Eighteenth-Century Paris: From Sin to Disorder"; Theo van der Meer, "The Prosecutions of Sodomites in Eighteenth-Century Amsterdam: Changing Perceptions of Sodomy."

8. Examples of this kind of study include James R. Dubro, "The Third Sex: Lord Hervey and his Coterie"; George E. Haggerty, "Literature and Homosexuality in the Late Eighteenth Century: Walpole, Beckford, and Lewis"; G. S. Rousseau, "The Sorrows of Priapus: Anticlericalism, Homo-social Desire, and Richard Payne Knight," "In the House of Madam Vander Tasse on the Long Bridge: A Homosocial University Club in Early Modern Europe"; Dennis Rubini, "Sexuality and Augustan England: Sodomy, Politics, Elite Circles and Society."

9. See, for example, the excellent essays collected in *Queering the Renaissance*, ed., Goldberg.

1. Sodomitical Practices

1. While this phrase is generally attributed to Blackstone's *Commentaries*, it is clearly a much older construction. Boswell, for example, translates a let-

ter of Pope Honorius III from 1227 in which Pope Honorius writes of the "sin which should neither be named nor committed" (*Christianity* 380).

2. Interestingly, Stirling "Englishes" aposiopesis as "A Concealing"; however, he lists it not as a scheme of omission, but under the heading "Figures for Amplifying."

3. For a discussion of the development of sodomy laws, see Bruce R. Smith, *Homosexual Desire in Shakespeare's England*, 41–52; and Jonathan Ned Katz, "The Age of Sodomitical Sin," 46–47.

4. *pathick (or pathic)*: refers to the passive partner in sodomy

5. *Poems on Affairs of State* will hereafter be designated as *POAS*.

6. These opinions belong, respectively, to Sir William Petty, William Petyt, Sir Francis Brewster, and Daniel Defoe.

7. This narrative in which sodomy appears as a dangerous, inverted form of sex which gives birth to death rather than life is currently recycled in many reactionary discussions of AIDS.

8. The modern equivalent—no doubt enabled in part by this historical construction—would be the demonization of Africa as the supposed origin of AIDS.

9. *butter'd buns*: whores; a woman who has just slept with another man

10. McIntosh, you will recall from the Introduction, defined the social role as a set of expectations/assumptions which constitutes a social "type" and which can circulate as credible regardless of whether the content of the role is actually fulfilled (see "The Homosexual Role"). Again, the "communist" and "Elizabethan Underworld" examples are instructive.

11. This construction in some ways prefigures the deficiencies of later models of "inversion" which similarly imposed a rhetorical hermaphrodism on same-sex desire in order to assert that it was really "heterosexual" but which ultimately could only account for desire moving in one direction. See Carol-Anne Tyler, "Boys Will Be Girls," 34–37.

12. Jonathan Wild's account of a "Company of *He-Whores*" (30) in *An Answer to a late Insolent Libel* similarly concludes with the disbanding of the "Company" as all of the sodomites are brought magnificently to justice.

2. The Sodomitical State

1. "The Women's Complaint to Venus," however, also implicates "heterosexual" debauchery in the state of the nation. The satirist represents the "Poor Whores" as looking back to a former Golden Age:

> In the Reign of good *Charles* the Second
> Full many a Jade

A Lady was made
And the Issue Right Noble was reckon'd.   (167)

2. While I do not find this interpretation convincing, it does at least have the virtue of recognizing that the sin of Sodom is more social than sexual.

3. The actual etymologies of these names are, in fact, unknown. See *The Interpreter's Bible*, 1:632–33.

4. One finds this process repeated in modern commentaries. In Gerhard Von Rad's *Genesis*, for example, Von Rad, perhaps understanding displacement better than he is aware of, makes the following comment on Gen. 19:5: "One must think of the heavenly messengers as young men in their prime, whose beauty particularly incited evil desire" (217). Even setting aside the desire that we are implicitly invited to invest in this scene, Von Rad here credits the agents of "good" with inciting the desire that is then denounced as "evil" and punished.

5. Relatedly, see Arthur N. Gilbert's "Sexual Deviance and Disaster" for an account of how prosecutions for sodomy increase during periods of social conflict.

6. "The frogs, tired of their easy life, petitioned Jupiter for a king. He good-humouredly obliged them by throwing a log into their pond. At first they were terrified by the splash, but in the course of time grew accustomed to and then contemptuous of the log. Then they petitioned Jupiter a second time, and he sent them a stork who proceeded to devour them. When they appealed to Jupiter a third time, he refused to remove the stork, since they suffered for their own folly" (*POAS* 1:189, note).

7. Susan Staves, making a more abstract, less topical, argument, suggests that *Sodom* can be read as a critique of the Hobbesian dictate that a sovereign's commands should be obligatory. See *Players' Scepters*, 266–68.

8. Bolloxinion, though, does get the last words: "Let heaven descend, and set the world on fire—/ We to some darker cavern will retire" (116). Doesn't this seem, strangely, to cast Bolloxinion as Lot?

9. Indeed, as Harold Weber has recently pointed out, *Sodom* "never presents two men satisfying themselves sexually. . . . It shows us women masturbating with dildoes, women bringing men to orgasm with their hands, a dance that dissolves into oral and genital intercourse, a sister seducing her brother; though it constantly insists on the joys and virtues of buggery, that act must always take place offstage" ("Carolinean Sexuality" 83).

10. Law subsequently escaped and fled to France where he went on to become a famous (or infamous) financier, initiating the Mississippi Scheme.

See Carswell, *The South Sea Bubble*; Hyde, *John Law*; Lande, *Introduction to John Law*; and Thiers, *The Mississippi Bubble*.

11. For a more complete discussion of this account, see Rousseau, "An Introduction." Rousseau asserts that Manley's narrative is the most plausible explanation for Wilson's wealth, though he gives no reason for doing so (63). Hyde, in his biography of John Law, also relates Manley's narrative — but without citing the source (26–28). And Lawrence Lande, though he does not say that Villiers had an affair with Wilson, also claims that she arranged Law's escape from jail but, again, he provides no source for this assertion (2). Villiers and Law do make an appearance in *Love Letters*: alarmed at rumors that she is the one who is supporting Wilson, "Mrs. V— ll—s" employs a spy, "Johnasco," to discover the source of Wilson's wealth. Johnasco, however, is bought off with Wilson's gold and Mrs. V—ll—s is duped (36–40).

12. See Addison's figuration of "Public Credit" in *Spectator* No. 3 as a virgin with what Pocock characterizes as "an excessively hysterical nervous system" (99). The virgin in Addison's allegory swells and diminishes, but never produces (Steele and Addison 430–33).

13. For example, in Hogarth's famous cartoon of the South Sea Bubble, reprinted in J. Langdon-Davies's *The South Sea Bubble: A Collection of Contemporary Documents*, the London Fire Monument appears with its antipapist inscription replaced with an anti-stockjobber inscription.

3. Sodomitical Smollett

1. See, for example, Donald Bruce, *Radical Doctor Smollett*; David Daiches, "Smollett Reconsidered"; Robert Giddings, *The Tradition of Smollett*; Tom Scott, "The Note of Protest in Smollett's Novels"; K. G. Simpson, "Tobias Smollett: The Scot as English Novelist."

2. Interestingly, this separating of the critical men from the boys (or, rather, men from the eunuchs) is not unlike the "theory" of homosexuality propounded by psychologist Gregory Rochlin in *The Masculine Dilemma*. Rochlin understands the homosexual to be incapable of entering the competitive world of male rivalry, and he cites an anonymous "youth" who states that gay men "can't meet the standards of manhood. That takes incredibly high performance, competitiveness, winning all. Being 'gay' gets you out of the competition of manhood" (discussed in Dollimore 265–67).

3. Cf. Tom Scott's "The Note of Protest in Smollett's Novels." Scott argues that the appearance of Captain Whiffle, "an exhibitionist homosexual," in *Roderick Random* should be taken as being on a par with "the

appalling human suffering and agonizing death" that Smollett ascribes to navy life: "we are treated to some camp, pansy scenes at which Smollett is not laughing with us—he is outraged" (113).

4. One might recall the *The Sodomites Shame and Doom*, discussed in chapter 1, claimed that what the sodomite lacked was a "steddy Resolution" (2).

5. George II apparently was actually in the habit of kicking and "rumping" people. See Maynard Mack's *The Garden and the City*, 130, 136*ff*.

6. This translation is from the "Notes" to *Peregrine Pickle* (789).

4. The Sodomitical Spectacle

1. Dollimore offers the example of the "malcontent" in Renaissance drama "who haunts the very power structure which has alienated him, seeking reinscription within it but at the same time demystifying it, operating within and subverting it at the same time" (285).

2. However, Rigby would not confess to the charge either. Instead he demurred the indictment, which means that he did not make a plea because he claimed that the case was insufficient and should not have been brought to court. Unfortunately, the judges found the case sufficient and, when a case was found to be sufficient, a demurrer was treated the same as a plea of "guilty." The *Account* treats Rigby's actions in court as a mere ploy to avoid disclosure. The broadside not only discloses Rigby, but also supplies the missing confession that justifies such a disclosure by representing him "confessing" his criminal intent over and over to Minton, if not to the judges.

3. For an argument that trial reports constitute a subgenre of eighteenth-century pornography, see Peter Wagner's "The Pornographer in the Courtroom" and *Eros Revived*, 113–32. Wagner focuses primarily on the so-called "Crim. Con." (criminal conversation: i.e., adultery) cases.

4. For an eroticized twist on this, see Gay's *The Beggar's Opera*. This is Mrs. Peachum: *"Beneath the left ear so fit but a cord/ (A rope so charming a zone is!),/ The youth in his cart hath the air of a lord,/ And we cry, There dies an Adonis!"* (152)

5. For more on the vulnerability of the "controlling gaze," see Scott Paul Gordon's "Voyeuristic Dreams: Mr. Spectator and the Power of Spectacle"; and Christopher Pye's "The Sovereign, the Theater, and the Kingdome of Darknesse: Hobbes and the Spectacle of Power."

6. Dollimore, in fact, suggests that fantasy may be a "principal medium" for transgressive reinscription (324).

7. For an overview of the most influential arguments in this respect, see Linda Williams's *Hard Core* 16–23.

8. However, we might interestingly apply Kaja Silverman's observations on the primal scene to the pornographic scene: "The mastering, sadistic variety of voyeurism . . . can perhaps best be understood as a psychic formation calculated to reverse the power relations of the primal scene—as a compensatory drama whereby passivity yields to activity through an instictual 'turning around' and reversal" (165).

9. See also, for example, John Illo's "The Idyll of Unreproved Pleasures Free"; Robert Markley's "Language, Power, and Sexuality in Cleland's *Fanny Hill*"; and Michael Shinagel's "*Memoirs of a Woman of Pleasure*: Pornography and the Mid-Eighteenth-Century English Novel."

10. The scene in which Harriet observes a man sporting in a river, perhaps one of the most erotic in the novel, goes farther than the scene in which Charles lays naked on the bed inasmuch as it focuses not only on the man's penis, but also on his buttocks: "Then the luxuriant swell of flesh that rose from the small of his back, and terminates its double cope at where the thighs are sent off, perfectly dazzl'd one with its watery glistening gloss" (102).

11. Again, Silverman's subject is the primal scene rather than the erotic spectacle. However, given the homoerotic dynamics we have already looked at, it does not seem like a great stretch to say the the sodomitical spectacle constitutes *Memoirs of a Woman of Pleasure*'s "primal scene."

12. Compare, for example, the description of the younger boy, "those globular, fleshy eminences . . . which now, with all the narrow vale that intersects them, stood display'd" with this description of Emily: "Her posteriours, plump, smooth, and prominent, . . . fill'd the eye, till it was commanded down the parting or separation of those exquisitely white cliffs, by their narrow vale, and was there stopt, and attracted by the embower'd bottom-cavity" (118–19).

13. Julia Epstein has interestingly noted that Fanny's being knocked senseless here "foretells the speechlessness with which she will be reunited with Charles, though here it follows rather than precedes a sexual act in the textual order. Having catalogued all possible erotic maneuvers and all marks of bodily desire, Fanny's task of speaking is effectively finished. This scene, one of the final sexual consummations in the novel, represents a perfective moment: not one phallus, but two" (146).

Conclusion

1. It should be pointed out, however, that it only remains inviolable for the *white* character; Wallace, a black man, is sodomized.

2. I am grateful to Lynn Wells for bringing this publication to my attention.

Bibliography

Abelove, Henry, Michèle Aina Barale, and David M. Halperin, eds. *The Lesbian and Gay Studies Reader*. New York: Routledge, 1993.

An Account of the PROCEEDINGS Against CAPT. EDWARD RIGBY, . . . for intending to Commit the Abominable SIN of SODOMY on the Body of one William Minton. London: 1698.

Almonds for Parrots: or, a Soft Answer to a Scurrilous Satyr, call'd, St. James's Park. With a Word or two in Praise of Condons. London: 1708.

Alter, Robert. "Sodom as Nexus: The Web of Design in Biblical Narrative," pp. 28–42. In Jonothan Goldberg, ed., *Reclaiming Sodom*. New York: Routledge, 1994. Originally published in Regina Schwartz, ed., *The Book and the Text*, pp. 146–60. Oxford: Blackwell, 1990.

Babcock, Barbara, ed. *The Reversible World: Symbolic Inversion in Art and Society*. Ithaca: Cornell University Press, 1978.

The Baboon A-la-Mode. A Satyr Against the French. London: 1704.

Bailey, Derrick Sherwin. *Homosexuality and the Western Christian Tradition*. 1955. Hamden, Conn.: Archon Books, 1975.

Barrett, Michèle. "The Concept of 'Difference.'" *Feminist Review* 26 (1987): 29–41.

Beattie, J. M. *Crime and the Courts in England, 1660–1800*. Princeton: Princeton University Press, 1986.

Beier, A. L. *Masterless Men: The Vagrancy Problem in England, 1560–1640*. London: Methuen, 1985.

Bersani, Leo. "Is the Rectum a Grave?" Originally published in *October* 43 (1987): 197–222. Reprinted in Jonathan Goldberg, ed., *Reclaiming Sodom*, pp. 249–64. New York: Routledge, 1994.

Bingham, Caroline. "Seventeenth-Century Attitudes Towards Deviant Sex." *Journal of Interdisciplinary History* 1 (1971): 447–68.

Boon, Leo J. "Those Damned Sodomites: Public Images of Sodomy in the Eighteenth-Century Netherlands," pp. 237–48. In Kent Gerard and Gert Hekma, eds., *The Pursuit of Sodomy: Male Homosexuality in Renaissance and Enlightenment Europe*. New York: Harrington Park, 1989.

Boswell, John. "Categories, Experience, and Sexuality," pp. 133–73. In Edward Stein, ed., *Forms of Desire: Sexual Orientation and the Social Constructionist Controversy*. New York: Routledge, 1992.

——. *Christianity, Social Tolerance, and Homosexuality: Gay People in Western Europe from the Beginning of the Christian Era to the Fourteenth Century*. Chicago: University of Chicago Press, 1980.

——. "Revolutions, Universals, and Sexual Categories," pp. 17–36. In Martin Bauml Duberman, Martha Vicinus, and George Chauncey Jr., eds., *Hidden From History: Reclaiming the Gay and Lesbian Past*. New York: New American Library, 1989. Originally published in *Salmagundi* 58/59 (1982–83): 89–114.

Boucé, Paul-Gabriel. "Aspects of Sexual Tolerance and Intolerance in Eighteenth-Century England." *British Journal of Eighteenth-Century Studies* 3 (1980): 173–92.

——. "Introduction," pp. ix–xxv. *The Adventures of Roderick Random*, by Tobias Smollett. Oxford: Oxford University Press, 1979.

——. *The Novels of Tobias Smollett*. Trans. Antonia White and Paul-Gabriel Boucé. New York: Longman, 1976.

——. "The Secret Nexus: Sex and Literature in Eighteenth-Century Britain," pp. 70–89. In Alan Bold, ed., *The Sexual Dimension in Literature*. Totowa, N.J.: Barnes and Noble, 1983.

Boucé, Paul-Gabriel, ed. *Sexuality in Eighteenth-Century Britain*. Manchester: Machester University Press, 1982.

Bourgeois, Susan. *Nervous Juyces and the Feeling Heart: The Growth of Sensibility in the Novels of Tobias Smollett*. New York: Peter Lang, 1986.

Braudy, Leo. "*Fanny Hill* and Materialism." *Eighteenth-Century Studies* 4 (1970): 21–40.

Bray, Alan. *Homosexuality in Renaissance England*. London: GMP, 1982.

Bredbeck, Gregory W. *Sodomy and Interpretation: Marlowe to Milton*. Ithaca: Cornell University Press, 1991.

Bristow, Edward J. *Vice and Vigilance: Purity Movements in Britain since 1700*. Totowa, N.J.: Rowan and Litttlefield, 1977.

Brown, Laura. *Ends of Empire: Women and Ideology in Early Eighteenth-Century Literature*. Ithaca: Cornell University Press, 1993.

Bruce, Donald. *Radical Doctor Smollett*. London: Victor Gollancz, 1964.

Bruhm, Steven. "Roderick Random's Closet." *English Studies in Canada* 19, no. 4 (December 1993): 401–16.

"The Bubblers Medley, or a Sketch of the Times: Being Europe's Memorial for the Year 1720." In J. Langdon-Davies, comp., *The South Sea Bubble: A Collection of Contemporary Documents*. London: Jonathan Cape, 1965.

Burg, B. R. "Ho Hum, Another Work of the Devil: Buggery and Sodomy in Early Stuart England." *Journal of Homosexuality* 6, no. 1/2 (1980–81): 69–78.

Butler, Judith. "The Force of Fantasy: Feminism, Mapplethorpe, and Discursive Excess." *Differences* 2, no. 2 (1990): 105–25.

——. *Gender Trouble: Feminism and the Subversion of Identity*. New York: Routledge, 1990.

[Carey, Henry]. *Faustina: or, the Roman Songstress, A Satyr on the Luxury and Effeminacy of the Age*. London: 1726.

Carswell, John. *The South Sea Bubble*. Stanford: Stanford University Press, 1960.

Chauncey, George, Jr. "From Sexual Inversion to Homosexuality: Medicine and the Changing Conceptualization of Female Deviance." *Salmagundi* 58/59 (1982): 114–46.

Cleland, John. *Memoirs of a Woman of Pleasure* (1748–49). Ed. Peter Sabor. Oxford: Oxford University Press, 1985.

Coward, D. A. "Attitudes to Homosexuality in Eighteenth-Century France." *Journal of European Studies* 10 (1980): 231–55.

Cowie, Elizabeth. "Pornography and Fantasy: Psychoanalytic Perspectives," pp. 132–52. In Lynne Segal and Mary McIntosh, eds., *Sex Exposed: Sexuality and the Pornography Debate*. London: Virago, 1992.

Daiches, David. "Smollett Reconsidered," pp. 13–46. In Alan Bold, ed., *Smollett: Author of the First Distinction*. Totowa, N.J.: Barnes and Noble, 1982.

Davidson, Arnold I. "Sex and the Emergence of Sexuality." *Critical Inquiry* 14 (1987): 16–48.

Day, Robert Adams. "Sex, Scatology, Smollett," pp. 225–43. In Paul-Gabriel Boucé, ed., *Sexuality in Eighteenth-Century Britain*. Manchester: Manchester University Press, 1982.

Dickson, P. G. M. *The Financial Revolution in England: A Study in the Development of Public Credit, 1688–1756*. Toronto: Macmillan, 1967.

Dollimore, Jonathan. *Sexual Dissidence: Augustine to Wilde, Freud to Foucault*. Oxford: Clarendon, 1991.

Dryden, John. *The Conquest of Granada, Parts I and II* (1669–70). Ed. George Saintsbury. New York: Mermaid, 1957.

Duberman, Martin Bauml, Martha Vicinus, and George Chauncey Jr., eds. *Hidden from History: Reclaiming the Gay and Lesbian Past*. New York: New American Library, 1989.

Dubro, James R. "The Third Sex: Lord Hervey and his Coterie." *Eighteenth-Century Life* 2 (1976): 89–95.

Dunton, John. "The HE-STRUMPETS: A Satyr on the Sodomite-Club," pp. 93–99. In *Athenianism: or, the New Projects of Mr John Dunton*, 2 vols. London: 1710.

Dynes, Wayne R. and Stephen Donaldson, eds. *History of Homosexuality in Europe and America*. New York: Garland, 1992.

Edelman, Lee. *Homographesis: Essays in Gay Literary and Cultural Theory*. New York: Routledge, 1994.

Elias, Richard. "Political Satire in *Sodom*." *Studies in English Literature* 18 (1978): 423–38.

Ellis, Jim. "Desire in Translation: Friendship in the Life and Work of Spenser." *English Studies in Canada* 20, no. 2 (June 1994): 171–86.

Epstein, Julia. "Fanny's Fanny: Epistolarity, Eroticism, and the Transsexual Text," pp. 135–53. In Elizabeth C. Goldsmith, ed., *Writing the Female Voice: Essay on Epistolary Literature*. London: Pinter, 1989.

Epstein, Steven. "Gay Politics, Ethnic Identity: The Limits of Social Constructionism," pp. 239–93. In Edward Stein, ed., *Forms of Desire: Sexual Orientation and the Social Constructionist Controversy*. New York: Routledge, 1992. Originally published in *Socialist Review* 93–94 (May–August 1987): 9–54.

Evelyn, John. *The Diary of John Evelyn*, vol. 5. Ed. E. S. de Beer. Oxford: Clarendon Press, 1955, 6 vols.

Falkus, Christopher. *The Life and Times of Charles II*. Ed. Antonia Fraser. London: George Weidenfeld and Nicolson, 1972.

Fokkelman, J. P. "Genesis," pp. 36–55. In Robert Alter and Frank Kermode, eds., *The Literary Guide to the Bible*. Cambridge: Harvard University Press, 1987.

Foucault, Michel. *Discipline and Punish: The Birth of the Prison* (1975). Trans. Alan Sheridan. New York: Pantheon, 1977.

——. *The History of Sexuality*, vol. 1: *An Introduction* (1976). Trans. Robert Hurley (1978). New York: Vintage, 1990.

A Full and True Account of the Discovery and Apprehending A Notorious Gang of Sodomites in St. James's. London: 1709.

Fuss, Diana. *Essentially Speaking: Feminism, Nature, and Difference*. New York: Routledge, 1989.

Fuss, Diana, ed. *Inside/Out: Lesbian Theories, Gay Theories*. New York: Routledge, 1991.

Gairdner, William D. "Economics, Keynes, and the Gay Ethic," *Speaking Out* 2, no. 2 (1995): 1–8.

Garber, Peter M. "Famous First Bubbles." *Journal of Economic Perspectives* 4, no. 2 (1990): 35–54.

Garde, Noel I. (pseud.). *Jonathan to Gide: The Homosexual in History*. New York: Vantage, 1964.

Gassman, Byron. "Introduction," pp. 3–21. In O. M. Brack, ed. and Leslie A. Chilton, assistant, *Poems, Plays, and The Briton, by Tobias Smollett*. Athens: University of Georgia Press, 1993.

Gay, John. *The Beggar's Opera* (1728), pp. 145–206. *The Beggar's Opera and Other Eighteenth-Century Plays*. Introduction by David W. Lindsay. London: J. M. Dent, 1993.

Giddings, Robert. *The Tradition of Smollett*. London: Methuen, 1967.

Gilbert, Arthur N. "Buggery and the British Navy, 1700–1861." *Journal of Social History* 10 (1976–77): 72–98.

———. "Conceptions of Homosexuality and Sodomy in Western History." *Journal of Homosexuality* 6, no. 1/2 (1980–81): 57–68.

———. "Sexual Deviance and Disaster During the Napoleonic Wars." *Albion* 9 (1977): 98–113.

———. "Sodomy and the Law in Eighteenth- and Early Nineteenth-Century Britain." *Societas* 8 (1978): 225–41.

Goldberg, Jonathan. *Sodometries: Renaissance Texts, Modern Sexualities*. Stanford: Stanford University Press, 1992.

Goldberg, Jonathan, ed. *Queering the Renaissance*. Durham: Duke University Press, 1994.

———. *Reclaiming Sodom*. New York: Routledge, 1994.

Gordon, Scott Paul. "Voyeuristic Dreams: Mr. Spectator and the Power of Spectacle." *The Eighteenth Century* 36, no. 1 (1995): 3–23.

[Gordon, Thomas] Britannicus. *The Conspirators; or the Case of Cataline*. London: 1721.

Greenberg, David F. *The Construction of Homosexuality*. Chicago: University of Chicago Press, 1988.

———. "The Socio-Sexual Milieu of the *Love Letters*." *Journal of Homosexuality* 19, no. 2 (1990): 93–104.

Haggerty, George E. "Literature and Homosexuality in the Late Eighteenth

Century: Walpole, Beckford, and Lewis," pp. 167–79. In Wayne R. Dynes and Stephen Donaldson, eds., *Homosexual Themes in Literary Studies*. New York: Garland, 1992.

Halley, Janet E. "*Bowers v. Hardwick* in the Renaissance," pp. 13–39. In Jonathan Goldberg, ed., *Queering the Renaissance*. Durham: Duke University Press, 1994.

——. "Misreading Sodomy: A Critique of the Classification of 'Homosexuals' in Federal Equal Protection Law," pp. 351–77. In Julia Epstein and Kristina Straub, eds., *Body Guards: The Cultural Politics of Gender Ambiguity*. New York: Routledge, 1991.

——. "The Politics of the Closet: Towards Equal Protection for Gay, Lesbian and Bisexual Identity," pp. 145–204. In Jonathan Goldberg, ed., *Reclaiming Sodom*. New York: Routledge, 1994. Originally published in *UCLA Law Review* 36 (1989): 915–76.

Harris, Tim. *Politics Under the Later Stuarts: Party Conflict in a Divided Society, 1660–1715*. London: Longman, 1993.

Harvey, A. D. "Prosecutions for Sodomy in England at the Beginning of the Nineteenth Century." *Historical Journal* 21 (1978): 939–48.

Haywood, Eliza. *The Unequal Conflict; or, Nature Triumphant*. London, 1725.

Heilman, Robert. "Some Fops and Some Versions of Foppery." *ELH* 49 (1982): 363–95.

Henry, Matthew. *An Exposition of the Old and New Testament*, vol. 1 (1706). London: James Nisbet, 1857. 9 vols.

Hentzi, Gary. " 'An Itch of Gaming': The South Sea Bubble and the Novels of Daniel Defoe." *Eighteenth-Century Life* 17 (February 1993): 32–45.

Hobbes, Thomas. *Leviathan* (1651). Ed. C. B. Macpherson. Harmondsworth: Penguin, 1968.

Hunt, Margaret. "Afterword," pp. 359–78. In Jonathan Goldberg, ed., *Queering the Renaissance*. Durham: Duke University Press, 1994.

Hunter, J. Paul. *Before Novels: The Cultural Contexts of Eighteenth-Century Fiction*. New York: Norton, 1990.

Huussen, Arend H., Jr. "Sodomy in the Dutch Republic During the Eighteenth Century," pp. 169–78. In Robert Purks Maccubin, ed., *'Tis Nature's Fault: Unauthorized Sexuality During the Enlightenment*. New York: Cambridge University Press, 1987.

Hyde, H. Montgomery. *John Law: The History of an Honest Adventurer*. London: W. H. Allen, 1969.

Illo, John. "The Idyll of Unreproved Pleasures Free." *Carolina Quarterly* 17 (1965): 18–26.

The Interpreter's Bible. Ed. George Arthur Buttrick et al. 12 vols. New York: Abindon Press, 1952.

"Jenny Cromwell's Complaint Against Sodomy." Reprinted in Dennis Rubini, "Sexuality and Augustan England: Sodomy, Politics, Elite Circles, and Society," pp. 349–82. In Kent Gerard and Gert Hekma, eds., *The Pursuit of Sodomy: Male Homosexuality in Renaissance and Enlightenment Europe.* New York: Harrington Park, 1989.

Johansson, Warren. "London's Medieval Sodomites," pp. 159–64. In Wayne R. Dynes and Stephen Donaldson, eds., *History of Homosexuality in Europe and America.* New York: Garland, 1992.

Johnson, J. W. "Did Lord Rochester Write *Sodom?*" *Papers of the Bibliographic Society of America* 81 (1987): 119–53.

Juvenal. *The Satires.* Trans. Niall Rudd. Introduction by William Barr. Oxford: Clarendon, 1991.

Kahn, Madeleine. *Narrative Transvestism: Rhetoric and Gender in the Eighteenth-Century English Novel.* Ithaca: Cornell University Press, 1991.

Katz, Jonathan Ned. "The Age of Sodomitical Sin, 1607–1740," pp. 249–64. In Jonathan Goldberg, ed., *Reclaiming Sodom.* New York: Routledge, 1994. Originally published in *Lesbian/Gay Almanac*, pp. 31–65. New York: Harper and Row, 1983.

Kayy, W. H. (pseud.). *The Gay Geniuses: Psychiatric and Literary Studies of Famous Homosexuals.* Glendale: Marvin Miller, 1965.

Kimmel, Michael S. "From Lord and Master to Cuckold and Fop: Masculinity in Seventeenth-Century England." *University of Dayton Review* 18, no. 2 (Winter-Spring 1986–87): 93–109.

——. " 'Greedy Kisses' and 'Melting Exstacy': Notes on the Homosexual World of Early Eighteenth-Century England in *Love Letters.*" *Journal of Homosexuality* 19, no. 2 (1990): 1–10.

Kishlansky, Mark A. "Turning Frogs Into Princes: Aesop's *Fables* and the Political Culture of Early Modern England," pp. 338–60. In Susan D. Amussen and Mark A. Kishlansky, eds., *Political Culture and Cultural Politics in Early Modern England.* Manchester: Manchester University Press, 1995.

Kopelson, Kevin. "Seeing Sodomy: *Fanny Hill*'s Blinding Vision." *Journal of Homosexuality* 23, no. 1/2 (1992): 173–83.

Landa, Louis A. "A *Modest Proposal* and Populousness," pp. 102–11. In
James L. Clifford, ed., *Eighteenth-Century English Literature: Modern
Essays in Criticism.* Oxford: Oxford University Press, 1959.

Lande, Lawrence. *Introduction to John Law.* Edinburgh: Centre of Canadian
Studies, 1990.

Langdon-Davies, J., comp. *The South Sea Bubble: A Collection of Contemporary Documents.* London: Jonathan Cape, 1965.

Laqueur, Thomas. *Making Sex: Body And Gender from the Greeks to Freud.*
Cambridge: Harvard University Press, 1990.

Lee, Nathaniel. *The Tragedy of Nero, Emperour of Rome,* vol. 1, pp. 21–74.
In Thomas B. Stroup and Arthur L. Cooke, eds., *The Works of Nathaniel
Lee,* 2 vols. New Brunswick, N.J.: Scarecrow Press, 1954.

Lord, George deF. "Introduction," p. xxiii–lvi. In George deF. Lord, ed.,
Poems on Affairs of State: Augustan Satirical Verse, 1660–1714, 7 vols.
New Haven: Yale University Press, 1963.

Love Letters Between a certain late Nobleman and the famous Mr. Wilson
(1723). Ed. Micheal S. Kimmel. *Journal of Homosexuality* 19, no. 2 (1990):
11–45.

Lovejoy, Arthur O. *Essays in the History of Ideas.* Baltimore: Johns Hopkins
University Press, 1948.

Maccubbin, Robert Purks, ed. *'Tis Nature's Fault: Unauthorized Sexuality
During the Enlightenment.* New York: Cambridge University Press, 1987.

Mack, Maynard. *The Garden and the City: Retirement and Politics in the
Later Poetry of Pope, 1731–1743.* Toronto: University of Toronto Press, 1969.

Manley, Delariviere. *The Lady's Pacquet of Letters.* Appended to *Memoirs
of the Court of England. In Two Parts. By the countess of Dunois. . . . Now
Made English.* London: 1707.

Markley, Robert. "Language, Power, and Sexuality in Cleland's *Fanny
Hill.*" *Philological Quarterly* 63 (1984): 343–56.

McClintock, Anne. "Gonad the Barbarian and the Venus Flytrap: Portraying
the Female and Male Orgasm," pp. 111-31. In Lynne Segal and Mary
McIntosh, eds., *Sex Exposed: Sexuality and the Pornography Debate.*
London: Virago, 1992.

McIntosh, Mary. "The Homosexual Role." *Social Problems* 16, no. 2
(1968): 182–92. Reprinted with postscript in Kenneth Plummer, ed.,
The Making of the Modern Homosexual, pp. 30–49. Totowa, N.J.:
Barnes and Noble, 1981.

Melville, Lewis. *The South Sea Bubble.* 1921. New York: Burt Franklin,
1968.

Mengay, Donald H. "The Sodomitical Muse: *Fanny Hill* and the Rhetoric of Crossdressing." *Journal of Homosexuality* 23, no. 1/2 (1992): 185–98.

Merck, Mandy. "Difference and Its Discontents." *Screen* 21, no. 1 (1987): 2–9.

Miller, D. A. *The Novel and the Police.* Berkeley: University of California Press, 1988.

Miller, John. *Popery and Politics in England, 1660–1688.* Cambridge: Cambridge University Press, 1973.

Miller, Nancy K. " 'I's' in Drag: The Sex of Recollection." *The Eighteenth Century* 22 (1981): 45–57.

Monter, E. William. "Sodomy and Heresy in Early Modern Switzerland," pp. 41–55. In Salvatore J. Licata and Robert P. Peterson, eds., *Historical Perspectives on Homosexuality.* New York: Haworth, 1981.

Morris, Polly. "Sodomy and Male Honour: The Case of Somerset, 1740–1850," pp. 383–406. In Kent Gerard and Gert Hekma, eds., *The Pursuit of Sodomy: Male Homosexuality in Renaissance and Enlightenment Europe.* New York: Harrington Park, 1989.

Morton, Donald. "The Politics of Queer Theory in the (Post) Modern Moment." *Genders* 17 (1993): 121–50.

Mulvey, Laura. "Visual Pleasure and Narrative Cinema." *Screen* 16, no. 3 (1975): 6–18.

Mundus Foppensis: or, The Fop Display'd (1691). Augustan Reprint Society, No. 248. Los Angeles: University of California, 1988.

Neale, Steve. "Masculinity As Spectacle," pp. 9–20. In Stephen Cohan and Ina Rae Hark, eds., *Screening the Male: Exploring Masculinities in Hollywood Cinema.* New York: Routledge, 1993.

Noordam, Dirk Jaap. "Sodomy in the Dutch Republic, 1600–1725," pp. 207–28. In Kent Gerard and Gert Hekma, eds., *The Pursuit of Sodomy: Male Homosexuality in Renaissance and Enlightenment Europe.* New York: Harrington Park, 1989.

Norton, Rictor. *Mother Clap's Molly House: The Gay Subculture in England, 1700–1830.* London: GMP, 1992.

Nussbaum, Felicity A. *The Autobiographical Subject: Gender and Ideology in Eighteenth-Century England.* Baltimore: Johns Hopkins University Press, 1990.

Oaks, Robert F. " 'Things Fearful to Name': Sodomy and Buggery in Seventeenth-Century New England." *Journal of Social History* 12 (1978): 268–81.

Oldham, John. *The Poems of John Oldham.* Ed. Harold F. Brooks and Raman Selden. Oxford: Clarendon, 1987.

O'Neill, John H. "Sexuality, Deviance, and Moral Character in the Personal Satire of the Restoration." *Eighteenth-Century Life* 2 (1975): 16–19.

Pawelczak, Andy. "Review of *Pulp Fiction*." *Films in Review* 46, no. 1/2 (January/February 1995): 56–57.

Pepys, Samuel. *The Diary of Samuel Pepys*, vol. 4. Ed. Robert Latham and William Mathews. Berkeley: University of California Press, 1970, 11 vols.

Pittenger, Elizabeth. " 'To Serve the Queere': Nicholas Udall, Master of Revels," pp. 162–89. In Jonathan Goldberg, ed., *Queering the Renaissance*. Durham: Duke University Press, 1994.

Plain Reasons for the Growth of Sodomy, In England. London: [1730?].

The Play of Sodom, A Tragedy. London: 1707.

Pocock, J. G. A. *Virtue, Commerce, and History: Essays on Political Thought and History, Chiefly in the Eighteenth Century*. Cambridge: Cambridge University Press, 1985.

Poems on Affairs of State: Augustan Satirical Verse, 1660–1714. Ed. George deF. Lord et al. 7 vols. New Haven: Yale University Press, 1963-

Pope, Alexander.*The Poems of Alexander Pope*. Ed. John Butt. New Haven: Yale University Press, 1963.

Pye, Christopher. "The Sovereign, the Theater, and the Kingdome of Darknesse: Hobbes and the Spectacle of Power," pp. 279–301. In Stephen Greenblatt, ed., *Representing the English Renaissance*. Berkeley: University of California Press, 1988.

Rajan, Tilottama. *The Supplement of Reading: Figures of Understanding in Romantic Theory and Practice*. Ithaca: Cornell University Press, 1990.

Reading, Gerald Rufus Isaacs, 2d Marquis of. *The South Sea Bubble* (1933). Westport, Conn.: Greenwood, 1978.

Rey, Michel. "Parisian Homosexuals Create a Lifestyle, 1700–1750: The Police Archives," pp. 179–91. Trans. Robert A. Day and Robert Welch. In Robert Purks Maccubbin, ed., *'Tis Nature's Fault: Unauthorized Sexuality During the Enlightenment*. New York: Cambridge University Press, 1985.

———. "Police and Sodomy in Eighteenth-Century Paris: From Sin to Disorder," pp. 129–46. In Kent Gerard and Gert Hekma, eds., *The Pursuit of Sodomy: Male Homosexuality in Renaissance and Enlightenment Europe*. New York: Harrington Park, 1989.

Rochester, John Wilmot, Earl of. *The Complete Poems of John Wilmot, Earl of Rochester*. Ed. David M. Vieth. New Haven: Yale University Press, 1968.

Roseveare, Henry. *The Financial Revolution, 1660–1760*. London: Longman, 1991.

Rothstein, Eric. "Scotophilia and *Humphrey Clinker*: The Politics of Beggary, Bugs, and Buttocks." *University of Toronto Quarterly* 52, no. 1 (Fall 1982): 63–78.

Rousseau, G. S. " 'In the House of Madam Vander Tasse, on the Long Bridge': A Homosocial University Club in Early Modern Europe," pp. 311–48. In Kent Gerard and Gert Hekma, eds., *The Pursuit of Sodomy: Male Homosexuality in Renaissance and Enlightenment Europe*. New York: Harrington Park, 1989.

———. "An Introduction to the *Love Letters*: Circumstances of Publication, Context, and Cultural Commentary." *Journal of Homosexuality* 19, no. 2 (1990): 47–92.

———. "The Pursuit of Homosexuality in the Eighteenth Century: 'Utterly Confused Category' and/or Rich Repository?" *Eighteenth-Century Life* 9, no. 3 (1985): 132–68.

———. "The Sorrows of Priapus: Anticlericalism, Homosocial Desire, and Richard Payne Knight," pp. 101–53. In G. S. Rousseau and Roy Porter, eds., *Sexual Underworlds of the Enlightenment*. Manchester: Manchester University Press, 1987.

Roussel, Roy. *The Conversation of the Sexes: Seduction and Equality in Selected Seventeenth- and Eighteenth-Century Texts*. Oxford: Oxford University Press, 1986.

Rowse, A. L. *Homosexuals in History: A Study in Ambivalence in Society, Literature, and the Arts*. New York: Macmillan, 1977.

Rubini, Dennis. "Sexuality and Augustan England: Sodomy, Politics, Elite Circles, and Society," pp. 349–82. In Kent Gerard and Gert Hekma, eds., *The Pursuit of Sodomy: Male Homosexuality in Renaissance and Enlightenment Europe*. New York: Harrington Park, 1989.

Ruggiero, Guido. *The Boundaries of Eros: Sex Crime and Sexuality in Renaissance Venice*. New York: Oxford University Press, 1985.

Sabor, Peter. "Introduction," pp. vii–xxvi. *Memoirs of a Woman of Pleasure* (1748–49), by John Cleland. Ed. Peter Sabor. Oxford: Oxford University Press, 1985.

Saslow, James M. "Homosexuality in the Renaissance: Behaviour, Identity, and Artistic Expression," pp. 90–105. In Martin Bauml Duberman, Martha Vicinus, and George Chauncey, Jr., eds., *Hidden From History: Reclaiming the Gay and Lesbian Past*. New York: New American Library, 1989.

——. " 'A Veil of Ice between my Heart and the Fire': Michelangelo's Sexual Identity and Early Modern Constructs of Homosexuality." *Genders* 2 (1988): 77–90.

Savoy, Eric. "You Can't Go Homo Again: Queer Theory and the Foreclosure of Gay Studies." *English Studies in Canada* 20, no. 2 (June 1994): 129–52.

Schubert, Eric S. "Innovations, Debts, and Bubbles: International Integration of Financial Markets in Western Europe, 1688–1720." *Journal of Economic History* 48, no. 2 (1988): 299–306.

Scott, Joan. "The Evidence of Experience," pp. 397–419. In Henry Abelove, Michèle Aina Barale, and David M. Halperin, eds., *The Lesbian and Gay Studies Reader*. New York: Routledge, 1993.

Scott, Tom. "The Note of Protest in Smollett's Novels," pp. 106–25. In Alan Bold, ed., *Smollett: Author of the First Distinction*. Totowa, N.J.: Barnes and Noble, 1982.

Sedgwick, Eve Kosofsky. *Between Men: English Literature and Male Homosocial Desire*. New York: Columbia University Press, 1985.

——. *Epistemology of the Closet*. Berkeley: University of California Press, 1990.

——. "Privilege of Unknowing." *Genders* 1(1988): 102–24.

Select Trials at the Sessions-House in the Old-Bailey. . . . In Four Volumes. From the Year 1720, to this Time. London: 1742.

Senelick, Laurence. "Mollies or Men of Mode? Sodomy and the Eighteenth-Century London Stage," pp. 287–322. In Wayne R. Dynes and Stephen Donaldson, eds., *History of Homosexuality in Europe and America*. New York: Garland, 1992.

Shapiro, Susan C. " 'Yon Plumed Dandeprat': Male 'Effeminacy' in English Satire and Criticism." *Review of English Studies* 39 n.s. (1988): 400–12.

Shinagel, Michael. "*Memoirs of a Woman of Pleasure*: Pornography and the Mid-Eighteenth-Century Novel," pp. 211–36. In Paul J. Korshin, ed., *Studies in Change and Revolution: Aspects of English Intellectual History*. Yorkshire: Menston, 1972.

Silverman, Kaja. *Male Subjectivity at the Margins*. New York: Routledge, 1992.

Simpson, K. G. "Tobias Smollett: The Scot as English Novelist," pp. 64–105. In Alan Bold, ed., *Smollett: Author of the First Distinction*. Totowa N.J.: Barnes and Noble, 1982.

Simpson, Mark. *Male Impersonators: Men Performing Masculinity*. New York: Routledge, 1994.

Smith, Bruce R. *Homosexual Desire in Shakespeare's England: A Cultural Poetics*. Chicago: University of Chicago Press, 1991.

Smollett, Tobias. *The Adventures of Peregrine Pickle, in which are included Memoirs of a Lady of Quality* (1751). Ed. James L. Clifford. Oxford: Oxford University Press, 1964.

———. *The Adventures of Roderick Random* (1748). Ed. Paul-Gabriel Boucé. Oxford: Oxford University Press, 1979.

———. *Poems, Plays, and The Briton*. Ed. O. M. Brack, Jr.; Introduction by Byron Gassman; Assistant, Leslie A. Chilton. Athens: University of Georgia Press, 1993.

Sodom: or, The Quintessence of Debauchery (c. 1672–1673). Introduction by Albert Ellis. North Hollywood: Brandon House, 1966.

The Sodomites Shame and Doom, Laid before them with great Grief and Compassion. By a Minister of the Church of England. London: 1702.

Spector, Robert D. *Smollett's Women: A Study in an Eighteenth-Century Masculine Sensibility*. Westport, Conn.: Greenwood, 1994.

———. *Tobias George Smollett*. Updated Edition. Boston: Twayne, 1989.

Stallybrass, Peter and Allon White. *The Politics and Poetics of Transgression*. Ithaca: Cornell University Press, 1986.

Staves, Susan. "Kind Words for the Fop." *Studies in English Literature* 22 (1982): 413–28.

———. *Players' Scepters: Fictions of Authority in the Restoration*. Lincoln: University of Nebraska Press, 1979.

Steele, Richard and Joseph Addison. *Selections from "The Tatler" and "The Spectator."* Ed. Angus Ross. Harmondsworth: Penguin, 1982.

Stein, Edward, ed. *Forms of Desire: Sexual Orientation and the Social Constructionist Controversy*. New York: Routledge, 1992.

Stirling, John. *A System of Rhetoric, in a Method Entirely New*. London: 1733.

Straub, Kristina. *Sexual Suspects: Eighteenth-Century Players and Sexual Ideology*. Princeton: Princeton University Press, 1992.

Taylor, Anne Robinson. *Male Novelists and Their Female Voices: Literary Masquerades*. Troy, N.Y.: Whitston, 1981.

Thiers, Adolph. *The Mississippi Bubble: A Memoir of John Law* (1859). Trans. Frank S. Fiske. New York: Greenwood, 1969.

Thompson, Roger. *Unfit for Modest Ears: A Study of Pornographic, Obscene, and Bawdy Works Written or Published in England in the Second Half of the Seventeenth Century*. London: Macmillan, 1979.

A Treatise wherin are Strict Observations upon That detestable and most shocking Sin of Sodomy, Blasphemy, and Atheism. London: 1728.

Trevelyan, G. M. *The English Revolution, 1688–1689*. 1938. Oxford: Oxford University Press, 1965.

Trumbach, Randolph. "The Birth of the Queen: Sodomy and the Emergence of Gender Equality in Modern Culture, 1660–1750," pp. 129–40. In Martin Bauml Duberman, Martha Vicinus, and George Chauncey Jr., eds., *Hidden From History: Reclaiming the Gay and Lesbian Past*. New York: New American Library, 1989.

——. "Gender and the Homosexual Role in Modern Western Culture: The 18th and 19th Centuries Compared," pp. 149–70. In Theo van der Meer and Anja van Kooten Niekerk, eds., *Homosexuality, Which Homosexuality?* London: GMP, 1989.

——. "London's Sodomites: Homosexual Behaviour and Western Culture in the Eighteenth Century." *Journal of Social History* 2 (1977): 1–33.

——. "Sodomitical Subcultures, Sodomitical Roles, and the Gender Revolution of the Eighteenth Century," pp. 109–21. In Robert Purks Maccubbin, ed., *'Tis Nature's Fault: Unauthorized Sexuality During the Enlightenment*. New York: Cambridge University Press, 1987.

——. "Sodomy Transformed: Aristocratic Libertinage, Public Reputation, and the Gender Revolution of the Eighteenth Century." *Journal of Homosexuality* 19, no. 2 (1990): 105–24.

The Tryal and Condemnation of Mervin, Lord Audley of Castle-Haven, at Westminster, April the 5th 1631. London: 1699.

Tyler, Carol-Anne. "Boys Will Be Girls: The Politics of Gay Drag," pp. 32–70. In Diana Fuss, ed., *Inside/Out: Lesbian Theories, Gay Theories*. New York: Routledge, 1991.

Vance, Carol S. "Social Construction Theory: Problems in the History of Sexuality," pp. 13–34. In Theo van der Meer and Anja van Kooten Niekerk, eds., *Homosexuality, Which Homosexuality?* London: GMP, 1989.

van der Meer, Theo. "The Persecutions of Sodomites in Eighteenth-Century Amsterdam: Changing Perceptions of Sodomy," pp. 263–310. In Kent Gerard and Gert Hekma, eds., *The Pursuit of Sodomy: Male Homosexuality in Renaissance and Enlightenment Europe*. New York: Harrington Park, 1989.

Vickers, Brian, ed. *English Science, Bacon to Newton*. Cambridge: Cambridge University Press, 1987.

Von Rad, Gerhard. *Genesis: A Commentary*. Trans. John H. Marks. Philadelphia: Westminster Press, 1972.

Wagner, Peter. *Eros Revived: Erotica of the Enlightenment in England and America*. London: Secker and Warburg, 1988.

———. "The Pornographer in the Courtroom: Trial Reports About Cases of Sexual Crimes and Delinquencies as a Genre of Eighteenth-Century Erotica," pp. 120–40. In Paul-Gabriel Boucé, ed., *Sexuality in Eighteenth-Century Britain*. Manchester: Manchester University Press, 1982.

Ward, Edward (Ned). *The Secret History of Clubs*. London: 1709.

Warner, Michael. "New English Sodom." *American Literature* 64, no. 1 (1992): 19–47.

Weber, Harold. "Carolinean Sexuality and the Restoration Stage: Reconstructing the Royal Phallus in *Sodom*," pp. 676–88. In J. Douglas Canfield and Deborah C. Payne, eds., *Cultural Readings of Restoration and Eighteenth-Century English Theatre*. Athens: University of Georgia Press, 1995.

———. "Charles II, George Pines, and Mr. Dorimant: The Politics of Sexual Power in Restoration England." *Criticism* 32, no. 2 (Spring 1990): 193–219.

———. " 'Drudging in Fair Aurelia's Womb': Constructing Homosexual Economies in Rochester's Poetry." *The Eighteenth Century* 33, no. 2 (1992): 99–117.

———. *The Restoration Rake-Hero: Transformations in Sexual Understanding in Seventeenth-Century England*. Madison: University of Wisconsin Press, 1986.

Weeks, Jeffrey. "Against Nature," pp. 199–213. In Theo van der Meer and Anja van Kooten Niekerk, eds., *Homosexuality, Which Homosexuality?* London: GMP, 1989.

Weinrich, James. "Reality or Social Construction?" pp. 175–200. In Edward Stein, ed., *Forms of Desire: Sexual Orientation and the Social Constructionist Controversy*. New York: Routledge, 1992. Originally published as part of *Sexual Landscapes: Why We Are What We Are, Why We Love Who We Love*. New York: Scribner's, 1987.

Western, J. P. *Monarchy and Revolution: The English State in the 1680s*. Totowa, N.J.: Rowman and Littlefield, 1972.

Whitley, Raymond K. "The Libertine Hero and Heroine in the Novels of John Cleland." *Studies in Eighteenth-Century Culture* 9 (1979): 387–404.

Wild, Jonathan. *An Answer to a late Insolent Libel*. London: 1718.

Williams, Linda. *Hard Core: Power, Pleasure, and the "Frenzy of the Visible."* London: Pandora, 1990.

———. "Pornographies On/Scene, or Diff'rent Strokes for Diff'rent Folks," pp. 233–65. In Lynne Segal and Mary McIntosh, eds., *Sex Exposed: Sexuality and the Pornography Debate*. London: Virago, 1992.

Williams, Raymond. *Keywords: A Vocabulary of Culture and Society* (1976). Revised ed. New York: Oxford University Press, 1983.

Witcombe, D. T. *Charles II and the Cavalier House of Commons, 1663–1674*. Manchester: Manchester University Press, 1966.

"The Women's Complaint to Venus" (1698), pp. 167–78. *The Penguin Book of Restoration Verse*. Ed. Harold Love. Harmondsworth: Penguin, 1968.

The Women-Hater's Lamentation. London: 1707.

Index

Between Men ~ Between Women
LESBIAN AND GAY STUDIES
Lillian Faderman and Larry Gross, Editors

Judith Roof, *Come As You Are: Sexuality and Narrative*

Judith Roof, *A Lure of Knowledge: Lesbian Sexuality and Theory*

Claudia Schoppmann, *Days of Masquerade: Life Stories of Lesbians During the Third Reich*

Alan Sinfield, *The Wilde Century: Effeminacy, Oscar Wilde, and the Queer Moment*

Jane McIntosh Snyder, *Lesbian Desire in the Lyrics of Sappho*

Chris Straayer, *Deviant Eyes, Deviant Bodies: Sexual Re-Orientations in Film and Video*

Dwayne C. Turner, *Risky Sex: Gay Men and HIV Prevention*

Thomas Waugh, *Hard to Imagine: Gay Male Eroticism in Photography and Film from Their Beginnings to Stonewall*

Kath Weston, *Families We Choose: Lesbians, Gays, Kinship*

Kath Weston, *Render me, Gender Me: Lesbians Talk Sex, Class, Color, Nation, Studmuffins . . .*

Carter Wilson, *Hidden in the Blood: A Personal Investigation of AIDS in the Yucatán*